JOHN OLDHAM
AND THE RENEWAL OF CLASSICAL CULTURE

JOHN OLDHAM

AND THE
RENEWAL OF CLASSICAL CULTURE

PAUL HAMMOND

CAMBRIDGE UNIVERSITY PRESS
CAMBRIDGE
LONDON   NEW YORK   NEW ROCHELLE
MELBOURNE   SYDNEY

Published by the Press Syndicate of the University of Cambridge
The Pitt Building, Trumpington Street, Cambridge CB2 1RP
32 East 57th Street, New York, NY 10022, USA
296 Beaconsfield Parade, Middle Park, Melbourne 3206, Australia

First published 1983

Printed in Great Britain at the University Press, Cambridge

Library of Congress catalogue card number: 82-14567

British Library cataloguing in publication data
Hammond, Paul
John Oldham and the renewal of classical culture.
1. Oldham John, 1653-1683 — Criticism and interpretation
I. Title
821'.4   PR3605.04
ISBN 0 521 24748 9

AG

To my parents

CONTENTS

PREFACE

This book is a revised and abbreviated version of the dissertation that I submitted in 1978 for a prize fellowship at Trinity College Cambridge, 'to which foundation', with Dryden, 'I gratefully acknowledge a great part of my Education'. It is a pleasure to be able to thank publicly those to whom I owe much, for their teaching, their example and their fostering of an ethos of humane learning at Trinity: Carl Baron, Theodore Redpath and Leo Salingar. My undergraduate work on Oldham was directed by Harold Mason, who shared with me his fresh and searching ideas on the place of classical culture and creative translation in this period. Richard Luckett supervised my research with his characteristic erudition, shrewdness and tact. Howard Erskine-Hill, too, has been a valuable critic and advocate. Harold Brooks, with a generous and unselfish concern for the subject, gave me access to his thesis, kept me in touch with his later work, and wrote a scrupulous critique of my last draft. Several friends have been unstinting of their time and their learning: my thanks to Michael Comber, John Mason and Richard Sharpe. Finally, I must record my gratitude for financial support from the Master and Fellows of Trinity College. Cambridge; the School of English of the University of Leeds; and the Department of Education and Science.

Trinity College, Cambridge   Paul Hammond
New Year's Eve 1981

A NOTE ON TEXTS

For the works of Oldham I have used the following texts and abbreviations:

SJ   *Satyrs upon the Jesuits*, second edition (1682)
SNP   *Some New Pieces* (1681)
PT   *Poems, and Translations* (1683)
R   *Remains* (1684)
RMS   Bodley MS Rawlinson Poet 123

In most cases I have given line numbers followed by page references. In my quotations from Oldham I have made a few silent corrections. Reference simply to 'Brooks' is to Professor Harold F. Brooks's doctoral thesis, which is to be the basis of his forthcoming edition.

Jonson is quoted from *Ben Jonson*, ed. C.H. Herford and Percy and Evelyn Simpson (11 vols., Oxford, 1925-52); Rochester from *The Complete Poems of John Wilmot, Earl of Rochester*, ed. David M. Vieth (New Haven, 1968); and Dryden from *The Poems of John Dryden*, ed. James Kinsley (4 vols., Oxford, 1958) or, for material that Kinsley does not include, from *The Works of John Dryden*, ed. H.T. Swedenberg *et al.* (20 vols., Berkeley, 1956–). Boileau is quoted from the *Oeuvres Diverses du Sieur D*** avec le Traité du Sublime* (Paris, 1675) because Boudhors's text is based upon a late revision, but I have given line numbers from Boudhors as well as page references from the edition of 1675. I have reproduced the contemporary conventions regarding accents. Horace is quoted from Schrevelius and Juvenal from Lubinus; where these quotations are translated by Oldham I have not added a further translation. Readers will find that these texts differ occasionally in substantives, and frequently in accidentals, from modern editions. Editions and translations of Horace and Juvenal are listed on pp. 230 and 235 respectively. Other classical writers are generally quoted from Loeb editions; I have added translations of these quotations, and of passages of Renaissance Latin. French has not been translated.

Besides standard abbreviations for journals, I have used the following abbreviations: BL for the British Library, *FQ* for *The Faerie Queene* and *PL* for *Paradise Lost*.

PROLOGUE

In Dryden's poem *To the Memory of Mr. Oldham* we come across an extraordinary claim:

> For sure our Souls were near ally'd; and thine
> Cast in the same Poetick mould with mine.

In a long career Dryden expressed his admiration for many writers, but to no one else does he offer such an intimate tribute. Nor is this mere idiosyncrasy on Dryden's part: Pope and Johnson were also careful readers of Oldham who paid him the double compliment of explicit reference and unacknowledged quotation. But in our own day Oldham's work has largely been left unread. Half a century has passed since Harold Brooks began his edition, and in those years few but he and Rachel Trickett have tried to free Oldham from a reputation that has discouraged many from disturbing the dust on seventeenth-century copies. He is still known as the poet of invective, of the crude *Satyrs upon the Jesuits*; the man who mistook violence for strength, and abuse for wit; harsh in metre, negligent in rhyme, casually obscene. All of which is true: if we add that these features are often carefully nurtured and are but part of his range. There must have been other qualities in Oldham to draw from Dryden a poem of classic serenity moulded from passionate regret.

In seeking to make a revaluation of Oldham I have deliberately not offered a conventional critical study. This book does indeed point to what I consider to be his best poems, but it is also particularly concerned with how those poems were composed. Oldham gives us a rare opportunity to observe the workings of a poet's mind. The Rawlinson manuscript preserves a large collection of drafts that allows us to study the development of certain poems in considerable detail: this is a survival almost unique in the seventeenth century. Besides, Oldham was a scholarly poet, one who as he composed habitually recalled other men's poems and his own earlier work; and when he translated he sat down, as Dryden was to do, with a pile of translations and commentaries. It is therefore possible to trace the process of composition and to watch him making choices between various possibilities.

I have quoted extensively from Oldham and his sources, partly because the poems will not be very familiar, nor perhaps always accessible, and therefore merit extracts that are long enough to provide pleasure as well as evidence. But the quotations are also extensive because that is the only way in which the main questions raised in this book can be illustrated: What habits of reading were formed by the seventeenth-century educational system? What guided Oldham's choice of Latin and French models? What could he take from them, and what did he miss? What temptations did he have to struggle with to attain maturity? Did he educate his age or pander to its demands? Is he part of a culture or a coterie? I offer texts not as decoration to a thesis, but as documents that invite us to ponder these problems.

Oldham's culture, unlike ours, was still essentially Latin-based, and the Restoration reader would have brought to English poetry methods of reading, literary tastes and moral assumptions that had their origin in the classroom study of classical texts. The publisher of the 1717 edition of Roscommon, for example, expected his customers not only to read the Earl's translations of Horace as English poems, but to compare them with the Latin texts printed on facing pages, and to come to some critical judgment about the poems after studying the accompanying notes, which were translated from the best available edition of Horace, that by Dacier. These are seventeenth-century habits of reading that we need to recover.

Good translation is occasional: the movement of one mind towards another for particular reasons. This study seeks to show why Oldham sought out certain poems and not others, and this should be of particular interest if Oldham was, as I believe, one of what Harold Mason has called the 'centripetal minds' — 'minds with some sort of homing instinct for inward-tending movements whenever they sense that they are being extravagant or affected'.[1] When Oldham attempted to redeem the extravagance of his early work by turning to Horace, to Juvenal and to Boileau, he could not adopt a ready-made 'classical' stance, but had to fight the centrifugal tendencies in himself to make such a stance his own. And there were only certain parts of the multivalent classical heritage that he could make his own, partly because of his personal limitations, but partly because he was having to break new ground for his generation. In saying this, I am not too concerned to claim priority for Oldham's classical translations, either in chronology or in quality, though these pages will offer evidence on both counts. Rather, I hope to show in detail how one man achieved a new relationship to the classical heritage, and in so doing contributed to the new relationship to their traditions that his contemporaries were attempting to forge. Such a task has to be tackled afresh for each period, and can only be done by the best spirits of the age at their best moments. We should not underestimate this exploration and conquest by subsuming its results under the literary history of the classical 'imitation', and I offer this book partly as a prolegomenon to a wider re-examination of the classically-based culture of the age.

Oldham, I suggest, was one of the few true critics of the Restoration. Such men, said Arnold, are concerned for 'the best ideas, on every matter which literature touches, current at the time'.[2] When Arnold said that 'English poetry ... with plenty of energy, plenty of creative force, did not know enough',[3] he was referring to the early nineteenth century, but the judgment applies equally to the Restoration. The songs, the plays, the satires and lampoons, these display energy in plenty, but offer little real thinking about where man's true values lie. It is the genuine and urgent thinking that takes place as Oldham composes his translations that establishes their independence from their models, their abiding value, and their function as a critical preparation for the work of Dryden, Pope and Johnson.

I shall begin by examining how Oldham's education encouraged habits of reading and thinking conducive to this critical and creative enterprise.

1

ORIGINS

John Oldham was born on 9 August 1653 into a clerical family living on the borders of Wiltshire and Gloucestershire. His grandfather, John, was rector of Shipton Moyne, and a man of Puritan inclinations. He had the care of forty families, and received an annual income of £90. A good scholar, he bequeathed to his son — another John — 'tenne of my best lattin bookes that may be most vsefull for his studye'. The poet's father, also said to have been 'no mean schollar', was vicar of nearby Long Newnton until deprived for nonconformity in 1662.[1]

Oldham's earliest biographer, Anthony à Wood, writes that he was

> bred in grammar learning under his father till he was nigh fit for the university, afterwards sent to the school at Tetbury, where he spent about two years under the tuition of Henry Heaven, occasion'd by the desire of one Yeat an alderman of Bristol, who had a son then there under the said master, whom Oldham accompanied purposely to advance him in his learning. This occasion'd his longer stay at school than else he needed, but conduced much to his after advantage.[2]

Since Oldham gained most of his education at the hands of his father, and only entered the grammar school late in order to help another boy, we can only guess about his formative education. There seems no point in repeating here the detailed findings of recent scholars about the curriculum of the sixteenth- and seventeenth-century grammar school, but a brief review of its common content may be apposite.[3]

Most teachers would still be using Lily's Grammar as the foundation for Latin.[4] Easy practice in reading Latin would be provided by Aesop's Fables and Cato, and as the children progressed up the school they would work through such authors as Mantuan, Terence, Ovid, Cicero, the Greek New Testament, Virgil, Isocrates, Horace, Seneca's Tragedies, Hesiod, Juvenal, Persius and Homer.[5] Besides reading from the poets, and easy historians such as Cornelius Nepos and Lucius Florus, children would have composed letters in Latin, so that they became well-practised in translating between Latin, Greek and English, and in composing both in prose and verse. As an example of how authors were taught, these are the suggestions for working with Horace that Charles Hoole made in his *New Discovery of the Old Art of Teaching Schoole* (1660):

> Their afternoons Lessons may be in *Horace*, wherein they should be emploied.
> 1. In commiting their Lessons to memory, as affording a rich mine of invention.
> 2. In construing and parsing, and giving the Tropes and Figures.
> 3. In scanning and proving verses.
> 4. Sometimes in turning an Ode, or Epistle, into other kind of verses, English, Latine, or Greeke; sometimes in paraphrasing or enlarging the words in an Oratorical style (pp. 197-8).

In which editions would these authors have been read? Hoole advises:

> *Mr Farnabie* or *Mr Bonds Notes* upon this Poet will encourage your Scholars to proceed in him: And after they have read what you best approve (for he that feeds cleanly, will pare his apple) in this Author, you may let them proceed to *Juvenall*, and read some select Satyres, by help of *Farnabies notes*, or *Lubines Commentarie*, and then let them read *Persius* quite through, which besides the notes upon him, *Mr Holydaies* English Translation will help them to understand. As for *Lucan, Seneca's Tragedies, Martiall*, and the rest of the finest Latine Poets, you may do well to give them a taste of each, and show them how and wherein they may imitate them, or borrow something out of them (p. 198).

The schoolmaster had the responsibility for prudent selection, as the statutes of Tetbury School make clear:

> he shall not read unto the Schollars any of ye obscene odes, satyres, or epigrams of Juvenal, Martial, or Horace, or any other, but pass them over, choosing ye best in the same authors, and in others; and y^t he shall not at all read in the Schoole *Ovid de arte amandi*.[6]

The editions used would have been complete texts with annotations. Farnaby and Bond offer marginal glosses, while Lubinus provides a phrase-by-phrase exposition in the case of Juvenal, and a lengthy prose paraphrase for Horace. All these annotations were of course in Latin. Their aim was

almost exclusively to clarify the meaning, and there is very little illus-
trative reference to Roman history and customs, which were exhaustively
covered in separate works. Only in the English translations such as Holyday's Juvenal does one find background annotations of this kind. The
texts themselves would normally be unexpurgated. Farnaby says in the
preface to his 1612 edition of Juvenal: 'Lines which are indelicate I have
deliberately drawn a veil over, and in some cases entirely omitted. For to
what purpose would you expound those things which it is not fitting that
anyone should know?'[7] Omissions there may be, but a check on some
likely places failed to reveal any. Two samples from Juvenal will illustrate
editorial procedure. In Satire IX Farnaby prints the full text of lines 43-6,
without glosses. He comments that 'This is one of those places on account
of whose obscenity J.C. Scaliger told all good men to abstain completely
from reading Juvenal.' Lubinus, however, both prints and glosses the
passage, even though he says that 'Because the subject is so thoroughly dis-
gusting, these lines neither can nor should be explained.' He remarks that
'Juvenal is indeed to be rebuked for describing such monstrous behaviour
so openly'; and yet he adds: 'truly such obscenities will not harm the pure
in heart'. Similarly with Satire VI.334, both editors print the text,
Farnaby without and Lubinus with glosses, the latter adding, 'O monstrous
and unbelievable lust!' So the young reader was presented both with the
full text, and with some rudimentary moral guidance in his reading.

The practice of constant translation and composition, and the
encouragement given pupils to memorise whole passages and useful
phrases seems to have been a valuable preparation for Oldham: we shall
see that his own poetry demonstrates a close familiarity not only with
classical poetry but with its translators and editors as well. We cannot be
at all sure how much English verse Oldham would have written at school.
Dryden had to translate Persius's Satire III into English verse at Westminster;[8] Oldham, while teaching at Croydon, set his pupils to write
poems on the Popish Plot,[9] and Joshua Poole dedicated his poet's handbook *The English Parnassus* to his pupils. But the composition of Latin
verse was more frequent. It helped to teach correct pronunciation, and the
exercise of paraphrasing the Psalms in Latin verse taught devotion too. It
is difficult to know when Oldham learned French. A gentleman would
have been taught French by his tutor, but we do not know whether
Oldham's father knew enough French to teach him, though some puritan
families had learned French in order to maintain contact with Huguenot
refugees.[10] But French and other modern languages were increasingly
available at Oxford from private tutors.[11]

While Oldham's own remains from his time at Oxford are few, there is enough evidence from his immediate contemporaries about their life and work for us to be able to form a fairly clear picture of his likely pursuits. Under Oxford's conservative Laudian statutes of 1636, all freshmen had to attend lectures on grammar and rhetoric, and later on logic and moral philosophy. (Greek was postponed until the third year, which is strange, considering the hold it now enjoyed in the grammar schools.[12] But undergraduates would have been more affected by college than university teaching, and instead of trying to give a general account of the Oxford of his day, I shall concentrate on the evidence that takes us closest to Oldham himself.[13]

Oldham matriculated at St Edmund Hall in June 1670.[14] It was an obvious college to choose, for its new principal, Dr Thomas Tullie, had been headmaster of the grammar school in Tetbury, and many of its undergraduates came from Wiltshire and Gloucestershire families. After a depleted existence during the Commonwealth, the Hall attracted an increasing number of undergraduates, and according to Andrew Allam, vice-principal under Tullie's successor, it had during Tullie's day 'flourish'd in proportion to its bigness equall wth any other in ye University; & this was effect'd by means of ye exercise of a strict, even, & regular discipline'.[15]

The best evidence we have as to life at the Hall while Oldham was there is provided by the papers of John Freind, who came up in 1672 and died a year later, and for whom Oldham, in company with several other students, wrote funeral verses. Freind's correspondence is similar to what we might expect Oldham's to have been: the former was younger, but both their fathers were schoolmasters with farming connections. Freind wrote frequently to his father Nathaniel — generally in Latin — and received advice from him about his reading. In return he bought and sent home several books that his father was interested in: a Lexicon, Galtruchius's 'History of the heathen Gods', and Gassendi's 'Astronomy', though he missed a bargain second-hand Hesiod. His father urged John to study herbs as a preparation for medicine, and recorded that he 'seemed little addicted to Reading History or the Mathematicks'. Work had also to be done during vacations: John asks his father 'to borrow Mr Godwin of Henbury his Ovids Metamorphosis of Sands Translation for mee against I come down', though journeys had to be timed to coincide with slack periods on the farm:

> I would desire yo^w in yor next to send mee word when William
> shall come up, the best time I suppose will be between hay
> harvest & Corn harvest.

'Mr Principall', however, 'doth not well approove of Schollers being much in the Country.' Looking back on John's prospects, his father thought that 'if the worst happened he might doe as I had done viz imploy himselfe in a schoole, which would afford him a livelyhood if he had nothing else to trust to'.[16]

Even though his father told him not to think 'yo^w have enough till yo^w have mastered all Authors in Greek & Latin', John Freind had to make some selections in his reading. One of his first letters home asks his father for books which he has discovered will be necessary for his work at the Hall:

> I shall need some other Bookes, which I have not put up, which
> are these, Godwins Antiquities, Claudian (which is in my
> Custody, & the Greek Bible without the Testament, having
> already my Greek Testament with mee ... alsoe I would request
> yo^w to send mee Erasmus his Adages which I find will bee a
> materiall Book for mee.

Nathaniel clearly had a good library at home, and sent his son both books and advice. He suggested Lipsius's *Epistles* and *De Constantia*, and apologised for not having at home a Quintus Curtius. John was also told by his tutor to send home for a 'Homers works & Clavis'.[17]

John's tutor guided his studies carefully, and gave him this timetable:

Monday	After morning prayers, both public and	From noon to five o' clock: on Monday, Tuesday
Tuesday	private, and the reading of a chapter of	and Wednesday diligent work is to be devoted
Wednesday	the Bible in English and Greek, the remainder of the time is to	to the Latin language (*Philologicis Latinis*),
Thursday	be employed in philosophical studies	and on Thursday and Friday to Greek Authors.
Friday	osophical studies (*studijs philosophicis*)	
Saturday	In term, exercises are to be prepared; in vacation grammar is to be revised, sometimes Greek, sometimes Latin.	Afternoon: on Saturdays and on other days after dinner whatever time is free from pleasant and decent recreations is to be devoted entirely to Latin poetry and Roman antiquities.[18]

What does this programme amount to? The initial stress on public and private prayer and the reading of the Bible is echoed in the rules drawn up towards the end of the Commonwealth by Dr James Duport, fellow of Trinity College Cambridge, for the guidance of his pupils.[19] Duport expects daily attendance at morning chapel and at evening prayers in the tutor's room. As at St Edmund Hall, the Bible was to be read with the aid of Diodati's notes. The entry on the timetable that reads 'studijs philosophicis' probably refers to courses in logic. When Freind arrived at Oxford 'the Schollers of that Class in which m^r March intended to put mee went into the Compendium of Logick'.[20] This appears to have been a standard procedure, for when Henry Fleming was at Queen's in 1678 he reported that 'My tutor reads to me once for ye most part every day, and sometimes twice, in Sandersons logick which booke is all he reads to me as yet'; later he wrote that 'haveing read all Sandersons logick I must begin y^{is} next week in Ethicks', and he later went on to Geometry and 'Physicks'.[21] Duport told his pupils: 'Use often to dispute & argue in Logic, and Phylosophy with your Chamberfellow, and acquaintances when you are together.'[22] It looks as if students could quickly pass on from logic to moral philosophy and do some reading for themselves. Oldham appears to have taken more than a temporary and enforced interest in this part of the work, for in *A Letter from the Country* he writes of reading Aristotle:

> Strait the great *Stagyrite* I take in hand,
> Seek Nature, and my Self to understand.
>
> (101-2; *SNP* 123)

The two moral philosophers whom Oldham represents as standard reading in *The Thirteenth Satyr of Juvenal, Imitated* are Plutarch and Seneca;[23] George Fleming took a 'Seneca's Rhetorick & Philosophy' with him when he went up to St Edmund Hall in 1688.[24] Plato does not figure at all in the reading of students at the Hall, nor in the fellows' library. Oldham bought a copy of *Platonis de rebus divinis dialogi selecti Graece et Latine* (Cambridge, 1673)[25] on 14 July 1674, six weeks after graduating. This was edited by John North of Trinity College Cambridge, and presented Ficino's Latin translation alongside the Greek. North says that he had recommended to the bookseller the publication of a Plato because he had discovered that copies were very rare and expensive, whereas Aristotle was plentifully available in student editions.[26]

As for the classical poets, a student's notebook preserved in Queens' College Cambridge reveals one method of study. The student begins his work on Horace's *Sermones* by quoting the first three lines of I.i and then translating them. The next four pages are given over to an introduction to the *Sermones*, on who was Horace, what is meant by *sermo*, 'satyre', and so on. Then he returns to the first three lines of I.i and begins his commentary. This consists of (a) *Grammatica analysis*, etymology, syntax; (b) *Rhetorica analysis*, figures of speech; (c) *Logica analysis*, the thought. This analysis continues for the remainder of the poem, and he examines Juvenal in the same way.[27]

Another item on Freind's timetable was the preparation of exercises. His father preserved John's verses, which are usually on moral subjects such as 'Avoid the wicked Siren Sloth' and 'He who was not wary at first, will grieve later.'[28] But John was also expected to write verses for family occasions: he was told that 'Yo^r Uncle Freind is newly marryed, on Munday last & if yo^w send an Epithalamium a Copy of verses wishing him prosperitie he will take it very kindly ... & doth expect a Latin epistle from yo^w as soon as may be.'[29] There were also declamations to be written, and one of Freind's survives on the subject 'Whether it was good for Nero to fiddle while Rome burned'.[30] One wonders whether this training in making the worse appear the better reason contributed to the methods of the *Satyrs upon the Jesuits* and the *Satyr against Virtue*, the latter of which includes praise of Nero's burning of Rome.

The composition of epistles was also important. Freind used to write to his father in Latin, and was told:

> Yo^r Latter Epistles give mee hopes that by using to write in Latin yo^w will refine yor style & come to some good perfection in the Tongue. I advise yo^w to be reading the best Latin such as Lipsius whose Epistles & de Constantia together, I have sent yo^w ...
> be carefull in reading Latin & much endeavour to be exquisite in writing & speaking in that Tongue (pp. 49-51).

Duport's advice on writing Latin is quite judicious:

> let your stile be clear, & perspicuous, smooth, & plaine, & full, not darke, & clowdy, curt, crabbed, & ragged, and let your stile be nervous, & vivid, & masculine, not inert, flat, & languid...
> Doe not stuffe & loade your Speeches and Declamations with Greek, & Latine sentences, Apothegmes, verses or scrapps of Poets.
> But for your Epistles I doe not altogether dislike Lipsius his way which is to chequer them sometimes with Greek words & Sentences Sayings of Poets and the like, now and then to intermingle some odd, old word, so it be sparingly, & when you write to your equalls (p. 10).

Drafts of two Latin letters survive amongst Oldham's papers. One is addressed to John Spencer in December 1678, and begins with an explanation of why he is using Latin:

> Mirare forsan cur Latine ad te scribo, idque putidum quid & nimis Grammaticum sapere putas: Rationem alius verbis sic habe: Etiam vulgari lingua scriptae testantur literae nos amicorum meminisse, sed aliena, nos de illis meditari (RMS 279).

> ('Perhaps you are wondering why I'm writing to you in Latin, and think it rather affected, and smacking too much of the Schools: Accept this reason — in the words of another: Letters even when written in our native language show that we have remembered our friends, but when written in a foreign language show that we have actually thought about them.')

The explanation, and the use of the anonymous authority ('alius verbis') suggest that this is an unusual event. Oldham subsequently takes the opportunity 'to intermingle some odd, old word',[31] and to talk about their friendship in terms that remind us that this was a favourite topic for epistles set as school exercises:[32]

> num te fori litigantis rixae & strepitus arrectum tenent? num domi Legum volumina lexis, & Themidis arcana scrutare? an cum lepidis sodalibus Gratijs et Risui litas, & vino curas domas? ... Adest propemodum (immo seculum abesse videtur) tempus, quo potestas presentis tui mihi fuerit. Peream, si quid uspiam in votis magis sit mihi (RMS 279-80).

> ('I wonder whether the quarrelling and din of the lawcourts hold you enthralled? Or have you been reading tomes of law at home — searching out the mysteries of Themis? Or perhaps you're in pleasant company, making offerings to the Graces and Laughter — overcoming cares with wine [as Horace would say]? ... The time is almost at hand — it seems, indeed, that you've been away for a hundred years — when the opportunity of your presence will be mine. Let me die if there is anything which I long for more than that.')

However widely classical studies ranged, there was a central core of authors who could be taken as models. Duport recommended:

> In the course of your studies, use to reade, among the antient classick Authors, the best, & of the best note, as Homer,

Aristotle, Virgill, Tully, Seneca, Plutarch, and the like ... In the reading of Authors observe the most remarkable passages, & note them with a black-lead-pen, and reserve them after ward to your Common-place book ... In reading of heathen Poets, especially Juvenal, & Martiall, suck the hony out of the flower, and passe by the weedes (pp. 3-4).

John Potenger, drawing on his Oxford education of the 1660s, advised his grandson 'to keep an intimate acquaintance with classical authors, especially Cicero, Livy, Caesar's Commentaries, Sallust, Quintus Curtius, &c. Let Virgil and Horace be your beloved poets; read others at your leisure, but let these be your constant directors in prose and verse.'[33] One hears very little explicitly about the educative value of the classics — what there was to be gained from them apart from an elegant style. There is plenty of advice on improving reading in the English divines, and on looking to one's tutor as the fount of moral wisdom,[34] but little is said about the great humanist conception of the classics as the vehicle for reaching mature thought about man and his society.

Certainly Erasmus still figures in the programmes of reading. George Fleming wrote home from school in 1686 to ask for 'any of Erasmus is workes except his Colloques, as De lingua or De copia virborum'.[35] But Erasmus seems to have survived in attenuated versions. The *Adages* in their final sixteenth-century form displayed an exceptionally creative use of classical literature. Time and again it is Erasmus's present social and moral concerns that are placed first, and examples from the classical and Christian world are adduced to support them. Quotations are extensive. But if we look at the *Adagiorum Epitome* published at Oxford in 1666 (a more likely book for John Freind to have used than the old and bulky *Adagiorum Chiliades*) it is evident that the process of selection has also been a process of trivialising the original enterprise, and reducing the long discussions to brief maxims. The bones of the humanist enterprise are still there: we are told 'Qualis vir, talis oratio' and 'Corrumpunt bonos mores colloquia praua'.[36] There is still some elementary work of moral definition:

> *Prora & puppis* ... Prora itaque et puppi summam consilii nostri significamus: ut, Pietas studiorum nostrorum prora & puppis esse debet. Quibusdam omnium rationum prora & puppis est pecunia. Consimili figura dictum est in Apocalypsi: Ἐγώ εἰμι a καὶ ω. Ego sum *a* & ω. Ego sum rerum omnium summa.[37]

There is sensible advice: 'Amicorum est admonere mutuum', 'Animo aegrotanti medicus est oratio',[38] and readers are introduced cautiously to examples of immorality:

> *Sardanapalus* ... Hujus cognomen ob insignem hominis mollitiem abiit in proverbium. Fuit autem Sardanapalus delitiis usque adeo effoeminatus, ut inter Eunuchos & puellas, ipse puellari cultu desidere sit solitus.[39]

Even if Oldham did not take the subject of his poem *Sardanapalus* from this adage, he is likely to have been influenced by this habit — no doubt shared by his teachers — of selecting such moral *exempla*.[40] The *Adagiorum Epitome* mentions Sardanapalus in the section headed 'Intemperantia, Libido', whose half-a-dozen pages are concerned chiefly with homosexuality and effeminacy, and offer entries of this kind:

> *Complura masculi canis cubilia* ... Sunt canis infinita cubicula masculi. Recte dicetur in hominem mulierosum: peculiariter in eum, qui non contentus certo thoro, passim per aliena cubilia voluntari gaudeat.[41]

But these miniature examples scarcely suffice to turn moral maxims into moral thought.

In some cases, the editing of the *Epitome* has distorted the whole temper of Erasmus's enterprise. Thus the reader of the *Epitome* is told bluntly that '*Foemina nihil pestilentius*. Hanc sententiam sic effert Homerus ... Usque adeo nihil improbius, muliereque pejus.'[42] But in the *Adagiorum Chiliades* the passage continues: 'Frequenter apud antiquos poetas male audit mulierum genus. Quae quidem & hodiernis temporibus strenue dant operam, ne poetae plane uaniloqui fuisse uideantur.'[43] What is exemplified here is not only the loss of the breadth and humour of Erasmus, but a willingness to accept truth in the crude form of extracted truths. However useful such prepared phrases were in prose composition, they suggest a reductive way of reading the classics, and it would not be surprising if a writer of sensitivity and intelligence came to feel that the only way of rescuing the wisdom of classical literature was to stop weaving these maxims into his own work, and to concentrate instead upon reviving entire the poems from which they had been severed.

Classical history was another subject on which undergraduates worked. Henry Fleming wrote in 1678 that 'in spaire hours from logick I read Lucius Florus, Sallus and such histories out of which I write collections' Eight months later he wrote again: 'I read History such as Lu. Florus, Salust, Historia ab urbe condito &c.' His brother George was also reading 'Justinians Institutions, being an Epitome of the Civil Law'.[44] Since history was read from primary sources, textbooks just provided background material on Roman customs and institutions. The two favourite books of this kind appear to have been Rosinus's *Antiquitatum Romanorum Corpus*, and the smaller English handbook by Thomas Godwyn, *Romanae Historiae Anthologia*.[45] Oldham bought an interleaved copy of the latter in 1672 and annotated it copiously,[46] and in a similar fashion John Potenger made his copy of Godwyn into a commonplace book by writing poems and declamations on the blank pages.[47] Godwyn discusses Roman religion and government, the organisation of the army, games and plays. But in reminding ourselves of what was common property amongst educated men in the Restoration, we should not forget that Oldham was, by the standards of the gentleman *littérateur*, a considerable scholar. A piquant example of this may be found in those manuscript copies of Oldham's poem *Sardanapalus* which preserve his marginal annotations.[48] These give precise references to Strabo's *Geography*, Clement of Alexandria's *Stromateis*, Augustine's *De Civitate Dei*, Justinus's *Historia Philippicae*, Orosius's *Historiae Adversum Paganos*, Suidas, Diodorus Siculus and Athenaeus. One does not often find pornography that cites Orosius.

How much of such an education would have stayed with a man afterwards, if he were not engaged in teaching? This is a question that could occupy a book by itself, but a few examples may be pertinent. An obvious source for information of this kind is Pepys, who records the purchase of a Hebrew grammar and Scapula's Lexicon. He read for pleasure a Latin comedy by Randolph, some Cicero, and the *Metamorphoses* with his wife. He tested his servant on the Latin New Testament, and had to use a grammar to refresh his memory. Pepys's brother John, at Cambridge, asked him for Rosinus's 'Roman antiquities' and Gassendi's 'Astronomy'. The latter Pepys was able to give him immediately, and the Pepys library now contains 1685 and 1683 editions of those books.[49] The library also includes the Cnipping variorum edition of Ovid (3 vols., 1683, the edition that Dryden preferred), Bond's edition of Horace (1663), and − very interestingly for our purposes − two French editions: *Les Poesies d'Anacreon et de Sappho* (1681) and Dacier's *Oeuvres d'Horace* (10 vols., 1691).[50] French editions of classical texts do appear to have been esteemed, and we find a dozen such books in the library of Sir George Etherege, who did not have a university education.[51] Congreve's library was extensive.[52] It was rich in the major classical texts, and included Stephanus's *Dictionarium historicum, geographicum, poeticum*, Scapula's Lexicon, a *Clavis Homerica* and *Graecae Grammatices Rudimenta*. He had Lipsius's *De Constantia* and Erasmus's *Adagiorum Epitome*. Amongst the French versions of the classics are d'Ablancourt's Lucian and Tacitus,

Cassandre's translation of Aristotle's *Poetics,* and versions by the Daciers of Anacreon and Sappho, Terence, Aristophanes, Homer, Sophocles, Aristotle and Horace. Congreve was also much interested in contemporary French literature, notably Arnauld and Nicole's *L'Art de Penser,* Bouhours' *Entretiens d'Ariste et d'Eugène,* Balzac, three copies of Boileau, Corneille, Saint-Évremond, La Fontaine, Gassendi in Bernier's abridgement, Montaigne, Molière, Racine, Rapin (*Oeuvres Diverses* and, in English, *Reflections on Aristotle's Treatise of Poesie*) and Voiture. Similar lists could be made from the libraries of Waller and Wren,[53] and from the known reading of Dryden.[54] Though a man of letters might continue to read his classics in the original, and to stock his library with new editions, translations were increasingly available, and we are told of Aubrey that 'though he read various Latin authors during his adolescence, it was English translations like Sandys' *Ovid* and Holland's *Livy* that he found the most "wonderfull helpe to my phansie"'.[55]

To what extent did the universities also encourage the reading of modern literature and the discussion of current affairs? Although tutors may, like Duport, have recommended Herbert for devotional purposes, official interest in English poetry probably did not extend beyond the setting of occasional exercises.[56] However, gentlemen who were at the university for a non-scholastic education would have been directed to Bacon, Browne, Burton, Thomas More and Herbert.[57] It is likely, too, that there was a lively interest in making and exchanging verses amongst the undergraduates themselves. The commonplace book of George Stanhope at Cambridge contains not only poems written by himself (chiefly addressed to friends and family) but a number of poems by eminent contemporaries: five by or ascribed to Rochester, *Mac Flecknoe,* and Richard Duke's *A Panegyrick upon Oats.*[58] William Doble at Oxford copied into his commonplace book (1669-74) Rochester's *Tunbridge Wells* and *Satire against Reason and Mankind.*[59] John Potenger records that not until he graduated was he free to pursue his own interests, reading Milton and Hobbes for example.[60] One man particularly alive to new events in politics and literature was White Kennett, who came up to St Edmund Hall in 1678, and was later its vice-principal. While still an undergraduate he published two political poems, and his diary notes the purchase of various satires and pamphlets, mostly after his graduation.[61]

Kennett was soon to use his freedom in a more adventurous way. In October 1682 he travelled to northern France and made a point of visiting the Jesuit College when he was in St Omer. He might have had misgivings as he saw the inscription over the door — 'Dieu convert Les Anglois' — but he was 'entertained wth a gentile breakfast', and was placed at ye same table where Oats sate at ye same time he swore to have been in England. Oats branded wth many bitter Epithets. his degree at Salamanca a notorious sham. He was such an untractable dunce y^t to get rid of him from St Omars they sent him of some message to Vallerdolid in Spain where he continued not long before he was expelld at wch time he run back to England... my objection of their occasionall if not intentionall idolatry replied to by an acknowledgement $y^t y^e$ common people were to be kept in a devout kind of ignorance & $y^t y^e$ neglect of this piece of policy must needs be repented of by y^e church of England. Many wheedling invitations & winning proposalls to tarry & be adopted into their society... Engaged in a dispute $w^{th} y^e$ Tutor to y^e Governours sons ... He was A very zealous Catholick yet freely confessed y^t many of y^e Jesuites had been too extravagant in their moralls & politicks.[62]

So this graduate of St Edmund Hall and future bishop was taking pains to understand the Jesuit point of view, and arguing with them over the disputed issues – discussing, indeed, some of the charges that Oldham had raised in his *Satyrs upon the Jesuits* the previous year.

Now this was also one of the chief activities amongst the fellows of St Edmund Hall. Not many of them may have been able to travel to St Omer – or thought it prudent – but the evidence that we have as to their reading points to them spending much of their time researching theological and ecclesiastical controversy.

The Hall's library was begun in the 1660s, exclusively for the use of fellows, and was evidently designed to supplement their own collections. The main emphasis was on philosophical, theological and controversial works. We know that Oldham's tutor, Will Stephens, borrowed the following books between 1667 and 1673: two of the four volumes of *Petri Gassendi Opera Omnia* (1658); *Corpus et Syntagma Confessionum Fidei* (1612), which collects confessions of faith from various Protestant churches; Francis Mason's *Vindiciae Ecclesiae Anglicanae* (1625), a defence of the Church of England against Bellarmine in particular; Ambrose Fisher's *A Defence of the Liturgie of the Church of England* (1630); volume III of Gassendi; Hooker's *Ecclesiastical Polity* and Hamon L'Estrange's *Alliance of Divine Offices*.[63] Mason, Fisher, Hooker and L'Estrange represent the central episcopalian strain in Anglicanism. Stephens's tastes in borrowing are similar to those of the other fellows. Gassendi was the most popular, being borrowed seven times. Suarez's

Metaphysicarum Disputationum (1619) was presented in 1665 and borrowed four times. Other books used include three more defences of the Church of England against Rome: Chillingworth's *The Religion of Protestants*, Richard Field's *Of the Church* and John White's *The Way to the True Church*. Interest in the same question is exemplified by a volume of anti-Roman tracts, the Tridentine *Canones et Decreta* and the *Index Librorum Prohibitorum*. While Suarez seems to have been read for his philosophy, the works of his fellow-Jesuit Bellarmine that the Hall owned were the *Disputationum . . . De Controversiis Christianae Fidei, Adversus Huius Temporis Haereticos*. We know of course that Donne made a special study of Bellarmine, but it is interesting that Henry Fleming at Queen's in 1683 paid 3s. 'For Bellarminus enarvatus in 2 vol.'[64]

The presence of Gassendi suggests that the fellows were also paying attention to one of the chief contemporary challenges to traditional Christian thought. Sometimes it was his *Astronomy* that people bought, but St Edmund Hall was given two sets of the complete works, and although these volumes contained treatises on logic and physics, the distinctive contribution of Gassendi was his revival of interest in Epicurus. His *Syntagma Philosophiae Epicuri* (1649) and *De Vita et Moribus Epicuri* (1647) stimulated an interest in Epicurus that took hold first of all in France but soon reached England.[65] In the popular mind both the amoral pragmatism associated with the Jesuits, and the materialist atheism of Epicurus tended towards the subversion of the inherited moral code. As we shall see later, both were challenges for Oldham.

I have assembled some indications of the content of an undergraduate's curriculum, of his likely extracurricular studies, and of the work done by graduates and fellows. It may be worth extending this sketch a little by considering the work of two Oxford publishers, Anthony Stephens and John Fell. Anthony Stephens set up shop around 1681, but ran into financial trouble, and his books were seized to pay off his debts in January 1687.[66] D.G. Vaisey says that 'by no stretch of the imagination could he be considered an important bookseller', but although Stephens's career was short, his choice of titles to publish was remarkably enlightened, and provides a sidelight upon another aspect of intellectual life in Oxford. The first book that Stephens published was one of the most successful of the age, Thomas Creech's translation of Lucretius. This was issued in 1682 and reprinted three times in 1683. One of the prefatory poems exclaims:

> How happy had our English Tongue been made
> Were but our Wit industrious as our Trade

Wou'd we from hence to distant Countries go?
What *Greece* or *Rome* e're yields in *England* sow
And teach th' Unlearned what the Learned know.
In this the *French* Excel, but we take Care
Not what they write, but only what they wear.[67]

The anonymous writer goes on to recommend Creech to translate
Theocritus, Virgil and Horace. The latter

we have in Paraphrastick Dress,
(They who enlarge his Poems, make 'em less).

Creech did indeed follow his Lucretius with versions of Horace and
Theocritus, both published by Stephens in 1684. Theocritus was prefaced
with a translation of Rapin's *De Carmine Pastorali*. There were two issues
of the Theocritus in 1684, and the astute Tonson had a stake in the
Horace as its London bookseller. But Creech's translations were just part
of Stephens's venture. In 1683 he published a translation of Anacreon
edited by Francis Willis and Thomas Wood, which was inspired by Cowley,
whose versions are included, as is Oldham's imitation of *The Cup*, which
appeared in his *Poems, and Translations* the same year.

Stephens's interests extended beyond poetry. In 1683 he commissioned
White Kennett to translate Erasmus's *Moriae Encomium,* which was
published as *Witt against Wisdom.* Only three days after delivering his copy
to Stephens, Kennett was invited by him to take part in a collaborative
translation of Cornelius Nepos.[68] Among Kennett's fellow-contributors
to Cornelius Nepos were Creech, Thomas Tullie and Matthew Morgan,
who had written a prefatory poem to Kennett's Erasmus that also praised
Creech's Lucretius, and claimed that the English had now surpassed the
French in the art of translation.[69] It looks very much as if we have here a
group of scholars with common interests, who were aware of the achievement of the French in making the classics available to the general reader
through translations, and who were beginning to do the same job
themselves.

But Stephens was not the only enterprising publisher in Oxford at this
time. From the early 1670s Dr Fell, the Dean of Christ Church, had actively
been establishing the concern that was to develop into the Oxford
University Press. His colleagues in the enterprise were Sir Leoline Jenkins,
Principal of Jesus, Dr Thomas Yates, Principal of Brasenose, and Sir
Joseph Williamson, Secretary of State. The early concerns of the group
were in producing classical and theological works, but of special interest
is a problem that arose in January 1672. The printers had run out of

copy, and in order 'not to keep them on play-wages', Fell and Yates found someone to make a rapid translation from Rapin. His *Reflections upon the Use of Eloquence of These Times* was soon followed by *A Comparison between the Eloquence of Demosthenes and Cicero*. It is curious that there is no mention of Rapin's name either in the extant correspondence between the publishers or on the title pages, which simply say: 'Translated from the French'. Was this in itself sufficient commendation to attract customers? It is also notable that the *Reflections* were being simultaneously and independently translated in London, and both versions appeared in the same year as the French original.[70]

There is one personal glimpse of Oldham at Oxford. The anonymous author of the biography in the 1722 edition of Oldham gives the following relation, which, though perhaps coloured by hindsight, is worth preserving:

> As to the Person of Mr. *Oldham*, Mr. *Slater*, a Bookseller now at *Eton*, who served his Apprentiship at *Oxford*, assured us he knew Him well, and was often happy in his Company. He said, his Stature was Tall, the Make of his Body very thin, his Face long, his Nose prominent, his Aspect unpromising, but *Satire* was in his *Eye*. He was Consumptive not a little, increased by Study and Application to Learned Authors, of whom He knew much, as is plain from his SATIRES *against the* JESUITS, where there is as much Learning as Wit discovered.[71]

Not bothering to complete his BA by determination, Oldham returned to Gloucestershire in 1674 – 'much against his humour and inclinations' says Wood – to help out in his father's school, and in 1676 moved to Croydon as an usher at Whitgift School. Thereafter he served as tutor in the households of Sir Edward Thurland and William Hicks, enjoyed or endured, *c.* 1681, a period of independence in London, and finally attracted the patronage of William Pierrepoint, Earl of Kingston, at whose house in Holme Pierrepoint, Nottinghamshire, he died in December 1683.[72]

It would not be sensible to attempt any precise equation between Oldham's education and the poems that he was to write. We can be certain, however, that at school and university he would have been introduced to a range of classical authors; told to be selective in his use of them; thoroughly drilled in language and literature by construing, translating and composing. Although there was a tendency to reduce literature into maxims, Oxford was becoming aware of the work of the French editors and critics who were reviving Erasmus's concern for the transmission of classical literature in a form accessible to non-specialist readers. Oxford men were beginning to translate the classics as never before, and by Oldham's death there were many translations of complete works and separate poems, whereas at his graduation ten years earlier this activity had barely begun. Oxford was also steeped in theological controversy. Oldham's education thus prepared the ground both for his translations and for the *Satyrs upon the Jesuits*. It was necessary, but it was not sufficient. New stimuli would be required to help Oldham to achieve the freedom to write and translate in a non-scholastic way, and the chief of these was to be Boileau. But before examining his discovery of Boileau, we must first consider Oldham's early poetry and two principal influences on it, Cowley and Rochester.

2

INDIRECTIONS

The Earl of Rochester is said to have admired Cowley the most among the English poets, and Boileau among the French.[1] These are the three writers who are the presiding geniuses of Oldham's early poetry. I shall be arguing later that it was in his *annus mirabilis* of 1678 that Oldham began to discover where his true talent lay, and that his discovery was in part due to a recognition of what Boileau had to teach him, particularly as a practitioner of recreative translation from classical poetry. But before 1678 Oldham's verse is largely influenced by Cowley and Rochester (themselves notable translators) and their influence upon his style and choice of subject never completely disappeared in the course of what was, after all, a very brief career.

Looking back on his life, Cowley reflected that 'a warlike, various, and a tragical age is best to *write of*, but worst to *write in*'.[2] From his schooldays times had been, if not tragic, at best unsettled. He was brought up in the 1630s, years which certainly seemed golden in retrospect to the Earl of Clarendon, but which even he had to admit were anxious to those who lived through them. There was no parliament; the king had sent the nobles back to their estates; prospects of political advancement were uncertain. But at least to the bedridden Ben Jonson the rising generation must have seemed promising. Apart from his own Sons, his talented young friends included Thomas Hobbes and the Tew Circle around Lucius Cary. Dissension and war did not entirely ruin those hopes, but the fruits were very different from what might once have been looked for. Hobbes's *De Cive* and *Leviathan* are more urgent and polemical than their Tevian original, *The Elements of Law*. Falkland died young and disillusioned, and the politics of Tew survived neither in Clarendon's firm royalism nor in Waller's enfeebled moderation. The Sons of Ben managed no achievement equivalent to Jonson's own, and their *Ionsonus Virbius* makes sad reading.[3] They left the next generation little to go by.

Cowley was born too late to be one of the Sons, but he did profess a

primary debt to Jonson, and in his *Poems* of 1656 we meet odd remi-
niscences of the pre-war culture. Cowley writes under a double burden.
Not only does he have an investment in vanished values: he also carries the
pressure of the expectations created by his own precosity. He admits that
his early works he felt obliged

> ... by Discretion to conceal and suppress ... as *Promises* and
> *Instruments* under my own hand, whereby I stood *engaged* for
> more then I have been able to *perform*; in which truly, if I have
> failed, I have the real excuse of the *honestest* sort of *Bankrupts*,
> which is, to have been made *Unsolvable*, not so much by their
> own *negligence* and *ill-husbandry*, as by some notorious accidents
> and publick disasters (The Preface (1668), *Poems*, p.9).

The significance of Cowley's motto, *Tentanda via est*, was made explicit
by Dryden when he too came to consider the legacy of Jonson's contemporaries: 'We acknowledge them our Fathers in wit, but they have ruin'd
their Estates themselves before they came to their childrens hands ...
There is no bayes to be expected in their Walks; *Tentanda via est qua me
quoque possum tollere humo*.'[4]

In his verses *To the Lord Falkland* Cowley celebrates a man who
embodied the virtues of this lost generation:

> There all the *Sciences* together meet,
> And every *Art* does all her *Kindred* greet,
> Yet justle not, nor quarrel; but as well
> Agree as in some *Common Principle*.
>   (*Poems*, p. 19)

There is a tranquil strength in this union of virtues and abilities in Falkland. These values are essentially Jonsonian. Very similar in this respect is
the poem *On the Death of Sir Henry Wootton*, which bears the clear
impress of Jonson's *Epigrammes*:

> He's gone to *Heav'n* on his *Fourth Embassie*.
> On earth he travell'd often; not to say
> H'had been abroad, or pass loose *Time* away.
> In whatsoever Land he chanc'd to come,
> He read the *Men* and *Manners*, bringing home
> Their *Wisdom*, *Learning*, and their *Pietie*,
> As if he went *to Conquer*, not to *See*.
>   (*Poems*, p. 20)

This recalls Jonson's poem to Sir William Roe:

ROE (and my ioy to name) th'art now, to goe
    Countries, and climes, manners, and men to know,
T'extract, and choose the best of all these knowne,
    And those to turne to bloud, and make thine owne:
May windes as soft as breath of kissing friends,
    Attend thee hence; and there, may all thy ends,
As the beginnings here, proue purely sweet,
    And perfect in a circle alwayes meet.
                    (*Epigrammes,* CXXVIII)

Cowley's lines are neatly turned, but they lack that supple rhythm of
Jonson's which marks his epigram as an expression of believed values.
Already in Cowley's

He did the utmost *Bounds* of *Knowledge* find,
He found them not so large as was his *Mind.*
               (*Poems*, p. 20)

there is a wooden movement that matches the banal thought. Jonson's
centripetal conception of an exploration that strengthens one's living
centre has become the centrifugal pursuit of 'the utmost *Bounds* of *Knowledge*', an empty phrase that anticipates the inflated rhetoric of Oldham's
Satyr against Vertue.

    I have no doubt that Cowley believed in the values expressed by Jonson
and exemplified by Falkland and Wotton, but they were the hallmark of a
past generation, of a vanished style and purpose. It does not seem that
Cowley was able to possess these values inwardly in such a way that they
might provide a real source for his own verse. When in these *Miscellanies*
of 1656 we do find poems that embody Cowley's own discoveries, they
are disturbingly different. Although *The Mistress* was one of the most
popular series of love poems in the century, there is in Cowley a strong
tendency to disparage love. It might be argued that what Cowley despises
in his *Ode* ('Here's to thee, *Dick*') is only 'whining Love', but sexuality is
presented by a reductive imagination:

With all thy servile pains what canst thou win,
But an *ill-favor'd*, and *uncleanly Sin?*
A thing so vile, and so short-liv'd,
That *Venus Joys* as well as she
With reason may be said to be
From the neglected *Foam* deriv'd. (*Poems*, p. 26)

This perspective anticipates the translations of pseudo-Petronius *Against*

Fruition that Oldham and others made in the Restoration, but it lacks their wit. This tendency is seen again in the poem *On the Death of Mr. Crashaw*:

> Still the old *Heathen Gods* in *Numbers* dwell,
> The *Heav'enliest* thing on Earth still keeps up *Hell* ...
> Nay with the worst of Heathen dotage We
> (Vain men!) the *Monster Woman Deifie*.
>
> *(Poems,* p. 48)

Undermining Cowley's language is the imperfect correlation between private feeling and public statement: the former remains imperfectly defined while the latter appears merely quirky, carrying little general truth.

Cowley considered that the composition of religious poetry was an important task that his age had neglected, yet he also recognised that his own attempt was inadequate, and abandoned the *Davideis* unfinished and imperfectly revised because of a lack both of 'Leisure' and 'Appetite':

> I am far from assuming to my self to have fulfilled the duty of
> this weighty undertaking: But sure I am, that there is nothing
> yet in our *Language* (nor perhaps in *any*) that is in any degree
> answerable to the *Idea* that I conceive of it *(Poems,* p. 14).

Why was it that there could be no achievement to match Cowley's conception? The *Davideis* was in design not only impossibly full of diverse incidents, but also an *exemplum* of an ideal progress from adversity to triumph, following the course of 'this young *Prince*; who from so small beginnings, through such infinite troubles and oppositions, by such miraculous virtues and excellencies, and with such incomparable variety of wonderful actions and accidents, became the greatest *Monarch* that ever sat on the most *famous* Throne of the whole Earth' *(Poems,* p. 12). Epic this might be — in the Hollywood sense — but one wonders whether any human materials for such a conception were to hand. Cowley had to abandon *The Civil War* when events became too intractable, and some of the verse was adapted for the heroic *Davideis*. Cowley had ideas about the fall of man, and about perfect kings, but did he have much insight into common human nature?

Aspiration — the 'Idea' that Cowley conceived of himself and his vocation — seems rarely to have issued in achieved poetry. In the case of the *Davideis* it may be because the poem was chiefly nourished by (and designed to nourish in its turn) the millenial yearnings of a man who was himself suffering 'troubles and oppositions'. The pressures of precocious

success, the desire to emulate Donne and Jonson, and the need for consolation in private and public adversity, all these conspired to persuade
him to accept intention for achievement.

Here are the opening lines of the *Davideis*:

> I Sing the *Man* who *Judahs Scepter* bore
> In that right hand which held the *Crook* before;
> Who from best *Poet*, best of *Kings* did grow;
> The two chief *gifts Heav'n* could on *Man* bestow.
> Much danger first, much toil did he sustain,
> Whilst *Saul* and *Hell* crost his strong fate in vain.
>
> (*Poems*, p. 242)

This is telling, not showing. The expository manner — which might have
been suitable for an opening — is laboured, and no imaginative grasp of the
material is ordering its presentation. Phrases such as 'that right hand
which' and 'did grow' are clumsy, while the insistence in '*Saul* and *Hell*'
and 'strong fate' seems a recourse of weakness. But in case we should be
tempted to dismiss the passage — or the poem — as of no importance, it is
worth recording that these very lines came into Oldham's mind when he
was trying to find an heroic model for the opening of *The Desk*.

But it would be wrong to suggest that the whole poem was written in
this doggedly dutiful spirit. The description of hell caught the imagination
of contemporaries, though even here we find both the fine verse-music of:

> Where their vast *Court* the *Mother-waters* keep,
> And undisturbed by *Moons* in silence sleep.
>
> (*Poems*, p. 244)

and the heavy-handed:

> Where he the growth of *fatal Gold* does see.

It was perhaps not wholly fortuitous that the passage was so much imitated
by the writers of lurid broadsides, or to mock effect. Cowley's presentation of Satan is crude:

> Thrice did he knock his Iron teeth, thrice howl,
> And into frowns his wrathful forehead rowl.
> His eyes dart forth red flames which scare the *Night*,
> And with worse *Fires* the trembling *Ghosts* affright.
>
> (*Poems*, p. 245)[5]

Cowley's Envy is also a disturbing creation, disturbing not because we feel
challenged to recognise our own experience of envy, but precisely because

there is so little of that penetration in the image, and so much interest on the part of the poet in the repulsive details — an interest that becomes wanton:

> *Envy* at last crawls forth from that dire throng,
> Of all the direful'st; her black locks hung long,
> Attir'd with curling *Serpents*; her pale skin
> Was almost dropt from the sharp bones within,
> And at her breast stuck *Vipers* which did prey
> Upon her panting heart, both night and day
> Sucking black *bloud* from thence, which to repair
> Both night and day they left fresh *poysons* there.
> Her garments were deep stain'd in humane gore,
> And torn by her own hands, in which she bore
> A knotted whip, and bowl, that to the brim
> Did with green gall, and juice of wormwood swim.
>
> (*Poems*, p. 246)

There may be an element of degenerate Spenser in this, but if so it is a mode that no longer carries its original moral purpose very clearly, for the apocalyptic strain becomes almost autonomous of the poem's overt intention:

> shall *Mighty We*
> The glory of our wrath to *him* afford?
> Are *We* not *Furies* still? and *you* our *Lord*?
> At thy dread anger the fixt *World* shall shake,
> And frighted *Nature* her own *Laws* forsake.
>
> (*Poems*, p. 246)

We begin to hear the rhetoric of Garnet and Loyola from the *Satyr upon the Jesuits*:

> Lives yet that hated *en'my* of our *cause*?
> Lives *He* our mighty projects to oppose?
> Can *His* weak innocence, and Heaven's care
> Be thought security from what *we* dare?
> Are you then *Jesuits*? are you so for nought?
>
> (*SJ* 6)

But if Cowley sometimes indulged an inflated and wanton rhetoric — a centrifugal impulse — he was nevertheless also one of those who possess what H.A. Mason has called '*centripetal minds*, minds with some sort of homing instinct for inward-tending movements whenever they sense that they are being extravagant or affected'.[6] In both impulses Cowley resembles Oldham.

The centripetal instinct in Cowley is most clearly shown in his writing on friendship and retirement, and here we do find that he is the heir to Jonsonian humanism. His poem *On the Death of Mr. William Hervey* achieves an imaginative and elegiac felicity:

> 6.
> Ye fields of *Cambridge*, our dear *Cambridge*, say,
> Have ye not seen us walking every day?
> Was there a *Tree* about which did not know
>   The *Love* betwixt us two?
> Henceforth, ye gentle *Trees*, for ever fade;
>   Or your sad branches thicker joyn,
>   And into darksome shades combine,
> *Dark* as the *Grave* wherein my *Friend* is laid.
>   (*Poems*, p. 34)

Yet in the same poem we find:

> 12.
> *Knowledge* he only sought, and so soon caught,
> As if for him *Knowledge* had rather *sought*.
> Nor did more *Learning* ever crowded lie
>   In such a short *Mortalitie*.
> When ere the skilful *Youth* discourst or writ,
>   Still did the *Notions* throng
>   About his eloquent Tongue,
> Nor could his *Ink* flow faster then his *Wit*.
>   (*Poems*, p. 35)

Here the wit is not felicitous but banal. But alongside this flat, expository manner we have the plain strength of:

> We'have lost in him *Arts* that not yet are *found*.

and the imaginative beauty of:

> Then down in peace and innocence he lay,
>   Like the *Suns* laborious light,
>   Which still in *Water* sets at Night,
> *Unsullied* with his *Journey* of the *Day*.
>   (*Poems*, p. 36)

The poem appears to try several modes because distrustful of its own effectiveness. This lack of confidence in his poetry also appears in Cowley's habit of bolstering the *Pindarique Odes* and *Davideis* with voluminous notes.

It was perhaps in the *Essays in Verse and Prose* that Cowley was most significantly a transmitter of the classical heritage, or at least that part of it which was used to celebrate and define 'The Happy Man'.[7] Cowley's versions of the key passages in Horace, Virgil, Seneca and Martial, though they reduce the poets to a uniform tone, do make the material current in English. It is possible that the very instability of Cowley's language made it easier for poets to use this material in their own work. Poems such as his *Ode Upon Liberty* have vital subjects but are not dauntingly coherent achievements:

> These ['the Great'] are by various Tyrants Captive lead.
> Now wild Ambition with imperious force
> Rides, raines, and spurs them like th'unruly Horse.
>   And servile Avarice yoakes them now
>   Like toilsome Oxen to the Plow.
> And sometimes Lust, like the Misguiding Light,
> Drawes them through all the Labyrinths of Night.[8]

Here the language veers from the imaginative to the expository, sometimes achieving an epigrammatic freshness:

> To thy bent Mind some relaxation give,
> And steal one day out of thy Life to Live.

Dryden turned to this poem when composing his translation of Horace's *Carm.* III. xxix, and Oldham used one of its lines, 'Unhappy Slave, and Pupil to a Bell!' in a context in which he examines liberty not in Cowley's discursive way but by depicting the miseries of a poor chaplain in a wealthy household, where such men are literally 'Slaves to an Hour, and Vassals to a Bell!' (*PT* 142). Cowley's influence lay in the transmission of large concerns and small turns of phrase.

Oldham found in Cowley a variety of forms and subjects that helped him to make a start on his own writing. *The Mistress* offered neat love verses whose expressions, like those of Waller, were sufficiently detachable to be appropriated in Oldham's poems to Cosmelia.[9] The scriptural verses that were part of many a poet's repertoire continued the practice of paraphrasing the Proverbs and Psalms that had been a standard school exercise. Oldham has paraphrases of Psalm 137 and the Te Deum, and his poem *David's Lamentation* is a late scion of the *Davideis*. Cowley's epic was the most influential attempt at that form between Spenser and Milton, and provided the Restoration with a model for the heroic manner, though not itself managing to incarnate heroic values. The *Miscellanies* were backward-looking to the age of Jonson, and their ethos could not be inherited. Cowley's genial grace was also hard to inherit. Oldham probably comes closest to doing this in those drinking-songs which approximate in spirit to Cowley's *Anacreontiques*. The wit of Cowley's *The Country Mouse* is more of a personal achievement than a commonly accessible 'mock-heroic' mode:

> At the large foot of a fair hollow tree,
> Close to plow'd ground, seated commodiously,
> His antient and Hereditary House,
> There dwelt a good substantial Country-Mouse . . .
> *(Essays*, p. 414)

If we compare this with the tone of Oldham's beast-fable in *A Satyr addressed to a Friend* we find that Oldham's tone is more astringent, the mark not only of a different private temper but of a generation with new interests. Cowley's selection from the classical heritage met his own needs, but that heritage is multivalent, and he had not looked to those parts of it which were to form the *points de repère* for Oldham and those others of his generation who took their cue from Boileau.

The use that Oldham made of Cowley's pindaric form exemplifies the strengths and limitations of Cowley as a model. Oldham's *To the Memory of Mr. Charles Morwent* derives from Cowley both in form and conceit, but (less demonstrably) may also depend upon Cowley's verse-music. The opening of stanza XXI perhaps has something of the movement of the lines on Hervey and on the mother-waters:

> Thy Soul within such silent Pomp did keep,
> As if Humanity were lull'd asleep.
> So gentle was thy Pilgrimage beneath,
>   Time's unheard Feet scarce make less Noise,
> Or the soft Journey which a Planet goes.
>   Life seem'd all calm as its last Breath.
> A still Tranquillity so husht thy Breast,
>   As if some *Halcyon* were its Guest,
>   And there had built her nest.
> (*R* 68)

Cowley always contributed to Oldham's language, but the truly creative springs of his poetry were elsewhere.

Until his death in 1680, Rochester's poetry circulated almost entirely in manuscript copies, this chancy and sometimes clandestine method no doubt helping to enhance the legend. Something of the poetry and the legend must have reached Oldham at Croydon, through contacts that we cannot now trace, for we find him writing verse that attempts to share some of Rochester's subjects and tones. But it appears that this interest was soon reciprocated, for it is reported that Rochester and other 'Wits' visited Oldham one day at Whitgift school.[10]

The poem that had chiefly attracted them was probably the one commonly known as the *Satyr against Vertue*, dated July 1676 in Oldham's fair copy, where it has the sub-title 'Suppos'd to be spoken by a Court-Hector at Breaking of yᵉ Dial in Privy-Garden' (RMS 2), a reference to the episode in June 1675 when Rochester and some friends smashed the glass sundial in the king's Privy Garden. This was one of Oldham's poems that most appealed to Pope; here is one of the many passages that Pope marked as specially fine:

> A true, and brave transgressor ought
> To sin with the same height of spirit, *Caesar* fought:
> Mean-Soul'd offenders now no honours gain,
> Only debauches of the nobler strain.
> Vice well-improv'd yields bliss, and fame beside,
> And some for sinning have been deifi'd.
> Thus the lewd Gods of old did move,
> By these brave methods to the seats above.
> Ev'n *Jove* himself, the Sovereign Deity,
> Father and King of all th' immortal Progeny,
> Ascended to that high Degree;
> By crimes above the reach of weak Mortality.
> He Heav'n one large Seraglio made,
> Each Goddess turn'd a glorious Punk o'th' trade;
> And all that Sacred place
> Was fill'd with Bastard Gods of his own race:
> Almighty Lech'ry got his first repute,
> And everlasting whoring was his chiefest Attribute.
> (*SJ* 103-4)[11]

If we compare this passage with, say, Pope's own relish of divine love-making in *Iliad* XIV, or Dryden's in *Sylvae* and the *Fables*, Oldham's ironic celebration of libertine extravagance appears narrow and joyless; his tone lacks the generous relish of the more mature Dryden and Pope. Sometimes Oldham imports his language ready-made from sources in Cowley; one such case is:

> 'Tis I the bold *Columbus*, only I,
>   Who must new Worlds in Vice descry,
>   And fix the pillars of unpassable iniquity.
>   (*SJ* 109)[12]

As that last phrase suggests, Oldham's constrained imagination relies heavily upon negatives and vagueness to express this wild indulgence:

> Somewhat compleatly wicked, some vast Gyant-crime,
>   Unknown, unheard, unthought of by all past and present time.
>   (*SJ* 108)

The poem's subtitle indicates that it was written 'In imitation of Mr *Cowley*' and Cowley may have led Oldham not only into the exclamatory mode, and the inflated language, but also into a flatness of verse-rhythm. Cowley himself had said that although the versification of his *Pindarique Odes* might appear to be rough, it would be found to be otherwise if the verse was properly pronounced. But Oldham seems not to have paid much attention to this point when borrowing the form, nor, indeed, to have heeded Cowley's warning that 'though the *Liberty* of them may incline a man to believe them easie to be composed, yet the undertaker will find it otherwise'.[13] Some of Oldham's characteristic lines in this poem are scarcely recognisable as verse.

The *Satyr against Vertue* was intended ironically, though some of Oldham's contemporaries evidently misunderstood this, as has one modern commentator.[14] Oldham assured his readers that the *Satyr against Vertue* was not given that title by him, and was meant 'to abuse those, who valued themselves upon their Wit and Parts in praising Vice, and to shew, that others of sober Principles, if they would take the same liberty in Poetry, could strain as high rants in Profaneness as they' (*SJ* A4r). Yet although we may accept that the poem was consciously designed as an ironic celebration of (and therefore a serious satire upon) libertine ways, irony is a complex matter, and it is by no means improbable that this ironic intention allowed Oldham to indulge in 'high rants in Profaneness' from which he would otherwise have considered himself bound to refrain.[15] Whatever his intention, Oldham has allowed his poetry to celebrate dissipation with a crudity of expression and rhythm that comes all too easily. The danger is that his poetic resource may become 'subdu'd / To what it workes in, like the Dyers hand'.

Curiously this instability extends also to the *Apology* that follows the *Satyr*. Anxious that we should not miss the apparently Erasmian purpose of the preceding poem,[16] the *Apology* insists that Oldham's muse 'only acted here in Masquerade'. But the tone of the *Apology* is confused. Oldham appears self-conscious, and perhaps self-righteous too:

> Our Poet has a different taste of Wit,
> Nor will to common Vogue himself submit.
> Let some admire the Fops whose Talents lie
> In venting dull insipid Blasphemy;
> He swears, he cannot with those terms dispense,
> Nor will be damn'd for the repute of sense.
> Wit's name was never to profaneness due,
> For then you see he could be witty too:
> He could Lampoon the State and Libel Kings,[17] ⎫
> But that he's Loyal, and knows better things, ⎬
> Than Fame, whose guilty Birth from Treason springs. ⎭
>
> (*SJ* 112)

This heavy-handed solemnity is oddly close to obscenity in the reference to 'our Nobles',

> Whose nauseous Poetry can reach no higher
> Than what the Codpiece, or its God inspire.
> So lewd, they spend at quill; you'd justly think,
> They wrote with something nastier than Ink.
>
> (*SJ* 113)

This humourless satire leads to an assertion of Oldham's poetic aims:

> To noble Satyr he'd direct his aim,
> And by't Mankind, and Poetry reclaim,
> He'd shoot his Quills just like a Porcupine
> At Vice, and make them stab in every Line.
>
> (*SJ* 114)

The instability of Oldham's manner as a moral satirist is also apparent in a poem which he never acknowledged in print, but which, like the *Satyr against Vertue*, appeared in the 1680 editions of Rochester.[18] *Upon the Author of a Play called 'Sodom'* is ostensibly an attack upon the perpetrator of an obscene play, but it uses such detailed sexual and scatological abuse that one can only suppose that it became an opportunity for Oldham to indulge his imagination with complete license, perhaps with some cathartic effect. Why the comparatively light-hearted obscenity of *Sodom* should have drawn such a reply from Oldham is mysterious.

Oldham indulged his imagination more readably in *Sardanapalus*, which is still unpublished.[19] It is a sexual fantasy dressed in quasi-heroic language, celebrating the exploits of a monarch with only one interest:

> Methinks I see the now in full *Seraglio* stand ⎫
>   With Love's great Scepter in thy hand – ⎬
> And over all the Spatious Realm thy power extend ⎭
> Ten Thousand Maids lye prostrate at thy feet
> Ready thy Pintle's high Commands to meet.

Probably *Sardanapalus* was intended in part as a satirical allusion to Charles II.[20] Burnet wrote that Charles, who at the outbreak of the great fire of London was found feasting, 'was compared to Nero, who sung while Rome was burning, and was made look worse than Sardanapalus',[21] so it may have been a current comparison. Several features of the poem suggest that Oldham may have been attempting to emulate Rochester's 'sceptre' lampoon on Charles, of which both the previous and the following quotation may be echoes:

> Another justly merits Subsidies
> At whose blest touch Imperial Pego do's vouchsafe to rise
> But happy Shee, & most of all rewarded is –
> Whoever can invent new motions to advance ye bliss –

But whether as satire or as fantasy, *Sardanapalus* is an unsophisticated piece.

We may note, however, that Oldham was taking a serious (if ambivalent) interest in erotic literature at this time, for on page 88 of the Rawlinson manuscript is the heading, 'In Aloi[si]ae Sigeae Toletanae Satyram Sotadicam', dated 7 May 1677, implying that he intended an attack on Nicholas Chorier's *Aloisiae Sigeae Toletanae Satyra Sotadica de arcanis Amoris et Veneris*, a pornographic book that was composed around 1660 and circulated in England in the mid-1670s.[22]

It may have been partly under the influence of Cowley and Rochester that Oldham tried his hand at this unstable mixture of erotic, heroic and invective verse. But Oldham took a more serious interest in the poetry of love in *The Passion of Byblis*, which owes its existence to the volume of *Ovid's Epistles* published in 1680 with contributions by Dryden, amongst others. Oldham's own account of its genesis is as follows:

> 'Twas occasion'd upon Reading the late Translations of *Ovid's Epistles*, which gave him a mind to try what he could do upon

a like Subject. Those being already forestal'd, he thought fit to make choice of this of the same Poet, whereon perhaps he has taken too much liberty. Had he seen Mr. *Sandys* his Translation before he begun, he never durst have ventur'd: Since he has, and finds reason enough to despair of his undertaking. But now 'tis done, he is loth to burn it ... 'Tis the first attempt, he ever made in this kind, and likely enough to be the last, his vein (if he may be thought to have any) lying another way (*SJ* A4*v*).[23]

It seems that the particular subject that caught Oldham's interest was the psychology of female passion. In part this leads him to a more explicit sensuality: with Ovid's

> Pro Venus, & tenera volucer cum matre Cupido,
> Gaudia quanta tuli! quam me manifesta libido
> Contigit! ut jacui totis resoluta medullis!
> > (IX.481-3)

and Sandys's close rendering:

> O *Venus*, and with thee, thou winged Boy!
> What pleasure, what content, had I that night!
> How lay I all dissolued in delight!
> > (p. 311)

compare Oldham:

> 'Gods! what a scene of joy was that! how fast
> 'I clasp'd the Vision to my panting breast!
> 'With what fierce bounds I sprung to meet my bliss,
> 'While my rapt soul flew out in every kiss!
> 'Till breathless, faint, and softly sunk away,
> 'I all dissolv'd in reeking pleasures lay!'
> > (*SJ* 123)

But to find the vocabulary to analyse Byblis's state of mind was not easy. Oldham's expansion of Ovid's 'dubia ... mente' (472) into a couplet offers a dichotomy that continues the crude drama:

> Now likes, and now abhors her guilty flame,
> By turns abandon'd to her Love, and Shame.
> > (*SJ* 122)

Yet Oldham imagines more subtly when writing of unperceived change: where Ovid has 'nullos intelligit ignes' (457) Oldham writes:

> At first her new-born Passion owns no name,
> A glim'ring Spark scarce kindling into flame;
>
> (*SJ* 120)

which shifts the metaphor from the fires of passion to the heart as a chaos in which sparks break out of the darkness. This is a concise version of the extended metaphor in *A Letter from the Country* (examined in Chapter 3) and the interest that Oldham shows there in unfelt, unperceived change is aptly revived for Byblis:

> Yet knows she not, she loves, but still does grow,
> Insensibly the thing, she does not know.
>
> (*SJ* 121)

In the *Letter* it is the Fancy that creates images from chaos; so too in *Byblis*, where the desires repressed by the conscious mind are given free rein by the unconscious in dreams:

> Nor dare she yet with waking Thoughts admit
> A wanton hope: but when returning night
> With Sleep's soft gentle spell her Senses charms,
> Kind fancy often brings him to her Arms.
>
> (*SJ* 121)

This presentation of female sexuality unnerved John Dennis, who read his Ovid differently:

> The Sentiments are so tender and yet so delicate, the expressions so fit and withal so easie, with that facility which is proper to express Love, and peculiar to this Charming Poet; the turns of Passion are so surprizing and yet so natural, and there seems to be something in the very sound of the Verse so soft and so pathetick, that a man who reads the Original, must have no sense of these matters if he is not transported with it.[24]

Introducing his own translation of this eminently decorous Ovid, Dennis censured Oldham for 'two or three Passages of her Letter ... in which she says some things that are by no means consistent with that Modesty, which she ought to have, as a Lady, a Virgin, and a Woman of Honor' (Sig. A2*v*). Some lines that Dennis singles out for rebuke are:

> 'Let neither awe of Fathers frowns, nor shame ⎫
> 'For ought that can be told by babbling fame, ⎬
> 'Nor any gastlier fantom, fear can frame, ⎭
> 'Frighten, or stop us in our way to bliss. (*SJ* 131)

Dennis objects that Oldham has allowed Byblis to propose so many difficulties that her brother will be too frightened even if he were inclined to comply. Perhaps so; Oldham, however, has not concerned himself with this kind of quasi-naturalistic plausibility but has adopted a different strategy. He has given Byblis a long passage of libertine rhetoric. The lines just quoted are similar both in vocabulary and rhetoric to what we find in the *Satyr against Vertue* and the *Satyrs upon the Jesuits*. Indeed, there are moments when Byblis's language comes straight from Rochester himself:

> 'Let doating age debate of Law, and Right,
> 'And gravely state the bounds of just, and fit;
> 'Whose wisdom's but their envy, to destroy
> 'And bar those pleasures, which they can't enjoy: ...
> 'Without dull thinking we enjoyment trace,
> 'And call that lawful, whatsoe're does please.
> (*SJ* 130)[25]

Though this might frighten Byblis's brother, it would also signal to Restoration readers that the subject cannot be distanced as mere mythology, but has a contemporary purchase. It may be a rhetoric that is difficult for Oldham to control, but it is nevertheless more subtle than Dennis's overtly moralising alternative, which is even less plausible in context:

> O what infernal flame! What fury's this!
> Gods! from what height I plunge, to what abyss!
> Eternally farewell, O Honor, Vertue, Bliss!
> (p. 9)

Oldham's other ventures into the poetry of love are not remarkable. He tried his hand at a few popular Latin pieces: some Ovidian elegies, Horace's *Carm.* III.ix, Catullus to Lesbia, 'Petronius' against fruition. Though he has energy, he has no distinctive vision to bring to the subject, and although he occasionally reaches for a fashionably rakish manner (as in the version of Voiture) he lacks most of Rochester's gifts in this mode: concision, controlled cynicism, lyrical grace. There is also in much of Rochester's love poetry a generous humour, which Dryden shares, but which Oldham often makes sour or prurient.

When Rochester died in 1680, Oldham composed a long memorial poem, a translation of the *Epitaphios Bionos* by the Greek poet Moschus. The poem had never been one of the central features of the classical heritage, but it seems to have aroused since the Renaissance a significant occasional interest. Along with Bion's *Epitaphios Adonidos*, which Oldham also translated, it reached its seventeenth-century audiences in collections of the Greek Bucolic poets, which were usually issued in parallel Greek and Latin texts, and often appended to editions of Theocritus.[26] Several poets turned to the *Epitaphios Bionos* as a model, particularly when composing elegies for fellow-poets.[27]

In the Advertisement to *Some New Pieces* Oldham explains how he came to compose *Bion* and *The Lamentation for Adonis*:

> ... they were occasion'd by a report, that some persons found
> fault with the roughness of my Satyrs formerly publisht, tho,
> upon what ground they should do it, I could be glad to be in-
> form'd. Unless I am mistaken, there are not many lines but will
> endure the reading without shocking any Hearer, that is not too
> nice, and censorious. I confess, I did not so much mind the
> Cadence, as the Sense and expressiveness of my words, and there-
> fore chose not those, which were best dispos'd to placing them-
> selves in Rhyme, but rather the most keen, and tuant, as being
> the suitablest to my Argument. And certainly no one that
> pretends to distinguish the several Colours of Poetry, would
> expect that *Juvenal*, when he is lashing of Vice, and Villany,
> should flow so smoothly, as *Ovid*, or *Tibullus*, when they are
> describing Amours and Gallantries, and have nothing to disturb
> and ruffle the evenness of their Stile.
>
> Howbeit, to shew that the way I took, was out of choice,
> not want of judgment, and that my Genius is not wholly
> uncapable of performing upon more gay and agreeable Subjects,
> if my humor inclin'd me to exercise it, I have pitch'd upon
> these two, which the greatest men of sense have allow'd to
> be some of the softest and tenderest of all Antiquity. Nay, if
> we will believe *Rapin*, one of the best Criticks which these
> latter Ages have produc'd; they have no other fault, than that
> they are too exquisitely delicate for the Character of Pastoral,
> which should not seem too labour'd, and whose chief beauty
> is an unaffected air of plainness and simplicity (*SNP* a2v-a3r).

Although Oldham speaks highly of Rochester, the choice of this kind of poem to celebrate him suggests that Oldham is attempting to establish his independence from Rochester, just as he is also demonstrating that his abilities are not circumscribed by his previous satirical and licentious poetry. It is also apparent from this preface that Oldham's primary interest is in

attempting a new area of poetry, rather than finding a way to pay tribute
to Rochester. It is interesting that this new departure, like others in Oldham's work, is made under the influence of a French critic. He must already
have valued Rapin highly to have worked through the treatise *De Carmine
Pastorali*.[28] There he would have found Rapin keen to stress that pastoral
is a civilised mode, fit for men of genuine taste. 'I suspect', he says, 'that
this whole genre may seem frivolous to those who are but little inclined by
an educated taste to explore these more delightful studies', and among the
pastoral writers he believes that 'Moschus shows so much more elegance
than Theocritus, a more cultured urbanity. For what could be better
wrought or more appealing than the epitaph for Bion, or the poem on
runaway Cupid?'[29] For Rapin, pastoral delights both the classical scholar
and the cultured layman who relishes good literature.

Oldham has certainly succeeded in creating a smooth verse:

> No more, alas! no more that lovely Swain
> Charms with his tuneful Pipe the wondring Plain:
> Ceast are those lays, ceast are those sprightly airs,
> That woo'd our Souls into our ravisht Ears:
> For which the list'ning streams forgot to run,
> And Trees lean'd their attentive branches down:
> While the glad Hills, loth the sweet sounds to lose,
> Lengthen'd in Echoes every heav'nly close.
> Down to the melancholy Shades he's gone,
> And there to *Lethe*'s Banks reports his moan:
> Nothing is heard upon the Mountains now
> But pensive Herds that for their Master low:
> Straggling and comfortless about they rove,
> Unmindful of their Pasture, and their Love.
> *Come all ye* Muses, *come, adorn the Shepherd's Herse,*
> *With never-fading Garlands, never-dying Verse.*
>   (*SNP* 75-6)

Indeed, Ezra Pound said of *Bion*:

> Rococo, by to-morrow you may be unable to remember a line
> of it BUT try to find in English another passage of melody
> sustained for so long, i.e. verse to SING ... You can hardly read
> it without singing, there is no let up in the cantabile quality
> unless it be in one strophe containing a condensed history of
> British poetry.[30]

This undoubted cantabile quality is hard to analyse, but one might remark
how the rhythm of each line varies from

Ceast are those lays, ceast are those sprightly airs

to

Straggling and comfortless about they rove

while many lines have the normative smoothness of:

And Trees lean'd their attentive branches down.

It is notable that Oldham manages in these couplets a song-like eloquence that one never finds in his Cowleian odes. Between 1676 and 1680 he gradually abandoned the pindaric ode in favour of the couplet, which he learned to employ in a variety of modes. Pound suggests that *Bion* must have been written by a man whose friends were in the habit of playing good music, and indeed a commonplace book survives, made up largely of song texts, which passed to Oldham from the family of his patron William Pierrepoint.[31]

But however deft Oldham's cantabile pastoral may be, the poem is also a tribute to an idiosyncratic and controversial writer. By preserving the classical dress of his model Oldham manages a sly understatement:

> Love ever was the subject of his lays,
> And his soft lays did *Venus* ever please.
> (*SNP* 82)

But Oldham also handles Rochester's biography tactfully: Moschus's παρθενικᾶν ἐρόεντα φιλήματα, χείλεα παίδων (66: 'the pleasing kisses of maidens, the lips of the boys') is translated simply as:

> Mute is thy Voice, which could all hearts command,
> Whose pow'r no Sheperdess could e're withstand:
> (*SNP* 80)

while παίδων ἐδίδασκε φιλήματα (83: 'he taught kissing of boys') is omitted. Oldham departs from his classical setting to name the most eminent English poets (Spenser, Chaucer, Milton, Cowley, Denham, Philips, Waller) but returns to this diplomatic veil when he reaches controversial ground. Moschus's figure of Pan presumably now represents Dryden:

> *Pan* only ere can equal thee in Song,
> That task does only to great *Pan* belong:
> But *Pan* himself perhaps will fear to try,
> Will fear perhaps to be out-done by thee.
> (*SNP* 79)

Although Rochester and Dryden had been on good terms, they were by the time of Rochester's death on opposite sides in the curiously protean literary feud in the Court circle. Perhaps Oldham felt it was only decent to make his reference to Dryden obliquely — and in a form that was at once compliment, doubt and challenge.[32] Rapin thought that pastoral could have a calming effect on people in thrall to the martial clamour of epics;[33] some similar effect may be aimed at by Oldham in his creation of an attractive pastoral occupying the middle ground of literary contention, offering an eloquent but impersonal tribute.

The passage that most deserves those last adjectives comes towards the end of *Bion*. As well as responding to the libertine element in Rochester's work, Oldham also seems to have absorbed the other side of that philosophy which traded in the Restoration under the name of Epicurus. The contemplation of death that Rochester managed in his translation from Seneca's *Troades* is achieved again here:

> Alas! by what ill Fate, to man unkind,
> Were we to so severe a lot design'd?
> The meanest Flowers which the Gardens yield,
> The vilest Weeds, that flourish in the Field,
> Which must ere long lie dead in Winter's Snow,
> Shall spring again, again more vigorous grow:
> Yon Sun, and this bright glory of the day, ⎫
> Which night is hasting now to snatch away, ⎬
> Shall rise anew more shining and more gay: ⎭
> But wretched we must harder measure find,
> The great'st, the brav'st, the witti'st of mankind,
> When Death has once put out their light, in vain
> Ever expect the dawn of Life again:
> In the dark Grave insensible they lie,
> And there sleep out endless eternity.
>
> (*SNP* 84)

Though Oldham has taken hints here from the Bible, *Othello* and Rochester's *Satyr against Reason and Mankind*, the eloquence is his own. The eloquence is less anguished and uneasy than in Rochester's lines from *Troades*, more expansive in feeling — though one of the prices Oldham pays for that is a tendency to tautology. He is writing rather against the grain.

In the poems discussed in this chapter, written between 1675 and 1680, we undoubtedly hear some of Oldham's distinctive voices; but when writing close to Cowley and Rochester he is not finding his own true centre. Important as these two poets were to him in suggesting both subjects and techniques, they had faults that were too similar to his own tendencies. In Cowley's poetry the drama of his language is often insecure, and the copiousness becomes slack; Rochester is often metrically negligent and has only an erratic sense of artistic decorum, as regards both poetic language and poetic structure. Neither can offer Oldham quite the discipline he needs, and while his own efforts at disciplining and extending his talents (as in *Byblis* and *Bion*) are impressive, they also seem slightly forced. But one can 'by indirections find directions out'; and there was, concurrently with these experiments, a more productive struggle, which must now be examined in the poems of 1678.

3

1678

It was during the year 1678 that Oldham began to discover where his true vocation lay, and the process by which he achieved this involved his realising both a personal maturity and a sense of his relation to the wider traditions of poetry, both English and European. To say that Oldham was overcoming certain adolescent traits would be impertinent if it were not a change for which the chief evidence lies in the poetry itself. As for the poetic tradition, his work during this year moves away from those poems indebted largely to Cowley which had hitherto dominated his output, and begins to use most of the new sources that are to be the springs of his poetry until his death. In most cases these sources are in 1678 only touched upon and their potential scarcely grasped. But this is not surprising: spiritual and intellectual progress is rarely linear, and we shall find Oldham turning back to the same authors, the same interests, even the same phrases, during the years ahead. It will be necessary to work in some detail through Oldham's struggles with his sources in order to reconstruct how he established a more mature relationship to his inheritance – and, indeed, to see what 'maturity' in this context amounts to.

We may begin with two poems in which Oldham first writes of the achievement of his predecessors, and the nature of poetic creativity. *Upon the Works of Ben. Johnson* was written in the first quarter of 1678, and *The Praise of Homer*, though we have no precise date for it, is closely connected. The work of Homer and Jonson has brought them immortality, and this idea inspires Oldham to a small but appealing act of imagination in describing the ending of all achievements:

> Not that vast universal Flame,
> Which at the final Doom
> This beauteous Work of Nature must consume,
> And Heav'n and all its Glories in one Urn entomb,
> Will burn a nobler, or more lasting Frame:
> (*Homer* 165-9; *SNP* 72)

or in a less grandiloquent but more poignant image:

> Till the last Scene of this great Theatre,
> Clos'd, and shut down,
> The numerous Actors all retire,
> And the grand Play of human Life be done.
> (*Johnson* 164-7;*PT* 79)

These are of course traditional images, but they are far from banal. A similarly simple diction and eloquent rhythm is used in these lines on Homer:

> Not Statues cast in solid Brass,
> Nor those, which Art in breathing Marble does express,
> Can boast an equal Life, or lastingness
> With their well-polish'd Images, which claim
> A Nich in thy majestick Monuments of Fame.
> Here their embalm'd incorruptible memories
> Can proudest *Louvres*, and *Escurials* despise,
> And all the needless helps of *Aegypts* costly Vanities.
> No Blasts of Heaven, or Ruin of the Spheres,
> Not all the washing Tides of rolling years,
> Nor the whole Race of batt'ring time shall e're wear out
> The great Inscriptions, which thy Hand has wrought.
> (138-49; *SNP* 70-1)

Oldham is drawing upon Horace:

> EXEGI monumentum aere perennius,
> Regalique situ Pyramidum altius;
> Quod non imber edax, non Aquilo impotens
> Possit diruere, aut innumerabilis
> Annorum series, & fuga temporum.[1]
> (*Carm.* III.xxx)

Horace contributes to Oldham's lines the monuments, brass and pyramids ('Pyramids of Wit' in the line preceding our quotation) and something of the effect of time and weather. Oldham has also remembered his Virgil:

> excudent alii spirantia mollius aera,
> (credo equidem), vivos ducent de marmore voltus.[2]
> (*Aeneid* VI. 847-8)

and the resulting 'breathing Marble' antedates the *OED*'s first example of 'breathing' in this sense. The 'Tides of rolling years' are also a classical conception, and again apparently introduce into English this use of 'rolling'.

So Oldham, though employing a Cowleian form, has turned to the Latin poets for expression of the permanence of Homer's work. But what of the nature of that work? Homer is claimed to be 'our sole Text, and Holy Writ ... the Canon of authentick Wit alone', and the sole source of 'sense'. This estimate of Homer, anticipating Pope's '*Nature* and *Homer* were, he found the *same*', had been expressed before – for example by Chapman,[3] but still seems remarkable in a period when the classical heritage upon which poets drew was largely Latin. But despite the use of 'holy Writ' and 'Canon', Oldham's notion of Homer's achievement and authority is by no means static. He is

> the unexhausted Ocean, whence
> Sprung first, and still do flow th' eternal Rills of sence.
> (19-20; *SNP* 63)[4]

and had an 'all-piercing Eye'. Homer made voyages and 'bold Discoveries', just as Jonson did, who made the 'full Discovery' that had only been sketchily charted by the ancients, and steered

> a course more unconfin'd, and free,
> Beyond the narrow bounds, that pent Antiquity.
> (25-6; *PT* 70)

In his conception of the classical achievement Oldham is not being servile, or using the more rigid language of 'rules' that was coming into fashion in England, but instead is closer to Jonson's own formulation in his *Discoveries*:

> I know *Nothing* can conduce more to letters, then to examine
> the writings of the *Ancients*, and not to rest in their sole Auth-
> ority, or take all upon trust from them ... It is true they open'd
> the gates, and made the way, that went before us; but as Guides,
> not Commanders (VIII, 567).

In both poems Oldham has his eye uneasily upon the French. Jonson is praised for work that is all of English staple without French 'tinsel', but in *The Praise of Homer* Oldham regrets that English poets have to write in an insular language. This lack of universality for English was not a new complaint: Waller had written that

> Poets that lasting marble seek,
> Must carve in LATIN, or in GREEK:

> We write in sand, our language grows,
> And, like the tide, our work o'er-flows.[5]

Oldham's worry is less the immortality of English, more the opinion of foreign poets about the English achievement — an anxiety to appear respectable in French eyes that can be seen elsewhere in the claim that the English have surpassed the French in translating the classics — a claim found, for example, in Roscommon's *Essay on Translated Verse* (1684) and the prefatory poems to Creech's Lucretius (1682-3).

A Letter from the Country to a Friend in Town

This poem, composed in July 1678, was prompted by a verse letter from John Spencer, who was studying at the Inner Temple.[6] Part of Spencer's letter was clearly directed at a common type of contemporary poetry:

> Witts now are grown so Critically nice,
> That Wholsome Cleanly diet wo'nt suffice,
> And therfore, be the subject ne'er so pure,
> Prophane, & Bawdy, make the Garniture.
>   (RMS 201)

No doubt this was particularly aimed at Oldham, for

> S^r, you see, that fools sometimes spy faults;
> And standers-by see better Gamesters blotts.
>   (RMS 203)

The good poet must also be a good man:

> Nor wou'd I ever to that stile attaine,
> Which speaks good poets but Ill natur'd men;
> Whose spightfull muses, passing by the good,
> Forrage on filth, & poyson choose for food.
>   (RMS 202)

Spencer has recognised the dubious morality of the motives to satire:

> For no one can in earnest rayle at ills,
> Unlesse within himself their stings he feels,
> Nor with delight malitious Satyr read,
> Except its bitter'st gaul with gaul does meet.

> In kenning vice, those most Quicksighted are,
> Who in their brests its counterpart do wear.
>
> (RMS 203)

Oldham may well have felt this to be particularly apposite to the poems that he had just been writing. For despite his claims to moral intention in such pieces as the *Satyr against Vertue*, something intimate to the man himself — his language, his rhythm, his rhetoric — had been devoted to licence and sensation.

In a letter to an old college friend written on the 'day after Midsummer 77' he wrote that he now found 'more real Pleasure in living within Bounds, then when I allow'd myself ye largest Swinge'.[7] He was sensitive about the admission, and afraid of the ridicule of his old companions: evidently Spencer's letter a year later touched on an area where he was still unsure of himself. The published *Letter from the Country* does not discuss the question of the morality of satire that Spencer had raised, though it does include this reference to his poetry in deprecating terms:

> Oft have I tried (Heav'n knows) to mortifie
> This vile, and wicked lust of Poetry:
> But still unconquer'd it remains within,
> Fixt as an Habit, or some darling Sin.
>
> (86-9; *SNP* 122)

This is overtly ironic — in context its tone is almost bantering — and yet in many statements intended to be accepted as irony there is an unconscious assent to the literal sense of the words too. The imagery is in itself significant. Some of the drafts of the poem suggest that it is specifically the Rochesterian influence that Oldham is reacting against:

> I envy not our witty bawdy Peer
> All ye loth'd wretched Fame he dos acquire
> Whom Hell, Debauches, Claps & Lust inspire.
>
> (RMS 95)

The lines:

> To be an Author, have thy posted Name
> Fix'd up with Bills of Quack & publick Sham.
>
> (RMS 94)

may be a sour memory of the Alexander Bendo episode.[8] In any case,

Oldham's drafts point to the debasement of poetry in the Rochester circle:

> Poet! once thought an honourable Name,
> And stood with First-rates in ye lists of Fame,
> Match'd Priests & Prophets, almost justled Kings,
> Is now debas'd amongst ye meanest things ...
> What is ye Credit, which he gains by it,
> The Credit of a damn'd confounded Wit:
> Tis what I know & think, but cannot tell.
>
> (RMS 95)[9]

Perhaps he was conscious too of the debasement of his own gifts:

> Wit, y^t luxurious Plant, is often found,
> To bear ye most & best (Fruit) in moderate Ground,
> If too much forc'd, it strait to rankness thrives
> And turns to Branches all, & empty Leaves.
>
> (RMS 96)

What might a suitable 'moderate Ground' be? Among the same drafts is a couplet that expresses a commonplace from Horace:[10]

> Who would both Ends of Poetry unite
> He equally must profit & delight.
>
> (RMS 95)

Horace was to figure importantly in the finished *Letter*, and in more creative fashion than this isolated tag might suggest.

This is the opening of *A Letter from the Country*:

> As to that *Poet* (if so great a one, as he,
> May suffer in comparison with me)
> When heretofore in *Scythian* exile pent,
> To which he by ungrateful *Rome* was sent,
> If a kind Paper from his Country came,
> And wore subscrib'd some known, and faithful Name;
> That like a pow'rful Cordial, did infuse
> New life into his speechless gasping Muse,
> And strait his Genius, which before did seem
> Bound up in Ice, and frozen as the Clime,
> By its warm force, and friendly influence thaw'd,
> Dissolv'd apace, and in soft numbers flow'd:
> Such welcome here, dear Sir, your Letter had

> With me shut up in close constraint as bad:
> Not eager Lovers, held in long suspence,
> With warmer Joy, and a more tender sence
> Meet those kind Lines, which all their wishes bless,
> And Sign, and Seal deliver'd Happiness:
> (1-18; SNP 118-19)

The poem begins with a comparison of Oldham's plight with that of Ovid in exile. The parallel goes beyond the circumstances of the arrival of a letter, for Ovid appears to have felt a compulsion for poetry from his youth, though intended by his father for a more profitable public career. Although he was well acquainted with the leading literary men of his day, such as Virgil, Tibullus and Propertius, his relation with the Roman aristocracy remained one of client to patron. In the *Tristia*, which would have been known to Oldham since his schooldays, Ovid expresses regret for his previous licentious work.

In fashioning the compliment to Spencer that is the burden of the opening paragraph, Oldham has borrowed two formulations, one from Cowley —

> A Cordial, that restores our fainting breath,
> And Keeps up Life even after Death

and one from Dryden —

> your Applause and favour did infuse
> New life to my condemn'd and dying Muse.[11]

But it would be a mystery why Oldham chose this compliment at all unless the whole passage were inspired by a similar elegant compliment in the *Epistolae Ho-Elianae*:

> I was plung'd in a deep Fit of melancholy, *Saturn* had cast his black Influence o'er all my Intellectuals ... when a Letter of yours ... was brought me, which presently begot new Spirits within me ... it became an Antidote, or rather a most sovereign Cordial to me ... as so many choice Flowers strew'd here and there, which did cast such an odoriferous Scent, that they reviv'd all my Senses and dispell'd those dull Fumes which had formerly o'er-clouded my Brain: Such was the Operation of your most ingenious and affectionate Letter, and so sweet an Entertainment it gave me.[12]

Roger Fleming, writing to his elder brother Daniel in 1651 had filled his letter with extracts from Howell:[13] it was evidently still a useful source for the fashionably-phrased letter. 'Infuse' was taken up from Dryden's couplet, but I doubt whether the notion of 'infuse / New life' would have been worth remembering if it had not carried hints of another context:

> Her soft embraces soon infuse desire,
> His bones and marrow suddain warmth inspire.[14]

Unlike more crass expressions of the idea that we shall meet later, 'infuse' in Oldham's use carries a suitably subtle hint of the metaphoric connection between poetic and sexual creation. Also neatly used is 'influence', which aptly combines the activity of the sun with that of the patron, and leads into 'and in soft numbers flowed'.[15] The whole impression given by the first paragraph is of the writer in easy and relaxed command of his material. The rhetorical structure is firm but unobtrusive: the passage does not fall apart into its constituent couplets, but has an appealing variety of movement.

The paragraph closes with the lines:

> My grateful Thoughts so throng to get abroad,
> They over-run each other in the crowd:
> To you with hasty flight they take their way,
> And hardly for the dress of words will stay.
>   (19-22; *SNP* 119)

That thoughts take the dress of words was a commonplace that Spencer had raised in his letter:

> Words are but Cloggs to sense, then why shou'd Man
> Affect the hardest words, the heavy'est chain?
> Those phrases to conception giue most ease,
> W^{ch} soonest bring the fairest Images.
> By those wee nearest to that state arrive,
> Wher all discourse shall bee Intuitive;
> Wher Spirits sha'n't their Joys by Proxy tell,
> But tho'ts reach tho'ts without a Vehicle.
>   (RMS 201-2)

In December 1678 Oldham returned to the subject in a letter to Spencer:

> Vellem ego quidem (si Dijs placuisset) expeditiorem sensus
> exprimendi viam, quam quae verbis fit: Vellem breviorem
> jungendi commercia, quam quae literis peragitur. Quam piget,
> animum meum qui toties amicum quantumvis dissitum adire

potest non posse etiam sine tabellario se legendum praebere. At hoc solum Angelis indultum: Nobis, quibus non licet esse tam beatis, hoc modo communicandi sunt animi (RMS 280).[16]

This was a condition of being human, as Raphael pointed out to Adam in his speech on the variety of living parts of creation:

So from the root

Springs lighter the green stalk, from thence the leaves
More aerie, last the bright consummate floure
Spirits odorous breathes: flours and thir fruit
Mans nourishment, by gradual scale sublim'd
To vital Spirits aspire, to animal,
To intellectual, give both life and sense,
Fansie and understanding, whence the Soule
Reason receives, and reason is her being,
Discursive, or Intuitive; discourse
Is oftest yours, the latter most is ours,
Differing but in degree, of kind the same . . .

time may come when men

With Angels may participate, and find
No inconvenient Diet, nor too light Fare:
And from these corporal nutriments perhaps
Your bodies may at least turn all to Spirit . . .

(*PL* v.479-97)

The passage is worth quoting at length because along with the question of the limitations of human converse it expresses the aspiration and growth of man in images that Oldham himself employs. In the drafts quoted earlier, he had used the image of a plant to register his own lack of fruitful growth. In the published poem the lines:

Praise, the fine Diet, which we're apt to love,
If given to excess, does hurtful prove:
Where it does weak, distemper'd Stomachs meet,
That surfeits, which should nourishment create.

(27-30; *SNP* 119)

are directed against reliance upon praise, but are couched in terms very close to those used by Davenant and Milton when warning of the dangers of knowledge:

For though Books serve as Diet of the Minde;
If knowledg, early got, self vallew breeds,

By false digestion it is turn'd to winde;
And what should nourish, on the Eater feeds.
(*Gondibert*, II.viii.22)

But Knowledge is as food, and needs no less
Her Temperance over Appetite, to know
In measure what the mind may well contain,
Oppresses else with Surfet, and soon turns
Wisdom to Folly, as Nourishment to Winde.
(*PL* VII.126-30)

The imagery of the drafts and of the finished poem suggests that Oldham has been thinking of his previous career as one that has brought 'empty Leaves' instead of the 'bright consummate floure' that is the result of a man cultivating the godlike qualities in him.

But the poem itself moves over these areas with a light tone, delivering a mild rebuke to Spencer in an urbane manner —

Consider, Sir, 'tis ill and dang'rous thus
To over-lay a young and tender Muse:
(25-6; *SNP* 119)[17]

— and proceeding to compliment him on his own facility in writing. Such a ploy was very much à *propos* when addressing a patron: witness Dryden's *Preface to the Rival Ladies* (one of the most important sources for a later part of this poem), which dwells on the works that Orrery had produced during moments of diversion from the cares of state.[18] The draft had brought in a grandiloquent account of Spencer's study:

What governs Kingdoms, & distributes Right,
And sets th'unerring Bounds of Just & Fit,
Is your great Task, a large & fruitful Soile
To exercise & pay your learned Toile:
(RMS 89)

which might have been suggested by Dryden's pages to Orrery, but may also echo Horace's *Carm.* III.xxix:

Tu civitatem quis deceat status,
Curas; & urbi sollicitus
(25-6)[19]

Again, however, although this gives us a clue as to the fundamental thoughts behind the poem, which emerge near the end, the poem continues on a lighter note than the draft, and in the self-critical phrase 'court ignoble ease'[20] the Miltonic echo carries no real moral weight.

The bantering deprecation of poetry includes, besides the occasional overstatement, many places where we touch on something serious in Oldham's poetic purpose. When he writes:

> Oft to divert the wild Caprice, I try ⎤
> If Sovereign Wisdom and Philosophy   ⎬
> Rightly applied, will give a remedy: ⎦
> Strait the great *Stagyrite* I take in hand,
> Seek Nature, and my Self to understand:
> (98-102; *SNP* 123)

he is following a tradition that frequently deferred to the authority of Aristotle, saying with Rapin, for example, that 'what is good on this Subject, is all taken from *Aristotle*, who is the only *Source* whence good Sense is to be drawn, when one goes about to Write',[21] but Oldham gives the impression not of following the master as a literary dictator, but of using him as a guide to understanding himself and his world.

In the next passage, a mocking denunciation of his own enslavement to poetry, Oldham turns to parallel passages in two past masters:[22]

> 'Enough, mad rhiming Sot, enough for shame,
> 'Give o're, and all thy Quills to Tooth-picks damn:
> 'Didst ever thou the Altar rob, or worse,   ⎤
> 'Kill the Priest there, and Maids Receiving force? ⎬
> 'What else could merit this so heavy Curse?   ⎦
> 'The greatest curse, I can, I wish on him,
> '(If there be any greater than to rhime)
> 'Who first did of the lewd invention think,
> 'First made two lines with sounds resembling clink,
> 'And, swerving from the easie paths of Prose,
> 'Fetters, and Chains did on free Sense impose:
> 'Curst too be all the fools, who since have went
> 'Misled in steps of that ill President:
> 'Want be entail'd their lot: − and on I go,
> Wreaking my spight on all the jingling Crew:
> (114-28; *SNP* 124)

Two poets have contributed to this: one is Horace, whose

>   utrum
> Minxerit in patrios cineres, an triste bidental
> Moverit incestus.   (*Ars Poetica*, 470-2)

(which might be translated as 'Has he pissed on his father's grave, or vandalised a shrine') has been adapted into 'Didst ever thou the altar rob ...?', where Oldham has for once found an appropriate use for his rhetoric of violence in urbanely reflexive mockery. Then he moves on to a version of some lines in Boileau's *Satire* II, where Boileau is discussing his vocation in a letter to Molière:

> Maudit soit le premier dont la verve insensee
> Dans les bornes d'un vers renferma sa pensee,
> Et donnant à ses mots une étroite prison,
> Voulut avec la rime enchainer la Raison.
>
> (53-6; p. 27)

That Oldham is thoroughly reworking the French may be gauged from Samuel Butler's version of the same passage:

> May he be damn'd, who first found out that Curse,
> T' imprison, and confine his Thoughts in Verse;
> To hang so dull a Clog upon his Wit,
> And make his Reason to his Rhime submit.[23]

In Butler the metaphors are latent, as they are in Boileau. In Oldham a lively re-imagining has taken place: 'lewd ... sounds resembling clink ... swerving' are more vigorously disrespectful than Boileau's seriousness permitted him, and they illustrate the new individuality and freedom in Oldham's use of his sources. It is at this point that Oldham begins that part of the poem which describes the activity of poetic creation, a remarkable passage that deserves detailed attention.

To what extent are we justified in considering Oldham's account of the mind to be a distinctive and original piece of thinking? It would clearly be beyond the scope of the present essay to survey the history of thinking about the working of the mind, but I believe it will be conceded that when Renaissance poets wrote about the origins of a work they placed little stress upon the mind of the creator.[24] It is largely a question of the images used: the source of a poem might be ascribed to a dream, to inspiration from heaven, from the poet's muse, from his mistress. Or from his master: a frequent image in the classical poetry that springs from Ben Jonson is of one poet taking his divine fire from his mentor, who like Prometheus was alone daring enough to steal it from heaven.[25] There was no language to cover the process of creation: we have already noted in Oldham's poem on Jonson the use of the image of the poet as architect and builder. From our standpoint we might say that this was congruent with pre-Romantic notions of poetry: or we might say that the mind itself was not understood in terms that encouraged thinking about creativity. L.L. Whyte has illustrated how, during the seventeenth century, there was a developing awareness of the unconscious, traceable at first only in passing references, given mystical and poetic form.[26] Whyte points to Ralph Cudworth as one who 'sought to disprove current scientific materialism by beating the atheistic scientists at their own game'. Oldham, I would contend, offers an account of the mind that also moves away from the mechanical philosophy of nature, and one that is more precise and detailed than anything quoted by Whyte. It is an imaginative, not scientific, precision, and to see how Oldham has achieved this it will be necessary to look first at the various images available to him.

Poetic creation is said to begin with the dual inspiration of wine and company. Boileau had written along similar lines that 'on a vu le vin et le hasard / Inspirer quelquefois une muse grossiere',[27] though the idea has a long history.[28] But in Oldham's case this was much more than a *topos*, for he seems to have inspired others in such circumstances. John Spencer opens his verse letter to Oldham by saying:

> I promisd poetry, t'is true,
> By wine embolden'd, & inspir'd by you,
> By you, who did mee with such notions store,
> I ne er soe much as dream'd of being Poor;
> Mine soe manur'd, all barren heads I scorn'd,
> Till sober I to my dull self return'd,
> And then I found my treasure was at most
> But tracts in waters, footsteps in the Dust.
>   (RMS 198)

and an anonymous poem in *Remains* records:

> I met the gentle Youth upon the Plain ...
> Then with *Assyrian* Nard our Heads did shine,
> While rich *Sabaean* Spice exalts the Wine;
> Which to a just Degree our Spirits fir'd;
> But he was by a greater God inspir'd:
> Wit was the Theme, which he did well describe,
> With Modesty unusual to his Tribe.
>   (*R* A6*r*)

When this happens, says Oldham,

> No sober good advice will then prevail,
> Nor from the raging Frenzy me recal:

Cool Reason's dictates me no more can move
Than men in Drink, in *Bedlam*, or in Love:
(140-3; *SNP* 125)[29]

Oldham develops the analogy of poet and lover, moving from their madness to their creativity. Spencer's letter had introduced one version of this image:

But as in Love, after the feirce attack,
The Spirits to their proper posts goe back,
And wher the bloody battail late was fought,
Ther's nothing left alive upon the Spot.
Soe my Dull Head, when hot, of Raptures full,
Is now vnfurnish'd left, an Empty Skull!
(RMS 199)

This probably helped Oldham to these lines:

Sometimes, after a tedious day half spent,
When Fancy long has hunted on cold Scent,
Tir'd in the dull, and fruitless chase of Thought,
Despairing I grow weary, and give out:
As a dry Lecher pump'd of all my store,
I loath the thing, 'cause I can do't no more:
But, when I once begin to find again,
Recruits of matter in my pregnant Brain,
Again more eager I the haunt pursue,
And with fresh vigor the lov'd sport renew:
Tickled with some strange pleasure, which I find,
And think a secresie to all mankind.
(148-59; *SNP* 125-6)

The presence here of the explicit sexual image probably owes more to its being fashionable (through the currency of the 'Imperfect Enjoyment' poems) than to its being enlightening: the sexual imagery in the rest of the passage is less obtrusive, more controlled.[30] Another image is of Fancy hunting, one that was probably suggested by Dryden's words in 'An account of the ensuing Poem' prefixed to *Annus Mirabilis*:

... wit in the Poet ... is no other then the faculty of imagination in the writer, which, like a nimble Spaniel, beats over and ranges through the field of Memory, till it springs the Quarry it hunted after; or, without metaphor, which searches over all the memory for the species or Idea's of those things which it designs to represent (*Poems*, p. 46).

It is disappointing that when Dryden proceeds to elaborate this idea he returns to a more conventional language:

> So then, the first happiness of the Poet's imagination is
> properly Invention, or finding of the thought; the second is
> Fancy, or the variation, deriving or moulding of that thought,
> as the judgment represents it proper to the subject; the third
> is Elocution, or the Art of clothing and adorning that thought
> so found and varied, in apt, significant and sounding words:
> the quickness of the Imagination is seen in the Invention, the
> fertility in the Fancy, and the accuracy in the Expression
> (pp. 46-7).

However, it is good to be reminded that the primary meaning of 'Invention' is 'finding' not 'unaided contrivance'. *Ex nihilo nihil fit*: a principle that Oldham's work itself exemplifies.

It used to be said that the world arose not from nothing, but from chaos. As an image of poetic creativity this had already been used by Oldham in his ode on Ben Jonson:

> Unform'd, and void was then its Poesie,
> Only some pre-existing Matter we
>   Perhaps could see,
>   That might foretell what was to be;
>   A rude, and undigested Lump it lay,
> Like the old *Chaos*, e're the birth of Light, and Day,
> Till thy brave Genius like a new Creator came,
>   And undertook the mighty Frame;
> No shuffled Atoms did the well-built work compose,
> It from no lucky hit of blund'ring Chance arose,
>   (As some of this great Fabrick idly dream)
> But wise, all-seeing Judgment did contrive,
>   And knowing Art its Graces give:
> No sooner did thy Soul with active Force and Fire
>   The dull and heavy Mass inspire,
>   But strait throughout it let us see
>   Proportion, Order, Harmony.
>   (33-49; *PT* 71-2)

Oldham had drawn on several versions of chaos to make this passage. The first line echoes 'Matter unform'd and void' from *Paradise Lost* (VII. 233), while later lines appear to draw on the same passage:

> vital vertue infus'd, and vital warmth
> Throughout the fluid Mass
>
> (236-7)

Besides this account of the creation of the world from chaos by God, Oldham has remembered Ovid's account at the beginning of the *Metamorphoses*, for 'rude, and undigested Lump' is Ovid's epithet for chaos, 'rudis indigestaque moles' (I.7).[31] This was not just a commonplace: the Lucretian vision was capable of capturing the imagination of the age (as the popularity of Creech's version suggests), even when it was also capable of being put to debased uses, as in this satire on women:

> And now within so boundless, huge a place,
> Whose vast immensity admits no space,
> To be call'd up or down, (gone to be lost)
> Thousands of Atoms eternally are tost;
> So that I do despair amidst them all,
> Of finding out Womans original.
> Thus spying Nature labouring, I find,
> The large frame begun within my larger mind,
> I see things coming gradually to perfection,
> At length compleated by coacervation:
> Nor had this Joynted Baby of my mind,
> Scarce all its shuffled parts combin'd;
> But straight some unforc'd Particles we see,
> That will with no part of the frame agree,
> Which hookt together by themselves, became
> The imperfect thing that Men do *Woman* name ... [32]

Here the anonymous hack has lifted a few touches from Milton, and possibly a few from Oldham, but the resulting passage has no coherent vision.

In contrast, this is the account of the poet's mind that Oldham produced by introspection guided imaginatively by the conventional analogy with chaos:

> 'Tis endless, Sir, to tell the many ways,
> Wherein my poor deluded self I please:
> How, when the Fancy lab'ring for a Birth,
> With unfelt Throws brings its rude issue forth:
> How after, when imperfect shapeless Thought
> Is by the Judgment into Fashion wrought.
> When at first search I traverse o're my mind,

> Nought but a dark, and empty Void I find:
> Some little hints at length, like sparks, break thence,
> And glimm'ring Thoughts just dawning into sence:
> Confus'd a while the mixt Idea's lie,
> With nought of mark to be discover'd by,
> Like colours undistinguisht in the night,
> Till the dusk images, mov'd to the light,
> Teach the discerning Faculty to chuse,
> Which it had best adopt, and which refuse.
>
> (162-77; *SNP* 126-7)

It was long ago recognised that the chief source for this passage is in Dryden's *Preface to The Rival Ladies*:

> My Lord, This worthless Present was design'd you, long before it was a Play; When it was only a confus'd Mass of Thoughts, tumbling over one another in the Dark: When the Fancy was yet in its first Work, moving the Sleeping Images of things towards the Light, there to be Distinguish'd, and then either chosen or rejected by the Judgment.[33]

Important as this passage was for Oldham (and it is remarkable that of all the material available to him he should have selected from one of Dryden's many prefaces one sentence that modern authorities have independently recognised as a significant contribution to the understanding of the mind),[34] it could not have inspired an account as long as Oldham's if it had not been re-imagined — if Oldham had not reworked the old metaphor by *imagining* his mind as chaos. To do that he turned to the magnificent new evocations of chaos in two parts of *Paradise Lost*: in Book II. 890-1038, where Satan traverses chaos, and in Book VII.210-60, where God creates the universe from chaos.

In both cases chaos is originally wild and furious, but Oldham's picture is calm, as in the moment when creation begins in Book VII, where 'on the waterie calme / His brooding wings the Spirit of God outspred' (234-5). When Oldham describes chaos as 'dark' and 'void' he is using epithets common to Ovid, Genesis and Milton. But other features have definitely been inspired by Milton. Oldham's 'Confus'd a while the mixt Idea's lie' draws not only on Dryden's 'confus'd Mass of Thoughts' but also on Milton's 'in thir pregnant causes mixt / Confus'dly' (II. 913-14). But perhaps the chief debt to Milton is in the establishment of a point from which creation can be viewed. In both Books II and VII we watch chaos, and move over and through it, first with Satan and then with the Spirit.

This sense of the spectator moving through chaos, but usually seeing it from above, unthreatened, may have helped Oldham to form his sense of movement: 'When at first search I traverse o're my mind'. There is movement in chaos too, not the random Epicurean collision of atoms, but purposive movement: Satan 'Springs upward like a Pyramid of fire' (II.1013) and later watches as

> the sacred influence
> Of light appears, and from the walls of Heav'n
> Shoots farr into the bosom of dim Night
> A glimmering dawn:
>
> (II.1034-7)

while during creation, after the Spirit of God has 'downward purg'd / The black tartareous cold Infernal dregs' (VII.237-8), God says 'Let ther be light',

> and forthwith Light
> Ethereal, first of things, quintessence pure
> Sprung from the Deep.
>
> (VII. 243-5)

So too in Oldham, with a vigour not present in Dryden's image,

> Some little hints at length, like sparks, break thence,
> And glimm'ring Thoughts just dawning into sence:

Although there is a verbal echo of Cowley here —

> As first a various unform'd *Hint* we find
> Rise in some god-like *Poets* fertile *Mind*.[35]

— the more dynamic language and movement is from Milton.

But we should not underestimate the originality of Oldham's final product. Much of Oldham's language has a sensitive precision that takes us further into the experience of creation than Dryden's account. Ideas are born with 'unfelt Throws' — their moment of coming remains a mystery; they 'lie . . . Confus'd' — a phrase that, unlike Dryden's 'tumbling . . . Confused', evokes the unconscious mind where ideas lie fused together; and this is an image greatly enhanced by the guiding conception of the mind as a dark abyss[36] from which ideas break of their own accord like sparks, rising upwards into consciousness.

Thoughts are then made into poetry, and it is at this stage that the poet as maker appears. Oldham says:

> Sometimes a stiff, unwieldy thought I meet,
> Which to my Laws will scarce be made submit:
> But, when, after expence of pains and time,
> 'Tis manag'd well, and taught to yoke in Rhime,
> I triumph more, than joyful Warriours wou'd,
> Had they some stout, and hardy Foe subdu'd:
> And idly think, less goes to their Command,
> That makes arm'd Troops in well-plac'd order stand,
> Than to the conduct of my words, when they
> March in due ranks, are set in just array.
>   (186-95; *SNP* 127-8)

Atoms in chaos are likened to armies by Milton, but the image had already been used of words in verse by Cowley:

> Till all the parts and words their places take,
> And with just marches *verse* and *musick* make;[37]

But although there are brief sources for many of the ideas in this passage, Oldham's account of how the mind works when creating poetry seems unmatched in length, coherence and precision. Moreover, because it is an imaginative passage it proved capable of feeding the imagination of Pope, as will be shown in the Epilogue.

In referring earlier to the drafts of this poem, I said that there were signs that Oldham was thinking not only about the subjects of his poetry but about the course of his past life. Now towards the end of the *Letter* comes a passage that confirms his dedication to poetry, and in so doing draws on a number of other poets in such a way as to suggest that they have helped him to make certain life-choices. This is the passage:

> 'What was't, I rashly vow'd? shall ever I
> 'Quit my beloved Mistress, Poetry?
> 'Thou sweet beguiler of my lonely hours,
> 'Which thus glide unperceiv'd with silent course:
> 'Thou gentle Spell, which undisturb'd do'st keep
> 'My Breast, and charm intruding care asleep:
> 'They say, thou'rt poor, and unendow'd, what tho?
> 'For thee I this vain, worthless world forego:
> 'Let Wealth, and Honor be for Fortunes slaves,
> 'The Alms of Fools, and prize of crafty Knaves:
> 'To me thou art, what ere th' ambitious crave,
> 'And all that greedy Misers want, or have:
> 'In Youth, or Age, in Travel, or at Home,

'Here, or in Town, at *London*, or at *Rome*,
'Rich, or a Beggar, free, or in the Fleet,
'What ere my fate is, 'tis my fate to write.

(211-26; *SNP* 128-9)

The opening questions may owe something to Donne's 'My Mistress
Truth, betray thee ...?'[38]; the next four lines draw on Cowley both for
their language and their verse-music:

Where their vast *Court* the *Mother-Waters* keep,
And undisturb'd by *Moons* in silence sleep ...

and Cowley's *Destinie* has perhaps contributed too:

Hate and *renounce* (said she)
Wealth, Honor, Pleasures, all the *World* for *Me*.
Thou neither great at *Court*, nor in the *War*,
Nor at th' *Exchange* shalt be, nor at the wrangling *Bar* ...

No Matter, *Cowley*, let proud *Fortune* see,
That *thou* canst *her* despise no less than *she* does *Thee*.
Let all her gifts the portion be
Of Folly, Lust, and Flattery,
Fraud, Extortion, Calumnie,
Murder, Infidelitie,
Rebellion and Hypocrisie ...

(*Poems*, pp. 193-4)

but this poem in itself could not invite Oldham to the warm and considered
statements that he is making. Cowley is a little too strident, and the self
looms too large in the poem for his philosophy to impress the reader with
a sense of general truth. Oldham, by contrast, does have here this power
of generalisation: his attitude to the gifts of Fortune is pointed but more
balanced. This, I suggest, is because Oldham has learnt for himself from
the poem which Cowley was drawing on:

Fortuna saevo laeta negotio, &
Ludum insolentem ludere pertinax,
Transmutat incertos honores;
Nunc mihi, nunc alii benigna.

Laudo manentem: si celeris quatit
Pennas, resigno quae dedit: & mea

Virtute me involvo, probamque
Pauperiem sine dote quaero.

Non est meum, si mugiat Africis
Malus procellis, ad miseras preces
Decurrere, & votis pacisci,
Ne Cypriae Tyriaeque merces

Addant avaro divitias mari.
Tunc me biremis praesidio scaphae
Tutum per Aegaeos tumultus
Aura feret, geminusque Pollux.
(Horace, *Carm*. III.xxix.49-64)[39]

Although 'poor, and unendow'd' probably stems directly from 'pauperiem sine dote quaero', and Oldham has retrieved something of Horace's economy of effect in the references to Fortune's gifts, such strength of thought is not repeated in Oldham, nor does it come unmediated. Boileau is paraphrasing Horace's attitude in *Satire* II:

Mon coeur exempt de soins, libre de passion,
Sait donner une borne à son ambition,
Et fuiant des grandeurs la presence importune,
Ie ne vais point au Louvre adorer la Fortune:
Et je serois heureux, si pour me consumer,
Vn Destin envieux ne m'avoit fait rimer.
(63-8; p. 28)

Oldham has lost his language of exploration, of pushing back the frontiers both of 'iniquity' and of poetry. In its place comes a more detailed account of poetic exploration, and a new note of acceptance of his vocation, and detachment from the frantic pursuit of material gratification. Oldham had written about his newly-found pleasure in 'living within bounds', which was a message extracted from Horace by his seventeenth-century readers. Milton, for example, when writing Raphael's speech to Adam in Book VIII had used *Carm*. III.xxix:[40]

Sollicit not thy thoughts with matters hid,
Leave them to God above, him serve and feare;
           ... joy thou
In what he gives to thee, this Paradise
And thy faire *Eve*; Heav'n is for thee too high
To know what passes there; be lowlie wise:
Think onely what concernes thee and thy being
(167-74)

and the seventeenth-century Horatian message sounds in other phrases: 'Live, in what state, condition or degree, / Contented'; 'taught to live, / The easiest way'; 'to know / That which before us lies in daily life, / Is the prime Wisdom' (176-7; 182-3; 192-4). Perhaps Oldham needed to read these sentiments in English before he could find the appropriate rhythms. In any case, the rhythm and music of the passage, and the conviction that they register, would not have been possible without contact with this strain of thought: a contact, that is, with the 'classics' that results not in verbal borrowings alone, but in a new direction for one's poetry, and one's life.

The Desk

After *A Letter from the Country* Oldham spent the autumn and winter of 1678 working on various modes of heroic poetry, first on his translation of Boileau's *Le Lutrin* and then on his initial poems on the Popish Plot. To be able to create an appropriate language for translating *Le Lutrin* depended in part upon having a sure grasp of what an epic or heroic poem would be like — and depended too upon having some belief still in the worth of epic and the values it endorsed. I need not rehearse here the reasons why Oldham had few usable examples of heroic poetry in English from which he could take his bearings in a translation of *Le Lutrin*. Though the epic remained prestigious, it was no longer achievable — in any expected form — after the events and philosophies of the civil war had splintered England's agreed image of its nationhood, and now that too many Restoration writers preferred to flatter a coterie rather than address a people. Nevertheless, the Dryden who was clear that the burlesque begets laughter while the heroic begets admiration,[41] is writing an heroic poetry of sorts in *Annus Mirabilis*, *Absalom and Achitophel* and *Mac Flecknoe*, for all three beget admiration in the reader. Wonder at the events in the last two poems is surely a more important reason why the reader returns to them than any laughter they may raise: and because admiration is aroused, the laughter is much subtler than that provoked by the anarchic procedures of burlesque. By 'burlesque' at this date (1667) Dryden would have meant a poem like Scarron's *Virgile Travestie*, a simply-conceived joke that pleases for a while but soon becomes tedious. This could not be said of the much subtler poem *Le Lutrin*. Scarron can be aped in English, but Boileau is harder to translate because his subtlety is distinctively a product of the Court of Louis XIV.

Louis was lavishly praised. Poetry, music and the visual arts combined to celebrate the sun-king, with Louis himself often taking a hand in the arrangements. In such circumstances, and when a writer's income was often derived from a royal pension, any attempt at criticism was unwise and even dangerous. Molière and La Fontaine managed occasionally to make carefully-phrased criticisms of Court life. Boileau in his *Satires* assumes an independence and a licence to be frank: *ea sola species adulandi supererat* ('that was the only form of flattery left').[42] But in England the case was different. A country that by the late 1670s had no compulsion to celebrate its monarch, and already enjoyed outspoken 'satire', did not have the restraint and subtlety — even in the movement of its verse line — to register the particular delight offered by *Le Lutrin*.

What is the nature of this delight? Certainly we enjoy the disparity between the quotidian action and the heroic form. There are also less obvious satirical modes: the recalling of medieval times and their *Rois Fainéants*, which both deflates slightly the pretensions of Louis and invites something approaching admiration for a state in which the kings devoted themselves to Mollesse,[43]

> S'endormoient sur le Trône, & me servant sans honte,
> Laissoient leur sceptre aux mains ou d'un Maire ou d'un Comte.
> Aucun soin n'approchoit de leur paisible Cour.
> On reposoit la nuit: On dormoit tout le jour.
>
> (II.125-8; p. 213)

Then again, the exchanges between the wig-maker and his wife in Chant II work partly by recalling Dido and Aeneas in *Aeneid* IV, but also by recalling Pauline and Polyeucte in Corneille's play.[44] The delight given by the episode will depend not only on our feelings about Virgil and Corneille, but on our attitude to — or involvement in — the Church of Rome as manifested in Louis's France. I imagine that the devout Catholic who was able to enjoy the blessing of the chanter's party at the end of Chant V as the glorious climax of the poem, was relishing something much finer than was the English Protestant to whom it was just a turn in the plot on a par with the battle of the books. Part of the feeling of appropriateness and release that the end of Chant V gives, must come from a feeling that the blessing of Mother Church is always available and always beyond petty disputes. When we see how complex is the mode of *Le Lutrin* and how vital to its survival as a living poem are the very positive responses that it evokes, we shall not be too hasty to talk about 'mock heroic' poetry as if it were *simplex et unum*, nor too surprised if the only way of translating the poem turns out to be by finding a whole new nexus of circumstances, associations and values: because translation has to be occasional, the only poems in English that come near to being living versions of *Le Lutrin* are *Mac Flecknoe* and *The Rape of the Lock*. Only Dryden and Pope had the depth and sensitivity to tap the roots of a society, and to control their tone so that idle mockery was avoided, and values emerged renewed. Even so, it might have to be conceded to the sceptical that neither English poem reaches beyond its engagement with the surface of a narrow area of life so successfully as *Le Lutrin*.

Oldham's translation of *Le Lutrin* survives in the Rawlinson manuscript in the form of rough drafts and a fair copy of Canto I, the title for Canto II, and a couplet from Canto IV.[45] The fair copy is dated '8r.78'. It is the first translation of *Le Lutrin* into English, and was followed in 1682 by a complete version signed 'N.O.'[46] The recurring problem for Oldham, that of finding the right tone, is illustrated from the start:

> Ie chante les combats, & ce Prelat terrible
> Qui par ses longs travaux, & sa force invincible,
> Dans P.... autrefois exerçant son grand coeur,
> Fit placer à la fin un Lutrin dans un Choeur.
> En vain deux fois le Chantre, appuié d'un vain titre,
> Contre ses hauts projets arma tout le Chapitre.
> Ce Prelat genereux aidé d'un Horloger,
> Soûtint jusques au bout l'honneur de son clocher.
> (I.1-8; p. 195)

>   I sing dire Battles & that sacred Wight
> 2 Who by long Hardship & undaunted Might
>   In Pourges erst, by his great Deeds made known,
> 4 Establisht in a Quire a Desk his Throne:
>   In vain against his high Designs ye Chanter twice
> 6 Made ye whole Chapter in Rebellion rise:
>   He, by his Sexton's Aid, did all withstand,
> 8 And to ye last his Chappel's Cause maintain'd:
>   (Draft: RMS 70)

> *Marginal revisions*: 1] a (for 'that'); 2] unconquer'd Prowess; 4] erected; 6] fierce bold Faction.

Oldham followed Boileau in using the sub-title 'An Heroique Poem' and began by looking for a serious heroic vocabulary to work with and against. The first three lines use a quasi-Spenserian language of knight-errantry: 'dire' is slipped in; 'Wight' had been archaic for nearly a century (contrast

Boileau's 'Prelat terrible'); 'erst', 'long Hardship', 'undaunted Might', 'unconquer'd Prowess' come from the same strain. The last two phrases may also echo Cowley's 'unwearied *Virtue*' from the opening of the *Davideis*, for from the same source Cowley's

> Whilst *Saul* and *Hell* crost his strong fate in vain
> (*Poems*, p. 242)

has influenced Oldham's

> In vain to cross his high designs . . .
> (Fair Copy, RMS 124)

while four lines later Oldham's

> what baneful Rage
> Could holy Men in such fierce Broils engage;
> (Draft, RMS 70)

has been shaped by Cowley's

> whom rage
> And thirst of *Empire* in fierce wars engage.

Besides Cowley, there was also Milton to hand. The line

> Establisht in a Quire a Desk his Throne.
> (Draft, RMS 70)

springs from

> Establisht in a safe unenvied Throne
> (*PL* ii.23)

Oldham's somewhat strange line disappears in revision, but the Miltonic echo is used again later, more appropriately, when the Dean, addressing his followers, speaks of being

> settled now in my establisht throne.
> (Fair Copy, RMS 131)

When writing that speech Oldham seems to have kept the Miltonic context in mind, for the line

> Him, whom your high & open suffrage chose
> (*Ibid.*)

derives from nothing in Boileau, but may be using another part of Satan's speech:

Mee though just right, and the fixt Laws of Heav'n
Did first create your Leader, next free choice ...
(*PL* II.18-19)

I do not suppose for one moment that Oldham intended his readers to recognise allusions to previous epics. Rather, these are attempts to find the right language, and some of the pre-cast phrases (such as 'dire', 'erst', 'undaunted', 'Deeds') disappear in revision:

I sing of Battels & y^t sacred Wight,
Who by long contests & unconquer'd might
In Pourges, fam'd by his great acts, at last
A fatal Desk within a Chappel plac't ...
(Fair Copy, RMS 124)

It appears that during his revisions Oldham realised that the joke was not simply one of applying epic epithets to the characters: he had to find a style whose seriousness was of a greater range than that. So it happens that instead of using that awkward grandiose idea in place of Boileau's fourth line —

Fit placer à la fin un Lutrin dans un Choeur

— Oldham catches the bathos of the French in his fair copy with:

A fatal Desk within a Chappel plac't.

But Oldham is perhaps more assured when he can produce a fairly straightforward kind of satire. The effect is, again, often cruder than Boileau's: his lines on the arrival of Discord in the Dean's apartments —

La Deesse en entrant, qui void la nappe mise
Admire un si bel ordre & reconnoist l' * * *,
(I. 69-70; p. 198)

— where the beautifully coy 'l' * * *' depends very much upon our feelings *for* the Church, are rendered by Oldham less deftly:

The Goddess entring finds ye Table spread
With Plates & Napkins in just order laid.
A while sh' admires in ye provisions there
The Churches well-known decency & Care.
(Draft, RMS 72)

There is more here than a difference in literary subtlety: the comparison points to the distance not only between French and English modes of satire, but between two cultures and religions. N.O. however, omits the reference to the Church altogether:

> The Goddess entring, saw the Table spread,
> And all within doors rarely ordered.
>
> (p. 5)

The description of the Dean is one of the more successful passages in Oldham's translation:

> Far back in an apartment wisely made,
> Where noise can ne're the privacy invade,
> Within an alcove's close obscure retreat,
> The scene of undisturbed ease & quiet,
> A bed with well-stuff'd pride it self dos raise,
> Rich with ye spoils of all ye feather'd race:
> Four stately curtains drawn exclude ye light,
> And in ye midst of day create a night:
> There, free at once from noise & care & pains
> Stretch'd wanton Sloth on downy empire reigns;
> There 'tis, ye Dean, with breakfast late refresht
> Waits dinner, & beguiles the time in rest:
> Plump Youth sits smiling in his cheerful face
> And o're his strutting cheeks her bloom displays:
> Two stories down his brace of chins advance,
> And strive to meet half way his rising paunch:
> (Fair Copy, RMS 126-7)

Some of this is stilted: 'wisely made' adds little, and 'it self dos raise' is a clumsily literal translation of 's'esleve'. But quite a lot of the passage has been freshly imagined, as a result, I think, of Oldham sharing something of Boileau's feeling *for* Mollesse. The first four lines translate the single line in Boileau:

> Dans le reduit obscur d'une alcove enfoncée
> (1.57; p. 198)

and the impulse towards the additional stress in Oldham upon undisturbed silence (2, 4) probably comes once more from Cowley's hell:

> Beneath the silent chambers of the earth ...
> Where their vast *Court* the *Mother-waters* keep,
> And undisturb'd by *Moons* in silence sleep ...
> (*Poems*, p. 244)

while line 8 may derive from part of the same passage:

> Here no dear glimpse of the *Suns* lovely face,
> Strikes through the *Solid* darkness of the place;
> No dawning *Morn* does her kind reds display;
> One slight weak beam would here be thought the *Day*.

But the evidence for Oldham having relished Mollesse is rather in the line

> Stretch'd wanton Sloth on downy empire reigns

in which the personification is much more active than in Boileau's

> Regne sur le duvet une heureuse Indolence.

and the same would be true of this comparison:

> La Ieunesse en sa fleur brille sur son visage:

> Plump Youth sits smiling in his cheerful face.

That Oldham has actually done *more* with these local personifications than Boileau may partly be due to his personal and national genius for the specific in poetry, but also points to his having seen something of the particular genius in *Le Lutrin*. Oldham was capable of confining himself to significant physical detail, as N.O. has done:

> A Stately Bed, the Posts most richly Gilt,
> Cover'd with Sumptuous Crimson Damask Quilt . . .
> (p. 5)

but instead he writes an heroic line:

> Rich with ye spoils of all ye feather'd race

which depends not on Cowley or Milton but is instead more Homeric.

But what of the technical processes of translating? Oldham usually keeps close to the French, often moving away into more idiomatic English in his revisions. He is an accurate reader of the French except for the one mistake of rendering 'J'eus beau prendre le Ciel & le Chantre à partie' (i.173) by 'I, who with Heav'n then took ye Chanters side' (Draft, RMS 77) instead of 'In vain I blamed Heaven and the Chanter.' The manuscript often reveals a struggle to shed constrictingly literal renderings, as when 'Vers cet endroit du Choeur' (159) is translated at first as 'Towards y^t place oth' Quire', then altered in the margins to 'In p[lace] oth' Q[uire] where . . .' and finally in the fair copy becomes 'Within ye Quire' (RMS 77 and 132). Oldham combines both close and free translation, as Discord's speech to the Dean illustrates:

> Tu dors? Prélat, tu dors? & là-haut à ta place,
> Le Chantre aux yeux du Choeur estale son audace,
> Chante les *Oremus*, fait des Processions,
> Et respand à grands flots les benedictions.
> Tu dors? attens-tu donc, que sans bulle & sans titre
> Il te ravisse encor le Rochet & la Mitre?
>   (1.73-8; p. 198)

> Sleepst thou? fond man, sleepst thou? while near ye place
> 2 The Chanter his bold Impudence displays?
> Sings ye Te deums, ye Processions gos
> 4 And lavishly his scatter'd Blessings throws:
> Sleepst thou? o sensless of approaching Fate,
> 6 Whilst Dangers thus surround thy threatned state?
> Whilst in dispute thy sacred Mitre stands
> 8 The likely spoils of bold usurping hands?
>   (Draft, RMS 72)

Marginal revisions: 6] tottring; 7] hallowd reverend; 8] Almost a prey to

'Near ye place' has been suggested by the French, but is awkward English, whereas the rest of the couplet works well enough. 'Y^e processions gos' may appear clumsy, but is a natural idiom of the period. The considerable expansion in lines 5-6, along with the general phrase 'fond man' instead of 'Prélat', suggests that Oldham wishes us to dwell briefly upon that very emotive moment in literature (we might for once use the word 'archetypal' to locate its power) when we watch someone asleep who is quite unaware of impending danger. In his revision of this passage Oldham makes lines 1-2 into a triplet, and by some changes of epithet strengthens his language:

> Sleepst thou? fond man, sleepst thou? while near ye place ⎫
> Ev'n now ye Chanter in full Quire displays   ⎬
> His harden'd impudence & thy disgrace?   ⎭
> Sings ye Te Deums, ye Processions gos,
> And show'rs of Blessings lavishly bestows?
> Sleepst thou? o sensless of approaching fate!
> Whilst dangers thus surround thy tottring state?
> Whilst in dispute thy threaten'd Miter stands,
> The likely Spoil of bold usurping hands?
>   (Fair Copy, RMS 127-8)

Sometimes Oldham's decisions are hard to account for. One might have imagined that Boileau's line, 'Ses Chanoines vermeils & brillans de santé' afforded better opportunities than 'Her healthful Canons in good plight & case' (RMS 125), where 'plight & case' are not only less vivid, but almost archaic, passing out of use in these positive senses. At another point we notice Oldham sacrificing a rhyme for the sake of a stronger word:

> As a fierce Bull, whom som ambitious Fly
> Durst sting; & with his life ye glory buy,
>   (Draft, RMS 74)

was his first thought, but in the fair copy (RMS 128) 'Fly' is dropped for the perhaps livelier and more colloquial 'Breeze',[47] with the result that the rhyme 'Breeze/buys' is imperfect. Oldham's idiomatic English also comes out in Gilotin's speech to the Dean, which Oldham makes twice the length of the French. There is the quasi-proverbial 'Dinner twice heated is not worth a groat', which Oldham contemplated changing to the more literal 'dos all its value lose' ('ne valut jamais rien') but happily decided not to; and the speech as a whole displays a grasp of simple language and effective verse-movement that create an impression of the speaking voice:

> Was it to pray that you were Prelat made? ...
> Is this a time for fasting? is it Lent,
> Ember, or Vigil to be abstinent?
> No, no, be wise ...
>   (Fair Copy, RMS 129)

At the same time the language is given an heroic rhetorical form by Miltonic syntactical inversions:

> When weightier matters your devotion call?
> When reeking dainties your attendance wait ...
>   ... all present feuds forego ... (RMS 129)

Without a translation of later parts of the poem, particularly the speeches of Mollesse, of the wig-maker and his wife, and the blessing of the opposition by the Dean, it is difficult to say how much of *Le Lutrin* Oldham appreciated, and how much of it could have been transposed into English. But it would not be surprising if Oldham abandoned *The Desk* because, after wrestling hard with the problem of an appropriate language, as we have seen him doing, he realised what a gap there still was between the two achievements. Professor Brooks remarks that Oldham's style is 'as lively as the original, if less polished',[48] but the distance between Oldham's verse and Boileau's is not a matter of polish, but of the difference between

French values and English values, between what French verse and English verse were capable of achieving, not to mention the difference between the two men in poise and sensitivity. Nor will it suffice to say that Boileau offered Oldham the proper machinery for heroical satire. Certainly Boileau, or the discipline of translating Boileau, helped Oldham to move away from two inadequate conceptions of the heroic: the 'ironic' rant of the *Satyr against Vertue*, and the rag-bag of phrases from previous epics. But turning to the *Satyrs upon the Jesuits* we find that the rant has not disappeared, and the 'machinery' is very different from Boileau's. A change to a more mature poetry could not be effected by a change of anything like machinery, but was dependent upon a change of values: perhaps, though, not so much a *change* of values as a stimulus to articulate and work from values that had hitherto not been much in evidence poetically. That, I take it, is happening in *A Letter from the Country*. To compare poems too readily in terms of genre is to risk losing sight of the inwardness and detail of the relations between them, and to use a label such as 'mock-heroic' for *Le Lutrin* would be to invite the reader to discover a lesser and simpler poem than is actually in front of him.

One might additionally exemplify the problems that Englishmen had in translating from French by examining the failures of Philips, Cotton and Otway in their renderings of Corneille and Racine: we would find again that French 'heroic' values cannot be transplanted, as there is no corresponding ethic in England. Cotton translated not only from Corneille but also from Scarron, and a brief comparison of the styles of Cotton and Scarron may be instructive. *Virgile Travestie* relies on a serious vocabulary, tinged with irony and sarcasm:

> Et que vostre beau Roy de vent
> Porte respect à mon trident.
> La mer n'est pas de son domaine,
> Qu'en sa demeure souterraine
> Il vous donne s'il veut la loy.

But Cotton is coarse:

> Go tell that farting Fool your Master,
> That such a whistling scab as he,
> Was ne'er cut out to rule the Sea;
> But that it to my Empire fell;
> Bid him go vapour in his Cell;
> There let him puff and domineer,
> But make no more such foisting here.

and his humour moves towards farce:

> No sooner landed we to bait us,
> But that the Rogues threw Cow-turds at us.[49]

There is here no chance (or intention) of a creative meeting between comedy or satire and an heroic mode. There is little intelligence about the poem as burlesque.

The translation of *Le Lutrin* by N.O. shares the tendency to the anarchic style that characterises not only *Scarronides* but also *Hudibras*. We can excerpt from N.O. some lines that stand by themselves with full seriousness:

> Enthron'd in borrowed lustre dares to Brave
> Thy *Soveraignty* ...
>
> (p. 9)

> More Worlds to satiate his Ambitious Mind ...
>
> (p. 21)

N.O. borrows from *Paradise Lost*:

> To tast the fruit of the forbidden Tree ...
>
> (p. 16)

> Hurl'd Headlong from high hopes ...
>
> (p. 2)

> Sluggard, awake, arise ...
>
> (p. 6)

and with equal freedom borrows the jokes of *Scarronides*:

> This Baggage once in her mad moods and tenses.
>
> (p. 14)[50]

But the result of these juxtapositions is a mongrel style where there is again no intelligent use made of the relation between heroic and comic modes. N.O. has seized upon Boileau's poem as a romp, little more. The complexity of *Le Lutrin* may have been beyond Oldham's reach too, but he was becoming too serious an artist to be tempted by the cheap effects of burlesque. But there were other kinds of cheap effect that he would not be able to resist.

Poems on the Popish Plot

While Oldham was working on *The Desk* in October 1678 the Popish Plot crisis erupted with the discovery of the body of Sir Edmondbury Godfrey, whose apparent murder gave alarming support to the fabrications that were being spread by Titus Oates, and he turned his attention to a political poem, trying out suitable forms borrowed from stock modes of the day. He first sketched some lines headed 'Advice to a Painter' in which he attacked one of the king's mistresses:

> Next our State Messalina represent,
> Whose taile's ye Rudder of our Government
> In which a drained King & Kingdom's spent,
> Damn'd Gulph of Lust!
>   (RMS 289)

A brief mention of 'their crimes' suggests that this was an early response to the Plot.

This attempt was quickly abandoned, but of another fragment, *The Vision*, Oldham felt sufficiently confident to make three drafts and a fair copy.[51] In the first draft the heading is simply 'Satyr'. The opening is rough:

> Dark was ye time, as ere new Light's first dawn
> And still, as ere motion it self began.
> In depth of Night & depth of silence drown'd,
>   (RMS 268)

and then occurs a line that justly survived unchanged into the fair copy:

> When sleep's soft magick had my sences bound.

Then follow twelve lines that work over possible descriptions of going to bed and falling asleep. The second and third drafts polish and add material, and the fair copy relates in full how the poet falls asleep and travels to hell, where Lucifer is about to begin a consult. There are sketches for some characters of villains, but the poem goes no further.

The device of falling asleep and dreaming was a common opening at this time, and many popular ballads had explored hell.[52] Three major poets had also made use of the setting.[53] Donne's *Ignatius his Conclave* places the Jesuits in hell, but he concentrates on satirising contemporary follies and does not exploit very far the setting and dramatic possibilities. The only detail that Oldham may have taken from Donne is the inclusion of Aretino in hell.[54] Cowley's *Davideis* added another character, Corah, and also contributed descriptive touches, for Oldham's

> Darkness thick-wove without one mingling ray,
> Compar'd to which our Night would be a day
>
> (RMS 268)

probably draws on Cowley's ever-useful description of hell. Cowley has suggested other details too. There seems little point in the opening phrase in these lines —

> Instead of Tapestry ye walls to grace,
> A well-wrought Imag'ry adorned ye place:
>
> (RMS 272)

unless Oldham was thinking of Saul's palace in *Davideis* II where

> Ten pieces of bright Tap'estry hung the room.
>
> (*Poems*, p. 290)

Cowley's 'Great *Belzebub* starts from his burning Throne' has been combined with Milton's 'High on a Throne of Royal State' to produce Oldham's

> high on a state
> Of glowing flames th' Infernal Monarch sate.[55]

But the Miltonic presence extends further:

> How he by subtle treachery did deceive
> The Mother of mankind, unwary Eve:
> In scaly foulds he hugs ye fatal Tree
> The root & stock of all our miserie.
>
> (RMS 272)

Much of the language of *The Vision*, while not obtrusively Miltonic, can be paralleled in *Paradise Lost*: 'wrack'd in sad despair', 'thrown headlong', 'vast', 'chaos', 'shades', 'band', 'Pillar of o^r Realm', 'durst his Heav'n invade', 'lively Portraitures', 'great exploits'.

Oldham was not alone in choosing a visionary visit to hell as the form for a topical satire. There is a broadside dating probably from 1681 called *The Deliquium: or, The Grievances of the Nation discovered in a Dream.* The author of this, after 'Evening's Coffee, lac'd with long argument' goes to bed where

> Thus lay I long, my Soul quite spent with Sighs,
> When Sleep insensibly stole o're my Eyes,

> From lump of Flesh unchain'd, methought my Soul
> Through Dark Unwholesome Foggy Mists did rowl,
> Horrour increasing still, methought I came
> To the dire Mansions of Eternal Flame
> The Gates of Brass transparent were, and thence
> Flew *Azure* Flames, with smoak of nauseous stench.

He sees the damned being tortured, and is then taken to the infernal parliament where two candidates are standing for election. One has tried to seduce Almanzor (i.e. James) to the conspiracy, but, failing, has had it rumoured that he agreed. The other has stirred up the Plot with Oates, Tonge and perhaps Shaftesbury ('Libertino'). The poem is clearly Tory, and takes over from Donne the motif of candidates rehearsing their credentials for an election in hell. Oldham's is the more skilful poem, but the coincidence of mode is notable.

Oldham began his attack on the Jesuits with the search for a form. When he abandoned the *Advice* and *Vision* modes and settled for the dramatic monologue of *Garnet's Ghost* he returned to a mode close to that of the *Satyr against Vertue*; beginning *in medias res* we have only the title to tell us how to read the poetry.

The evidence of the drafts suggests that Oldham had difficulty in finding anything to say, even though he was becoming a competent craftsman in verse. His first attempt opens with 'Garnet's Ghost. Addressing to ye Conspirators met in privat Cabal':

> From Hell's dread Monarch sent I envoy come
> To you great Homagers of Him & Rome ...
> First to your Royal Highness in due place
> H' ascribes all Merit, Honour, Glory, Praise ...
>   (RMS 246)

It is a strong opening: the use of the liturgical ascription is particularly telling. It is also a natural opening considering the stage of the Plot at which it was written. Godfrey's body was found on 17 October; at the beginning of November the papers of the Duke of York's secretary, Coleman, were being passed backwards and forwards between Lords and Commons, and as Roger North wrote: 'The discovery of Coleman's papers made as much noise in and about London, and indeed over all the nation, as if the very Cabinet of Hell had been laid open.'[56] Coleman's involvement naturally increased suspicion of James. Indeed, Oldham's imagination has come close to what was one of the best-kept secrets of the reign: that the Jesuits' consult of 1678 had been held in James's apartments.

These lines, with another brief draft ('Let Lazy Princes wait, / Till their slow Crowns be given by Fate')[57] and some marginal jottings are all that remain of Oldham's first impulse, fiercely Whiggish and topical. He did not pursue this tack: he heavily obliterated the stronger lines against James, and in the published *Satyrs* speaks not as a party man but as a champion of the nation and Protestantism against foreign subversion and superstition.

The lines that follow this first attempt in the manuscript (whether or not they were composed immediately afterwards) come from an early stage and illustrate how ideas are crystallising out into odd lines and couplets, only later being worked together into coherent passages. Oldham is playing with generalised statements about good and evil, which lack force and astringency:

> Right lies remote & wide from Interest
> Farther then Heav'n from Hell, or East from West.

> (RMS 246)

Marking time, he worries at this idea without developing it:

> Far as 'twas ever distant from my Brest
> Remov'd as far as tis from Pole to Pole
> Distant as Good was ever from this Soul.

Casting round for grounds of attack upon the Jesuits, Oldham tries:

> Except some few
> Whom silly inbred Honesty cajoles
> Or that dull piece ye holy Legend gulls
> Believ'd by none but Hereticks & Fools.

These lines are expanded and ordered three pages later, where Oldham now has the dramatic voice shaping the passage:

> But say, what is't y^t binds your hands? dos Fear
> From such a glorious Action you deter?
> Or is Religion? but you sure disclaim
> That frivolous Pretence, y^t empty name,
> Vain Bugbear-Word!

> (RMS 249)

The verse has gathered momentum, and has a firm rhetorical shape.

When considering the potential villainy of the conspirators, Oldham notes down ideas in independent couplets:

> Ravish at th' Altar, kill when you have done
> Make them your Guilt ye Victims to attone.

All sence of good ye very motions kill
Left only free to act & covet Ill:
    May it marks & tracks of Good deface
And true substantial Wickedness take place.
Let fired Cities to your Plots give light,
And those by greater Ruins be extinguisht quite
Dash heresy together with Brains
Out of their miter'd Heads. — Divan
                                    (RMS 260)

Lines 3-4 and 5-6 are two ways of turning the same idea. The other couplets relate one crime apiece. Several of the lines are not metrical. Two pages later these ideas are expanded. First the note 'Divan' is used:

How long will you endure y^t curst Divan
That damn'd Committee, whom ye Fates ordain
Of all our well-laid Plots to be ye Bane:
Unkennel those State-foxes, where they ly
                                    (RMS 262)

and there the passage breaks off. Then the last two lines of the previous passage are worked up:

Lug by ye ears ye Doting Prelates thence,
Dash Heresy together with their brains
Out of their miter'd Heads.
                            (*Ibid.*)

It is notable that when sketching the long list of prospective crimes that begins here and continues to the end of the poem Oldham does not rely upon his unaided imagination but turns instead to the heroic drama for ideas.[58] Page 265 of the manuscript has its margins filled with lines from Lee's *Mithridates* and *Sophonisba*, Otway's *Don Carlos* and Dryden's *All for Love*, while in the text lines from the drama are being given a new shape. From *Sophonisba* Oldham turns 'not one shall dare . . . / Nor for his soul whisper a dying Prayer' into: 'let them not dare / To mutter for their Souls a gasping Prayer.' From *Mithridates*, 'hurl Infants puling / From the lug'd breast' becomes: 'Pitty not Infants lugging at ye Breast', and is later modified to: 'Spare not young *Infants* smiling at the breast' (*SJ* 20). Another source at this point is Jonson's *Catiline*:[59]

No age was spar'd, no sexe. — Nay, no degree . . .
    'Twas crime inough, that they had liues.
                                    (I.239-44)

which becomes:

> spare
> No Age, Degree, or Sex; only to dare
> To own a Life, only a Soul to wear,
> Be Crime enough to los't;
> (RMS 265)

This is also substantively the reading of the pirated broadside *Garnet's Ghost* ([1679]), so it must have satisfied Oldham as a finished version for a while. But he finally tightened the structure of the lines, removing the clumsy 'to dare / To own', and the authorised printed version reads:

> spare
> No Age, Degree, or Sex; onely to wear
> A Soul, only to own a Life, be here
> Thought crime enough to lose't.
> (*SJ* 19-20)

Lines are not lifted from other writers and pushed unassimilated into the final poem. At one point Oldham recalled

> Submission, which way got it entrance here!
> — Perhaps it came e're Treason was aware

from *Don Carlos* and noted it in the manuscript in the form,

> Let no dull Virtue get Entrance there,
> but when Treason is not aware
> (RMS 250)

and then via 'Virtue intrudes with her lean holy face', from *Conquest of Granada,* arrived finally at:

> Let never bold incroaching Virtue dare
> With her grim holy face to enter there,
> No, not in very *Dream.*
> (*SJ* 11)

His common practice here is to use other poets' material to suggest his own ideas; revision often reduces or eliminates the parallels.

On the whole, the drafts show Oldham's detailed if sporadic care as a craftsman. Frequently the early drafts are weak, conceived without much pressure, and in need of working-up. This is particularly likely to happen where there is no clear overall direction of the design, and small pieces are recorded as they occur. Thus on page 250 in a passage of eighteen lines on the crimes of Catholics and sectaries there are four triplets, which are a sign not of strong but of slack poetry: there is more in each idea than can conveniently be shaped into a couplet, but not enough to generate a whole passage. In the printed texts all of the triplets survive, but the passage has been filled out with couplets. Similarly at the opening of the poem in the printed texts four couplets separate the first triplet from the second one, but two of these couplets are late additions. In an earlier version the closer proximity of these two triplets shows up more clearly how Oldham was finding it hard to get started. The third line of this triplet, for example, is just marking time:

> Like thine? we scorn so mean a Sacrament
> To seal & consecrate our high intent
> We scorn base blood should our high league cement.
>
> (RMS 248)

But there are examples of Oldham making a line stronger by repeated revision. On page 249 of the manuscript he writes:

> Well may such Fools be subject to controul
> Vassals to every thing y^t dares but rule.

and notes in the margin the alternatives 'The slaves', 'scepter'd Ass. y^t loads a throne'. The pirated printing of *Garnet's Ghost* has a couplet that looks as if it comes from an Oldham manuscript in which 'scepter'd' was taken up:

> Well may such fools be subject to controul;
> To every scepter'd wretch that dares but rule:

But in *Satyrs upon the Jesuits* (1681) we find:

> Well may such Fools a base Subjection own,
> Vassals to every *Ass*, that loads a Throne.
>
> (*SJ* 9)

which is the most accomplished version. It looks as if the broadside text derives from an early fair copy in which Oldham took from his marginalia the word 'scepter'd' but not the phrase 'Ass y^t loads a throne' which by 1681 he had come to recognise as the stronger reading.

It is beyond the scope of this book to examine in detail the *Satyrs upon the Jesuits*, for they are not part of Oldham's best work and have already attracted a disproportionate amount of attention from others; nor can I survey the literature of the Popish Plot at all comprehensively. But a brief sketch of this subject is necessary here to establish a context for Oldham's poems and to use that context to suggest an estimate of his contribution.[60]

It is clear from the Advertisement to the *Satyrs upon the Jesuits*, and amply confirmed by Professor Brooks's annotations, that Oldham composed these poems only after much research in primary sources for the history of the Jesuits and of the various persecutions. We saw in Chapter 1 that people with a sincere interest in religious controversy were prepared to take Catholic apologetic seriously and attempt to understand the opposing viewpoint. It is possible to find men in the Restoration period who were capable of taking a calm and balanced attitude: Halifax in *The Character of a Trimmer*, Sprat in his *History of the Royal Society*. Even at the height of the panic caused by the death of Godfrey it was possible to produce a dispassionate and non-partisan account of the murder that eschewed speculation about who was responsible.[61] In calmer times men could laugh at fears of popery coming in, and by 1681 one could write of

> many a witless, scribbling Tool;
> Who now sit mute, pick Teeth, and scratch the Head,
> Now th' Idol-Mother-Plot of Plots is dead.[62]

But at the time the fear was real enough, and good sense in short supply. An example of the staple fare is Henry Care's *Weekly Pacquet of Advice from Rome*, which he started on 3 December 1678. Each issue has two parts, 'The History of Popery', a serious refutation of Roman claims, and 'The Popish Courant', a satirical newsletter from Rome. The former seems designed for the intelligent reader who has no access to, or leisure for, the primary controversial texts. The first issues of 'The History of Popery' discuss the claim of papal authority by clear arguments about St Peter and the early Church, the authority of the Bishop of Rome under Constantine, the Council of Nicea. References are cited; there are quotations in Greek. But not all the argument is on this level; on page 94 we find:

> Pope *Paul* the 5th, who died but in the year 1621, caused
> his Picture to be put in the first page of divers Books dedi-
> cated unto him, with this Inscription: Paulo V Vice=deo;
> *To Paul* the 5th, a *Vice-god*: where note, that the *Numeral
> letters* of the Latine, exactly gives you the Number of the
> Beast, *Rev*. 13. *viz*. 666.

Well, they do; but like Care's frequent use of anagrams this will only convince the converted.

The poems written on the Popish Plot are a wild and various collection,

most of them very naive. One reacts to Godfrey's death with the cry of
'O Murder! Murder! Let this Shreik fly round.' Another makes capital out
of Oates's homosexuality and is adorned with a crude woodcut. Others
seize the chance to pay off old scores and attack the Presbyterians. Many
of the pieces are crabbed and obscure to the point of being unintelligible
today.[63] By contrast, Richard Duke's *A Panegyric upon Oates* has a light
touch that refreshingly takes the heat out of the subject, while remaining
an effective comment:

> Let's then, in honour of the name
> Of *Oates enact* some *Solemn Game*,
> Where *Oaten Pipe* shall us inspire
> Beyond the *Charms* of *Orpheus' Lyre*;
> *Stones*, *Stocks*, and every *Senceless thing*
> To Oates shall *dance*, to Oates shall *sing*,
> Whilst *Woods amaz'd* to th'Echoes ring.[64]

Apart from all this fun and fury, what were the real issues? *The Country-
mans Complaint, and Advice to the King* (1681) expresses a simple
concern about the loss of honesty:

> Vows and Religions are but bare pretence,   ⎫
> Oaths are found out to shackle Innocence,   ⎬
> And laws must serve a perjur'd Impudence ... ⎭
> All Truth and Justice, blushingly withdraw,
> Leaving us nothing but the Form of Law.

Equivocation, encouraged by the practice of casuistry, was similarly the
target of *The Priviledge of our Saints in the business of Perjury* (1681),
a cento of lines from *Hudibras* selected to make the point that 'Saints may
claim a Dispensation / To Swear and Forswear on occasion.'[65] Some of the
attitudes are reminiscent of Oldham's Garnet:

> Oaths are but words, and words but wind,
> Too feeble Implements to bind ...
> Oaths were not purpos'd more than Law,
> To keep the Good and Just in awe ...
> Is't not ridiculous and non-sense
> A Saint should be a slave to Conscience?

Links were also being made between the evils of popery and the Francophile
culture of Charles's Court. One pamphlet attacked Tories as lovers of
luxury, Rome and things French, of swearing and extravagant behaviour.[66]
The main threat, however, was seen to be one of violent subversion

based on a moral philosophy that encouraged equivocation. These ideas are not confined to those poems which announce themselves to be topical satire: they are also present in the drama. Adaptations of Shakespeare in the Restoration often prove to be a useful index to contemporary commonplaces. Crowne's *Henry the Sixth, The First Part* (1681), an adaptation of Shakespeare's *The second Part of Henry the Sixt*, features the murder of the Duke of Gloucester at the instigation of a cardinal. The Prologue offers the play as 'A little Vinegar against the Pope'. The scene between the cardinal and the murderers makes explicit the popular view of Catholic morality, and the same subject is treated by Crowne again in *The Misery of Civil-War* (1680; a version of *The third Part of Henry the Sixt*) in speeches such as:

> What then his Holiness will be your pardon?
> A very excellent office for a Pope!
> To be the Universal Bawd of Christendom!
> A very excellent Shepherd, that will give
> His Sheep a dispensation to be rotten!
>
> (p. 55)

and again:

> Do you think it easie to cheat priests,
> Who by the help, but of some barbarous words,
> As, *Entity*, *Unity*, *Verity*, *Bonity*,
> *Quiddity*, *Quantity*, *Quality*, *Causality*,
> Have conjur'd all you Kings out of their Kingdoms?
>
> (p. 61)

Part of the anxiety about casuistry may have come from a strong but vague association of it with the philosophy of Hobbes. Hobbes, of course, would have derided '*Entity*', '*Bonity*' and the rest, but his nominalism and his work of careful, even sly, definition may have unsettled men who knew what they meant by 'good' and 'evil'. Oldham's Garnet calls religion an 'empty name'. Besides, Hobbes's attack on popish superstition was uncomfortably close to an attack on all religion. Shadwell's *The History of Timon of Athens* (1678) acquires its frisson partly by being an instance of stage Hobbism, but good Protestants would also wish to attack Roman practices on the same grounds:

> I thought the Images of *Mercury* had only been
> The Favourites of the Rabble, and the rites of
> *Proserpine*: These things are a mockery to men

Of sence. What folly 'tis to worship Statues when
You'd kick the Rogues that made 'em!

(p. 58)

The Jesuits were a threat because Restoration England was vulnerable and confused both politically and philosophically.

As happened in the case of the *Satyr against Vertue*, Oldham allows his rhetoric to partake of the cheap sensationalism that thrilled the multitude, and the serious charges that he makes fail to convince in calmer times. He does point to the dangers to national and personal safety caused by the Jesuits' violent disregard for morality: specifically he is concerned for the rights of the king, for the sanctity of oaths and of the Bible. He thus appeals to common values shared by lovers of the Protestant Restoration whatever their party. Many of Oldham's points are made with force, but not with wit; much is crude, some is obscene. It did not have to be that way: in 1680 Sir Roger L'Estrange published *Twenty Select Colloquies out of Erasmus* and asked his readers 'to distinguish betwixt the *Romish Doctors* themselves; and not to involve *All Papists* under the same *Condemnation*. You will perhaps find matter of Diversion enough besides, to mollifie the *Evil Spirit*, and to turn some Part of the *Rage* and *Bitterness* that is now in Course, into *Pitty*, and *Laughter*' (Sig. A2r). Even when we make allowances for an element of disingenuousness in L'Estrange's claim (he was, after all, a propagandist) there remains to his contribution to the affray a genuinely humanist quality.

But a humanist element in Oldham's pieces is not much in evidence. Certainly he claims to be writing within the classical tradition, and acknowledges that Persius, Horace and Jonson were his models. But in spirit and intelligence there is nothing classical about these pieces. There are indeed moments when Oldham manages a subtler manner, as in the wittily reduced beast-fable in *Satyr* I:

> Grave bearded *Lions* manag'd the dispute,
> And reverend *Bears* their doctrins did confute:
> And all, who would stand out in stiff defence,
> They gently *claw'd*, and *worried* into sence:
>
> (178-81: *SJ* 14)

If only Oldham had been a closer student of the *Praise of Folly*! He lacked two gifts that Dryden possessed supremely: the ability to reason interestingly in verse, and the knack of transcending a particular crisis by translating it — finding a myth that made eternal the issues of the moment. Buckingham and Shadwell were almost irrecoverably translated, like

Bottom into the form of an ass, in Zimri and Mac Flecknoe. But Oldham's images do not have this power, which can only be the product of a highly disciplined artistic imagination. Though the finished *Satyrs* have been carefully organised, and their language is the language that Oldham considered appropriate, this *ad hoc* decorum cannot satisfy once the crisis is past. Oldham, in these poems, lacks 'true wit'; he is still learning.

4

HORACE

The *Satyrs upon the Jesuits*, which have only a notional relationship with classical satire, were composed during 1679 and published in November of 1680. A year after that volume appeared, Oldham published *Some New Pieces*, which included the first genuine fruits of his contact with classical poetry and with Boileau: imitations of Bion and Moschus, *A Letter from the Country* and four translations from Horace – of the *Ars Poetica*, *Serm.* I.ix, *Carm.* I.xxxi and II.xiv. The versions from Horace are his first formal adaptations from the classics, and deserve detailed consideration because we can observe Oldham tackling very different aspects of Horace and thereby extending his own range. By looking at the way in which he used the commentaries, translations and other sources we can follow an artist at work.[1]

Horace His Art of Poetry

In the first chapter it was suggested that while Oldham's education through the English grammar school curriculum and then at Oxford made him a competent classical scholar, well versed in interpreting Latin and Greek poetry, this education, though necessary for his later work, was not sufficient, and there was some other stimulus needed before Oldham took to translation in the way he did. And we have also seen how during 1678 Oldham turned to Boileau for guidance on how to write the sort of poetry that would really matter, both to himself and his age. Boileau's influence was to be important too in the translation of Horace's *Ars Poetica*, which he made probably in the spring of 1681. But Boileau was not the only Frenchman to enjoy a reputation in England, and to examine briefly the characteristic contributions to literary criticism made not only by Boileau but by Rapin and Bouhours as well may help to sketch a context for Oldham's version of Horace, and may also cast some light retrospectively upon the general character of the undertakings in which Oldham engaged during 1678, and upon the extent to which the discovery of his vocation depended upon his discovery of French thinking.

Through English eyes, French literary criticism of the later seventeenth century can appear narrowly hidebound by its insistence on 'rules' which have been abstracted from Aristotle (and twisted in the process by being muddled with Horace and sixteenth-century Italians) and which no longer have any organic relation to the procedures of living literature. Indeed, this would in many cases be a fair judgment. It is perhaps hard to follow Rapin with any interest when he writes to Bussy-Rabutin that 'On ne va à la perfection que par les règles.'[2] Certainly one has to be prepared for long stretches of Rapin and his colleagues to remain stubbornly inert for us, but since Dryden wrote that Rapin 'is alone sufficient, were all other Critiques lost, to teach anew the rules of writing',[3] and Oldham thought Rapin 'one of the best Criticks which these latter Ages have produc'd',[4] some inquiry is essential.

When Oldham wrote in *A Letter from the Country*:

> Strait the great *Stagyrite* I take in hand,
> Seek Nature, and my Self to understand :
> (101-2; *SNP* 123)

he was not voicing the last gasp of Oxonian scholasticism, but responding to the new and lively interest in Aristotle propagated, above all, by Rapin. The nature of this interest may be gauged through this quotation:

> ... il est bon de puiser dans les sources, d'étudier à fond les
> Anciens, principalement ceux qui sont Originaux : & sur tout
> se faire un sujet d'une meditation perpetuelle de la Rhetorique
> d'Aristote, qui a pris le soin d'exposer si exactement tout le
> détail des mouvements du coeur de l'homme.[5]

This is a note that recurs through Rapin's writing: knowledge of the 'heart' is the fundamental rule:

> La grande regle de traiter les moeurs, est de les copier sur la nature,
> & surtout, de bien étudier le coeur de l'homme, pour en sçavoir dis-
> tinguer tous les mouvements. C'est ce qu'on ne sçait point: le coeur
> humain est un abysme d'une profondeur, où la sonde ne peut aller,
> c'est un mystere impenetrable aux plus éclairez.[6]

In his *Reflexions sur l'Usage de l'Eloquence de ce Temps* Rapin has an impressive passage on the need for preachers to understand something of the constant self-deception and self-evasion in which the human heart indulges. The writer too needs to equip himself for his task not only by understanding the ways of the heart in general, but also by under-standing himself in order to perceive how his art needs both to develop and restrain his natural inclinations:

> Mais ce n'est pas tant pour sçavoir ses forces, qu'il faut connoistre
> son genie, que pour estre attentif à le former par le secours de
> l'art, & ne pas se méprendre dans les voyes qu'il faut tenir pour
> le perfectionner ... C'est donc par une longue reflexion sur soy-
> mesme, & par une perpetuelle meditation sur son naturel, jointe
> à l'étude, & à l'exercice de la composition qu'on se perfectionne,
> en perfectionnant son genie.[7]

These, I suggest, were the sorts of inquiry that Oldham had in mind in the
phrase 'Seek Nature, and my Self to understand'; besides, this passage
forms an apt summary of the exploration that we have observed Oldham
conducting during 1678.

Another contemporary French critic, Dominique Bouhours, reminds us
that the man of letters has to be learned but not pedantic; natural ability
and acquired scholarship have to be tempered by the education that only
familiarity with polite society can provide:

> Quoy qu'il en soit, continua Eugene, il est certain que la nature
> ne fait pas toute seule un bel esprit. La plus heureuse naissance a
> besoin d'une bonne education, & de ce bel usage du monde, qui
> rafine l'intelligence, & qui subtilise le bon sens. De la vient que les
> sçavans de profession ne sont pas d'ordinaire de beaux esprits:
> comme ils sont toûjours ensevelis dans l'étude, & qu'ils ont peu
> de commerce avec les honnestes gens, ils n'ont pas dans l'esprit
> une certaine politesse, & je ne sçay quel agrément qu'il y faut
> avoir. Ce n'est pas que la science soit contraire d'elle-mesme à la
> beauté de l'esprit; mais c'est que les grands Docteurs & ceux qui
> sçavent le plus de Grec & de Latin, ne sçavent pas le plus souvent
> bien user de leur science.[8]

In this *rapprochement* between classical texts and modern readers
the poets of Greece and Rome were taken out of the hands of the professional scholars and made to form (and, equally, to conform to) contemporary *mores*. Oldham shares this concern, though while he takes his cue
from Boileau in practising recreative translation, his work does not approximate at all closely to the ethos of Boileau's own culture.

There was at least one of Oldham's contemporaries who thought that a
careful study of Horace and Boileau was exactly what Oldham needed.
In one of the British Library texts of *Sardanapalus* the poem is followed
by these verses:

To the Author of Sardanapalus
upon That & his other Writeings.
S^r. William Some.

Thoe teaching thy peculiar Busness be
Learn this one Lesson, (School-master) of me
Where ere Sence fails, ye best Description's Vile
And a rough Verse the noblest Thought will spoil
Think it not Genius, to know how to scan
Nor Great to Shew a Monster for a Man
Wound not the Ear, with ill-turn'd Prose in Rhyme
Nor mistake furious Fustian for Sublime
Beleive this Truth, & thy vain Rumbling quit
What is not Reason, never can be Wit
From the Boys hands take *Horace* into Thine
And thy rude Satyrs by his Rules refine
See thy gross Faults in *Boileau's* faithfull glass
And get the Sence to know thy Self an Ass.[9]

Oldham was by no means the only poet interested at that time in the *Ars Poetica*. The poem had first been translated into English in 1567 by Thomas Drant, but the first influential version was Ben Jonson's, printed in the 1640 Folio, and separately as a Duodecimo in the same year. The Folio text (which Oldham used) was reprinted by Brome in his composite Horace of 1666 and 1671, 'borrowed', as he said, 'to crown the rest'.[10] Jonson's translation is very close to Horace, syntactically crabbed, but by no means without its occasional felicities. Still, it is surprising that it persisted into the Restoration, and in the 1680 revision Brome substituted a translation by 'S.P.' [Samuel Pordage]. In the same year Roscommon published his translation, and in 1684 there appeared Soames's own version of Boileau's *Art Poétique*, slightly revised by Dryden. In 1684 too Creech published a version in his complete translation of Horace. A brief glance at Roscommon and Soames is necessary as a preliminary to Oldham's translation, in order to gauge some of the difficulties of translating the poem known as the *Ars Poetica*.

One of the problems is signalled by the use of that title instead of *Epistola ad Pisones*, for if the Latin piece does hang together as a poem it is partly due to the epistolary mode, which allows informality, a constant wheeling round and backtracking in the way subjects are handled. Aesthetic principles emerge piecemeal. An important requirement for a poetic translation that follows the order of the original will be a mode that carries the discussion with ease; and one of the chief dangers, that the whole may fall apart into isolated rules and antiquarian examples.

The weakness of Roscommon's translation is of this kind. Roscommon is brief: he takes only 542 lines to Horace's 476. His compression, laconic style and excision of detail make for a collection of *sententiae* that are often admirably pithy when quoted in isolation, but are not always clearly related one to another as we read through the poem. There are times when it is hard to see how the poem is moving:

> A Poet should instruct, or please, or both;
> Let all your precepts be succinct and clear,
> That ready wits may comprehend them soon,
> And faithful memories retain them long;
> For superfluities are soon forgot.
> Never be so conceited of your Parts,
> To think you may perswade us what you please,
> Or venture to bring in a Child alive,
> That Canibals have murther'd and devour'd;
> Old age explodes all but Morality;
> Austerity offends aspiring Youths,
> But he that joyns instructions with delight,
> Profit with pleasure, carries all the Votes.
>
> (pp. 23-4)

This pared-down style makes it hard to grasp the *raison d'être* of the poem: there is little individuality, no distinctive mind at work with which we can make contact, and since Roscommon keeps the Roman references there are few connections into the literary experience of the Restoration.

Boileau made a radical transposition of the *Ars Poetica* when he wrote his *Art Poétique*, and it is the cautiousness of Soames when making his translation of Boileau that accounts for the disappointment we feel as we begin the first canto. Consider this:

> What-e're you write of Pleasant or Sublime,
> Always let sence accompany your Rhyme:
> Falsely they seem each other to oppose;
> Rhyme must be made with Reason's Laws to close:
> And when to conquer her you bend your force,
> The Mind will Triumph in the Noble Course;
> To Reason's yoke she quickly will incline,
> Which, far from hurting, renders her Divine:

But, if neglected, will as easily stray,
And master Reason, which she should obey.
Love Reason then: and let what e're you Write
Borrow from her its Beauty, Force, and Light.
(27-38)

There is hardly a line in this passage that is not a travesty of the best thought of the age. Not that it is literally unfaithful to Boileau:

Quelque sujet qu'on traite ou plaisant, ou sublime,
Que toûjours le Bon sens s'accorde avec la Rime.
L'un l'autre vainement ils semblent se haïr,
La Rime est une esclave, & ne doit qu'obeïr.
Lors qu'à la bien chercher d'abord on s'évertuë,
L'esprit à la trouver aisément s'habituë,
Au joug de la Raison sans peine elle fléchit,
Et loin de la gesner, la sert & l'enrichit.
Mais lors qu'on la neglige, elle devient rebelle,
Et pour la rattraper, le sens court aprés elle.
Aimés donc la Raison: que toûjours vos escrits
Empruntent d'elle seule & leur lustre & leur prix.
(1.27-38; pp. 138-9)

There are many instances even in these few lines of Soames not thinking out the implications of the Boileau. He thinks that 'Reason' (or 'the Mind' — and these are not necessarily equivalent?) has to reduce rhyme to submission: it sounds as if *rhyme* is being made 'Divine' by her submission to Reason's yoke, but in Boileau's

Et loin de la gesner, la sert & l'enrichit

'la' is 'la raison'. In Boileau it is reason that is not constrained but served and enriched by rhyme. To translate 'le bon sens' by 'sence' is not a mistranslation in the same way, but 'sence' does not carry the implication of a wide-ranging social, moral and literary decorum in the way that 'le bon sens' does — though Oldham's use of 'sense' in the same way suggests that Soames was hoping that his word would do the work of 'le bon sens'. But there was insufficient relevant achievement in English by the early 1680s for that to be possible. As a result Soames's line is remarkably banal: 'Always let sence accompany your Rhyme.' 'Accompany' here has none of the challenge implied in Boileau's 's'accorde'. It may appear that 'sublime' is performing an identical function in Boileau and Soames, but Boileau can trust his readers to understand the word because he had devoted a whole treatise to its illustration, the general tenor of which we may recall through a few fragments:

> ... si nous avons quelque voye pour nous rendre semblables aux Dieux; c'est de *faire plaisir* & de *dire la verité* ... le Sublime est en effet ce qui forme l'excellence & la souveraine perfection du Discours: ... il ne persuade pas proprement, mais il ravit, il transporte, & produit en nous une certaine admiration meslée d'étonnement & de surprise.[11]

Boileau has earned his right to use the word 'sublime'. We trust Soames less than we do Boileau not only because he has borrowed someone else's word, but because there is nothing in Soames's own writing to lead us to imagine that he could produce an account as fresh and enthusiastic as Boileau's. The failing is not just Soames's: 'sublime' has not been made part of the English critical enterprise (by Dryden, for example)[12] and it is fated to become a mere counter, as in these lines by Robert Gould:

> But, if in what's *sublime* you take delight,
> Lay *Shakespear*, *Ben*, and *Fletcher* in your sight:
> Where Human Actions are with Life exprest,
> *Vertue* extoll'd, and Vice as much deprest.[13]

If the second couplet is a clue to what Gould means here by 'sublime' then that word no longer has any traces of the living significance that it had for Boileau. Soames, not being a poet, merely borrows the big words, 'Reason', 'Sense', 'Sublime' in the hope that they will do his work for him, but they have lost their resonance. You can steal a talisman, but not command its power.

And this Dryden must have recognised. His tribute to Boileau in 1693 speaks of finding in France 'a living *Horace* and a *Juvenal*, in the Person of the admirable Boileau ... What he borrows from the Ancients, he repays with Usury of his own: in Coin as good, and almost as Universally valuable.'[14] It is in his person that Boileau recreates Horace; it is his own stamp that he puts upon his verse. We cannot say the same of Soames. Dryden seems to have done what he could, short of complete rewriting, to rescue Soames's *Art of Poetry*. Recognising that these precepts could not have much felt value for English readers unless they were cast in an English idiom (referring to English conditions, and enacted in English poetry) he changed the names and improved the first part of Canto IV. But as this was chiefly cosmetic, the poem's success remains limited. Neither Soames nor Roscommon matches the achievement of Boileau's *Art Poétique* because neither is re-imagining and re-valuing the Horace with the same urgency and involvement. I conjecture that it was because Roscommon's version has little of the personal and cultural energy of Boileau's (and none of its satirical edge) that Oldham thought that the task of interpreting Horace for his times was still to be done. A passage from Roscommon on the aims of education illustrates the effect of leaving the poem in its Roman dress:

> *Greece* had a Genious, *Greece* had Eloquence,
> For her ambition and her end was Fame;
> Our *Roman* Youth is bred another way,
> And taught no arts but those of Usury;
> And the glad Father glories in his Child,
> When he can subdivide a Fraction:
> Can Souls, who by their Parents from their birth
> Have been devoted thus to rust and gain,
> Be capable of high and generous thoughts?
> Can Verses writ by such an Author live?
> (pp. 22-3)

This has an impressive generality, a strong restrained force. The phrase 'high and generous thoughts' and the word 'devoted' (stronger then than now) make a general moral point. But compare Horace:

> Grajis ingenium, Grajis dedit ore rotundo
> Musa loqui, praeter laudem, nullius avaris.
> Romani pueri longis rationibus assem
> Discunt in parteis centum diducere. dicat
> Filius Albani, si de quincunce remota est
> Uncia, quid superat? poteras dixisse, Triens. eu,
> Rem poteris servare tuam. redit uncia: quid fit?
> Semis. at haec animos aerugo & cura peculi
> Cum semel imbuerit; speramus carmina fingi
> Posse linenda cedro, & levi servanda cupresso?
> (323-32)

There, in the same number of lines, is a dramatic sketch, and selection of significant detail that enforces a social point – about the aims of education, relative values in Rome, the choice of life. This is a familiar procedure, a poetic and satiric procedure, but not one that has much to do with the conception of poetry that leads Roscommon to instruct: 'Let all your precepts be succinct and clear.' The tendency for his translation to come apart into single-line precepts is aggravated by his unfortunate choice of blank verse as his medium. In Roscommon's hands it reads as unrhymed couplets, and has none of the powerful and flexible movement that blank verse can afford. Oldham allows himself more space and often translates more closely than Roscommon. He has a firm rhetorical control and command of verse paragraphs. In his hands the poem falls not into precepts but into passages where he was interested and passages where he was not. Here he clearly is engaged:

> *Greece* had command of Language, Wit and Sence,
> For cultivating which she spar'd no pains:
> Glory her sole design, and all her aim
> Was how to gain her self immortal Fame:
> Our *English* Youth another way are bred,
> They're fitted for a Prentiship, and Trade,
> And *Wingate*'s all the Authors, which they've read.
> *The Boy has been a year at Writing-School,*
> *Has learnt Division, and the Golden Rule;*
> *Scholar enough!* cries the old doating Fool,
> *I'le hold a piece, he'l prove an Alderman,*
> *And come to sit at Church with's Furs and Chain.*
> This is the top design, the only praise,
> And sole ambition of the booby Race:
> While this base spirit in the Age does reign,
> And men mind nought but Wealth and sordid gain,
> Can we expect or hope it should bring forth
> A work in Poetry of any worth,
> Fit for the learned *Bodley* to admit
> Among its Sacred Monuments of Wit?
>
> (516-35; *SNP* 26-7)

Oldham's reliance here upon commentators and previous translators is slight. There are few problems for him. 'Language, Wit and Sence' are hallmarks of modern culture, so these are retrospectively attributed to the exemplary classical civilisation. He places the narrow-minded businessman with that talent for monologue and hatred for enslavement by riches which are seen time and again in his satire. It is almost too easy. There is a colloquial turn to the grammar of

> And *Wingate*'s all the Authors, which they've read

and he has tossed off

> While this base spirit in the Age does reign,
> And men mind nought but Wealth and sordid gain,

without heeding the overinsistence in the adjective 'sordid' and the rhythm of 'Age does reign'. But on the whole the verse works well, with a vigorous rhythmic variety and deft manipulation of the couplet; often the unit of sense is extended to two-and-a-half or three lines. The colloquial attack on contemporary values takes off from, and returns to, some weighty lines encapsulating permanent classical ideas:

> *Greece* had command of Language, Wit and Sence . . .

> Fit for the learned *Bodley* to admit
> Among its Sacred Monuments of Wit?

This is one place where Oldham really could not have failed — the point of contact between Rome and London, the moment when the classics have a direct purchase upon the *mores* of his contemporaries, and upon an issue that rankled with him all his life.

In contrast to this, it may be instructive to see in detail how Oldham went about translating a passage that had no particular claims upon him — the account of the rise of tragic drama:

> Ignotum Tragicae genus invenisse Camoenae
> Dicitur, & plaustris vexisse Poemata Thespis:
> Quae canerent agerentque peruncti faecibus ora.
> Post hunc personae pallaeque repertor honestac
> Æschylus, & modicis instravit pulpita tignis,
> Et docuit magnumque loqui, nitique cothurno.
> (275-80)

> *Thespis* ('tis said) did Tragedy devise,
> Unknown before, and rude at its first rise:
> In Carts the Gypsie Actors strowl'd about, ⎫
> With faces smear'd with Lees of Wine and Soot, ⎬
> And through the Towns amus'd the wondring rout: ⎭
> Till *Aeschylus* appearing to the Age,
> Contriv'd a Play-house, and convenient Stage,
> Found out the use of Vizards, and a Dress
> (A handsomer, and more gentile Disguise)
> And taught the Actors with a stately Air, ⎫
> And Meen to speak, and Tread, and whatsoe're ⎬
> Gave Port, and Grandeur to the Theater. ⎭
> (427-38; *SNP* 22-3)

Open in front of him Oldham had the three previous seventeenth-century translations in English, those by Jonson, Pordage and Roscommon. There is no evidence to suggest that he knew Thomas Drant's version of 1567, or the Soames-Dryden translation of Boileau (which would be in manuscript), but the fourth book open before him was the *Art Poétique*:

> *Thespis* is said to be the first found out
> The Tragedie, and carried it about,
> Till then unknowne, in Carts, wherein did ride
> Those that did sing, and act: their faces dy'd
> With lees of Wine. Next *Eschylus*, more late,
> Brought in the Visor, and the robe of State,
> Built a small-timbred Stage, and taught them talke
> Loftie, and grave; and in the buskin stalke.
> 1640, Jonson (311-18)

> Thespis fut le premier qui, barboüillé de lie,
> Promena par les Bourgs cette heureuse folie,
> Et d'Acteurs mal ornés chargeant un tombereau,
> Amusa les Passans d'un spectacle nouveau.
> Eschyle dans le Choeur jetta les personnages:
> D'un masque plus honneste habilla les visages:
> Sur les ais d'un theatre en public exhaussé,
> Fit paroistre l'Acteur d'un brodequin chaussé.
> 1674, Boileau (III.67-74; p. 160)

> Once *Tragedy* was rude, and without Art
> When 'twas by *Thespis* carried in a Cart;
> Acting and singing they about did ride,
> With Lees of Wine, having their Faces dy'd.
> Vizards and Cloaths then Æschylus brought in,
> And was the first that did a Stage begin;
> Taught them to speak, with a more lofty Muse
> To tread the Stage, and Buskins how to use:
> 1680, Pordage (p. 402)

> When *Thespis* first expos'd the Tragick Muse,
> Rude were the Actors, and a Cart the Scene,
> Where ghastly faces stain'd with lees of Wine,
> Frighted the Children, and amus'd the Croud;
> This *Aeschilus* (with indignation) saw,
> And built a Stage, found out a decent dress,
> Brought Vizards in (a Civiler disguise)
> And taught men how to speak, and how to Act.
> 1680, Roscommon (p. 19)

Oldham's opening '*Thespis* ('tis said)' is a literal translation of 'dicitur ... Thespis', but the structure of the line is supplied by Jonson's '*Thespis* is said'. 'Tragicae genus ... Camoenae' is simply 'Tragedy' ('the Tragedie' (J)), whereas Roscommon has recovered the root meaning of 'Camoenae', the native Italian equivalent of the Greek Muse, in his 'Tragick Muse'. Oldham and Jonson keep close to 'invenisse' with 'devise' and 'found out'. Roscommon with 'expos'd' thinks more concretely of the stage. For 'ignotum' Oldham could not improve upon Jonson's 'unknowne'. Oldham's 'rude at its first rise' picks up 'rude' from Roscommon and Pordage. All four agree that 'carts' is the only English possibility for 'plaustris', and since it is an obvious one we cannot speculate upon whether it was (chiefly for Jonson) affected by folk memories of medieval and early Tudor styles of production, though Roscommon's 'a Cart the Scene' may be a different conception from Jonson's 'Carts, wherein did ride / Those that did sing, and act'. Roscommon's actors are 'rude', Oldham's are 'Gypsie'. The *OED* offers no help with 'Gypsie', so I can only assume that it is loosely used here for any uncultivated wandering people. 'Strowl'd' came into the language in the early seventeenth century and quickly acquired its familiar association with players. In Oldham's mind it was also associated with gypsies, for in the *Satyrs upon the Jesuits* he had written of

> The Church's *Hawkers in Divinity*,
> Who 'stead of *Lace*, and *Ribbons*, *Doctrine* cry:
> *Rome's Strowlers*, who survey each Continent,
> Its *trinkets*, and *commodities* to vent.
>
> (*SJ* 26)

'About' as a line ending was suggested by Jonson. 'Canerent agerentque' is translated literally by Jonson, but more freely by Roscommon ('Frighted the Children, and amus'd the Croud'), which, with Boileau's 'amusa', helped Oldham to 'amus'd the wondring rout'. If he needed a source for 'through the towns' he could have found it in 'par les Bourgs'. 'Peruncti faecibus ora' seems to admit of no wide solution: 'faces dy'd / With lees of Wine' (J), 'With Lees of Wine, having their Faces dy'd' (P), 'ghastly faces stain'd with lees of Wine' (R) and 'faces smear'd with Lees of Wine and Soot' (O), Oldham's imagination getting a little closer to what might actually have been the practice. The transitional 'post hunc', rendered 'next' (J) or 'till' (O) is omitted by Roscommon, who improvises 'with indignation'. Oldham's 'appearing to the Age' is simply a filler padding out a line that Roscommon had already begun for him by fitting Æschylus into a useful metrical position. There may be a hint of the different experiences of the Jacobean dramatist and the Restoration play-goer in Jonson's translation of 'modicis instravit pulpita tignis', 'Built a small-timbred Stage', compared with Oldham's 'Contriv'd a Play-house, and convenient Stage'. For 'repertor' Oldham uses Roscommon's 'found out'. 'Pallae' appears to be a special ceremonial garment for men, so Jonson's 'robe of State' is fair, and Roscommon's 'decent dress' is consonant with the general idea of a civilising reform, but Oldham's simple 'Dress' does not seem adequate. 'Disguise' also comes from Roscommon. 'Handsomer, and more gentile', for 'honestae' may take its comparative form partly from Roscommon, but also from Boileau's 'plus honneste', and the French influence may have led Oldham to 'gentile', a word re-adopted at the end of the sixteenth century from French, as this spelling reminds us. 'Docuit magnumque loqui' is naturally 'taught men how to speak' (R), which Oldham embroiders with 'Stately Air ... Meen ... Tread', catching for us the artificiality of Restoration tragedy. 'Port' is 'dignified carriage; stately bearing' (*OED, Port*₄ 1*d*, a 'rare' usage).

I trust that this sample demonstration will be sufficient to give the reader an idea of the mechanics of Oldham's translation. It is probably a fair illustration of how he uses his predecessors in passages that make no special claim on him (and in a fairly technical description such as this there is comparatively little room for originality). Where he is more interested there is often less use of previous versions, and profitable discussion needs to proceed at a different level.[15] In the remainder of this account of *Horace His Art of Poetry* I shall concentrate on passages that illustrate wider issues.

One of the themes of Horace's poem is the necessity for proportion and decorum in art, and in illustration he discusses the traits that are appropriate to characters at different stages of life. This passage derives chiefly from Aristotle's description in his *Rhetoric* of three ages of man: youth, old age, and maturity, which is the mean between the two. Horace adds another, the child:

> Reddere qui voces jam scit puer, & pede certo
> Signat humum: gestit paribus colludere, & iram
> Colligit ac ponit temere, & mutatur in horas.   (158-60)

> A Child, who newly has to Speech attain'd,
> And now can go without the Nurses hand,
> To play with those of his own growth is pleas'd,
> Suddenly angry, and as soon appeas'd,

Fond of new Trifles, and as quickly cloy'd,
And loaths next hour what he th'last enjoy'd.
(266-71; *SNP* 14)

Pordage and Roscommon are both too brief here:

A Child at first does childish things pursue,
Idly each hour a changed mind doth show,
Is quickly pleas'd, and soon does angry grow.
(Pordage)

One that hath newly learn'd to speak and go,
Loves childish Plays, is soon provok'd and pleas'd,
And changes every hour his wavering mind.
(Roscommon)

Had either of them ever watched a child walking with its newly-found firmness — 'pede certo signat humum'? Oldham does at least offer an equivalent vignette: 'And now can go without the Nurses hand'. Horace's 'iram / Colligit ac ponit temere, & mutatur in horas' is a rather summary account, and the greater feeling in the Oldham might derive from that in Aristotle:

εὐμετάβολοι δὲ καὶ ἀψίκοροι πρὸς τὰς ἐπιθυμίας, καὶ σφόδρα
μὲν ἐπιθυμοῦσι, ταχέως δὲ παύονται ὀξεῖαι γὰρ αἱ βουλήσεις
καὶ οὐ μεγάλαι, ὥσπερ αἱ τῶν καμνόντων δίψαι καὶ πεῖναι.
(II.xii.4)

('Changeable in their desires and soon tiring of them, they desire with extreme ardour, but soon cool; for their will, like the hunger and thirst of the sick, is keen rather than strong'.)

But I think rather that the reason why Oldham's translation gathers force from line to line is that he is drawing here on a sense of restlessness and dissatisfaction that we find not only elsewhere in his verse, but in that of Rochester as well. As an example from Oldham we may recall:

Tost by a thousand gusts of wavering doubt,
His restless mind still rolls from thought to thought:
In each resolve unsteddy, and unfixt,
And what he one day loaths, desires the next.
(*PT* 4)

Returning to the child, 'cloy'd' and 'loaths' are stronger words than we might expect in this context. While keeping the sketch appropriate to the child, Oldham is also hinting at a wider application.

Next comes the youth:

> Imberbis juvenis, tandem custode remoto,
> Gaudet equis canibusque, & aprici gramine campi;
> Cereus in vitium flecti, monitoribus asper;
> Utilium tardus provisor, prodigus aeris,
> Sublimis, cupidusque & amata relinquere pernix.
>
> (161-5)

> The beardless Youth from Pedagogue got loose,
> Does Dogs and Horses for his pleasures choose;
> Yielding, and soft to every print of vice,
> Resty to those who would his faults chastise,
> Careless of profit, of expences vain,   ⎫
> Haughty, and eager his desires t'obtain,   ⎬
> And swift to quit the same desires again.   ⎭
>
> (272-8; *SNP* 14-15)

'Pedagogue' may come from the gloss 'pedagogo' for 'custode', which most editors repeat from Pseudo-Acro, but Oldham may also be thinking of the hapless country youth in Rochester's *Artemisa to Chloe*, who was 'From pedagogue and mother just set free' (line 211). No translator shares Lubinus's optimism that a young man 'animum applicat vel ad Philosophiam, vel ad equos'! 'Cereus in vitium flecti' is literally, as Pordage has it, 'like wax, he yields to vice', and it should not be rendered as baldly as Roscommon's 'Prone to all vice' or Boileau's 'promt à recevoir l'impression des vices'. Oldham's 'Yielding, and soft to every print of vice' keeps the metaphor, but by changing Pordage's 'yields' to the more active 'yielding', adding 'soft' after the fashion of 'All the proud shees are soft to my Embrace' (*PT* 145), and suggesting the play of fingers in 'print', he gives the line a clear sensual charge. 'Careless of profit' may come from Pordage's 'cares not for profit' ('careless': J, R) and takes the severer view of Horace rather than the more indulgent view of Aristotle, who thought the young 'lovers of honour more than of profit'.[16] The two other strong words in this passage, 'Haughty' (ignoring the 'high-minded' element in 'sublimis') and 'swift', both come from Jonson.

In the account of middle age Oldham seems not to have been much interested:

> Conversis studiis, aetas animusque virilis
> Quaerit opes & amicitias: inservit honori:

Commisisse cavet, quod mox mutare laboret.

(166-8)

Those, who to manly years, and sense are grown,
Seek Wealth and Friendship, Honor and Renown:
And are discreet, and fearful how to act
What after they must alter and correct.

(279-82; *SNP* 15)

'Manly years' stays closer to 'aetas ... virilis' than the cautious 'riper years' of Pordage and Roscommon. 'Sense' and 'discreet' recur in Oldham's translation to denote the Horatian decorum in writing, but here seem to have no particular force.

But in the passage on old age Oldham really does seem engaged:

Multa senem circumveniunt incommoda: vel quod
Quaerit, & inventis miser abstinet, ac timet uti;
Vel quod res omneis timide gelideque ministrat,
Dilator, spe longus, iners, avidusque futuri:
Difficilis, querulus, laudator temporis acti
Se puero, censor, castigatorque minorum.

(169-74)

Diseases, Ills, and Troubles numberless
Attend old Men, and with their Age increase:
In painful toil they spend their wretched years,
Still heaping Wealth, and with that wealth new cares:
Fond to possess, and fearful to enjoy,
Slow, and suspicious in their managry,
Full of Delays, and Hopes, lovers of ease,
Greedy of life, morose, and hard to please,
Envious at Pleasures of the young and gay,
Where they themselves now want a stock to play:
Ill natur'd Censors of the present Age,
And what has past since they have quit the Stage:
But loud Admirers of Queen *Besse's* time,
And what was done when they were in their prime.

(283-96; *SNP* 15-16)

Roscommon has an inappropriate drama in his 'Old Men are only walking Hospitals.'[17] Pordage saw the combination of an abstract noun and potentially dramatic verb in

Multa senem circumveniunt incommoda

> A thousand ills, an old man do beset,

and Oldham likewise, though with a more precise choice of words, and more effective verse-movement. We can see from where Oldham has drawn some of the details for this passage. 'Still heaping Wealth, and with that wealth new cares' has been suggested by Boileau:

> La Vieillesse chagrine incessament ammasse,
> Garde, non pas pour soy, les tresors qu'elle entasse.

'Suspicious' may come ultimately from Aristotle, whose old men are 'always suspicious owing to mistrust, and mistrustful owing to experience'.[18] 'Full of Delays' is shared by Pordage and Roscommon. 'Lovers of ease, / Greedy of life' appears to come from Jonson's 'greedy ... of what's to come' and Aristotle's φιλόζωοι, probably via the gloss 'vitae cupidus, φιλόζωος'.[19] 'Morose' is from Pordage and Roscommon.[20]

But, having said this, Oldham's method of translation is shown up not as a mindless pillaging, but as a craftsman's careful selection of effective words, and once again the restraint and flow of the rhythm bear an aptly weighty reflectiveness. The extent to which Oldham's verse-movement matches the thought may be gauged by recalling Roscommon:

> Old Men are only walking Hospitals,
> Where all defects, and all diseases croud
> With restless pain, and more tormenting fear,
> Lazy, morose, full of delays and hopes,
> Opprest with Riches which they dare not use;

and then returning to the rhythms of Oldham.

The concluding *sententia*:

> Multa ferunt anni venientes commoda secum,
> Multa recedentes adimunt.

> Thus, what our tide of flowing years brings in,
> Still with our ebb of life goes out agen.

is culled from Pordage:

> The many Goods, our flowing years bring in,
> Decaying life bears from us, back ag'en.

and Roscommon:

> Thus all the treasure of our flowing Years,
> Our ebb of life for ever takes away.

As it stands, Oldham's couplet is an acceptable elegiac close, but this note was never one of his strengths, and it is no surprise to see how these lines were arrived at. Creech has a touch of inspiration in his last lines:

> The *Flow* of Life brings in a wealthy Store,
> The *Ebb* draws back, what e're was brought before,
> And leaves a *barren* Sand, and *naked* Shore.
>
> (p. 556)

The miseries of old age were of course a *topos*; what makes Oldham's account of particular interest is that he is performing (albeit briefly) what was for him the chief function of the poet – to make a commentary on the values of man. The greater power of the paragraph on old age may be due to the opportunity that it affords for contemplating man in the face of death, and thus for enforcing a value-judgment on the pursuit of wealth. The ostensible point of the Latin – instructions to the poet for the drawing of character – does not intrude.

A further implication of 'proportion' is that only if a style fits its subject can the poet hope to produce in his readers or audience the effect that he desires. When Dryden discusses this subject in the *Essay of Dramatic Poesy* he engages in some special pleading on behalf of rhymed plays:

> Tragedy we know is wont to image to us the minds and fortunes of noble persons, and to portray these exactly, Heroick Rhime is nearest Nature, as being the noblest kind of modern verse.
> *Indignatur enim privatis, & prope socco,*
> *Dignis carminibus narrari coena Thyestae,*
> (sayes *Horace*). And in another place,
> *Effutire leveis indigna tragoedia versus.*
> Blank Verse is acknowledg'd to be too low for a Poem, nay more, for a paper of verses; but if too low for an ordinary Sonnet, how much more for Tragedy, which is by *Aristotle* in the dispute betwixt the Epique Poesie and the Dramatick, for many reasons he there alledges, rank'd above it.[21]

Dryden is avoiding here the crucial issue – the relation of the language used to the feelings it expresses in the characters and designs to instill in the audience. The question was faced by Rapin in his account of the failure of contemporary tragedy:

> On ne parle pas assez au coeur des spectacteurs, qui est le seul art du theatre, où rien n'est capable de plaire, que ce qui remuë les

affections, & ce qui fait impression sur l'ame: on ne connoist point cette Rhetorique, qui sçait déveloper les passions par tous les degrez naturels de leur naissance & de leur progrés.[22]

Rapin's words speak to the condition of the English dramatists, who found it hard to forge a simple style that was not banal, and a passionate language that was not bombast. Horace's advice might therefore be apt:

> ... tragicus plerumque dolet sermone pedestri.
> Telephus & Peleus, cum pauper & exul uterque,
> Projicit ampullas & sesquipedalia verba,
> Si curat cor spectantis tetigisse querela.
>
> (95-8)

'Sermone pedestri' seems to have been a hard idea to pin down. Roscommon, reading back from 'Projicit', tries it negatively: 'Tragedians too lay by their State to grieve', and Oldham follows with:

> And Tragedy alike sometimes has leave
> To throw off Majesty, when 'tis to grieve.
>
> (165-6; *SNP* 9)

Roscommon has rendered 'Projicit ampullas & sesquipedalia verba' with neat literalness as 'Forget their swelling, and Gygantick Words.' Oldham with 'Lay their big words, and blust'ring language by' is approaching in 'blust'ring' a little closer to the actual language of Restoration drama. With 'si curat cor spectantis tetigisse querela' Roscommon's 'He that would have Spectators share his Grief' is to the point, while Oldham has been sidetracked, in 'If they expect to make their Audience cry', onto the external effect, possibly by following Porphyrio and Pseudo-Acro's 'si id agit ut adtente spectantem flere cogat' ('if he so arranges it that he carefully compels the spectator to weep').

But this happens not to matter, as Oldham now offers a few lines that do attempt to account for how that effect is produced. Horace is once again summary, and neither Pordage nor Roscommon stop to work out what he might mean:

> Non satis est pulcra esse Poemata: dulcia sunto,
> Et quocumque volent animum auditoris agunto.
>
> (99-100)

Your Poems must be soft, as well as fair,
To move their minds ev'n to what pitch you please.
                                            (Pordage)

He that would have Spectators share his Grief,
Must write not only well, but movingly,
And raise Mens Passions to what height he will.
                                            (Roscommon)

That leaves everything unsaid. In contrast to 'well' and 'fair', Oldham's 'elegant' does point to the superficial charms of Restoration drama, which need to be carried off by a deeper liveliness:

'Tis not enough to have your Plays succeed;
That they be elegant: they must not need
Those warm and moving touches which impart ⎫
A kind concernment to each Hearers heart,   ⎬
And ravish it which way they please with art. ⎭
                        (170-4; *SNP* 9-10)

This is the language that we have been missing – of an audience warming with concernment. It happens also to be the language of Dryden's discussion of whether an audience will be moved by reported incidents:

They therefore who imagine these relations would make no
concernment in the Audience, are deceiv'd, by confounding
them with the other, which are of things antecedent to the
Play; those are made often in cold blood (as I may say) to the
audience; but these are warm'd with our concernments, which
were before awaken'd in the Play ... the soul being already
mov'd with the Characters and Fortunes of those imaginary
persons, continues going of its own accord.[23]

(This is very much consonant with Rapin's critical interests.) Horace now has some lines (101-7) on the topic of:

Ut ridentibus arrident, ita flentibus adsunt
Humani vultus. Si vis me flere; dolendum est
Primum ipsi tibi ...

and then returns to our responses to drama:

> Format enim natura prius nos intus ad omnem
> Fortunarum habitum:
>
> (108-9)

Jonson offers: 'For Nature, first, within doth fashion us / To every state of fortune,' on which Pordage cannot improve:

> Nature doth first of all with us begin,
> And every change of Fortune forms within.

Roscommon, perhaps recalling 'cereus' from line 163 has: 'For Nature forms, and softens us within', which Oldham takes up and makes more concrete:

> For Nature works, and moulds our Frame within,
> To take all manner of Impressions in.

His next line, 'Now makes us hot, and ready to take fire', comes not from Horace's 'juvat aut impellit ad iram' (109), but from the line of Cicero quoted at this point by Pseudo-Acro: 'Ardeat orator si uult iudicem incendere' ('let the orator burn if he wishes to kindle the judge'); after which Oldham gives us a simple summary, 'Now hope, now joy, now sorrow does inspire.' But there is little here that amounts to a helpful account of our response, or a critique with some relevance to the contemporary drama. Oldham is often tied too closely to the literal sense and form of the Latin poem to be able to give his own work more than an intermittent hold on significant moral and artistic issues of his day.

Now, one such issue that literature and sub-literature of the Restoration compel us to consider is that of the morality of satire. Little attempt was made in the period to be clear about which forms of satire were healthy and which obnoxious, or about which style might be proper for a particular purpose. John Sheffield's remarks on the subject are too general to be of use:

> *Satyr* well writ has most successful prov'd
> And cures because the remedy is lov'd ...
>
> But 'tis mens *Foibles* nicely to unfold,
> Which makes a Satyr different from a Scold.
> Rage you must hide, and prejudice lay down,
> A Satyr's Smile is sharper than his Frown.[24]

Robert Wolseley attacked Sheffield in his preface to *Valentinian*, but concentrated on exposing muddle in Sheffield's reflections on bawdy songs. Wolseley also recognised, however, that as for satire, 'that most needful part of our Poetry, it has of late been more abus'd, and is grown more degenerate than any other; most commonly like a Sword in the hands of a Mad-man, it runs a Tilt at all manner of Persons without any sort of distinction or reason'.[25] Wolseley weighs in with some vigour against those who make indiscriminate satires against women, and then turns to a fault 'of a more serious Cast', which 'falling in with the baseness of a corrupt Age, does infinitely more mischief; this is made to wound where it ought to defend, and cover where it shou'd expose, to contradict the very first Elements of Morality, and bid defiance to the unalterable Essence of things, by calling *Good Evil, and Evil Good*'.[26] This could properly be alleged not only by partisans against their opponents' political satire, but by any disinterested reader of Oldham's *Satyr against Vertue*. Wolseley, however, has only proposed the heads of a discussion.

We have observed Oldham avoiding the question of the morality and decorum of satire when preparing *A Letter from the Country*. There were good reasons then for him being unprepared to tackle the issue, but now, with the *Satyrs upon the Jesuits* written, and the work of 1678 behind him, he had a wealth of relevant experience to bring to bear upon the 'Art of Rallying':

> But he, that would in this Mock-way excel,
> And exercise the Art of Rallying well,
> Had need with diligence observe this Rule
> In turning serious things to ridicule:
> If he an Hero, or a God bring in,
> With Kingly Robes, and Scepter lately seen,
> Let them not speak, like Burlesque Characters,
> The wit of *Billinsgate* and *Temple-stairs*:
> Nor, while they of those meannesses beware,
> In tearing lines of *Bajazet* appear.
> (370-9; *SNP* 19-20)

This is fairly elementary. But Oldham now seizes an opportunity to avoid a discussion of satire by retaining Horace's satyrs, even though Casaubon had long since dispelled the supposed origin of satire from satyrs in a book that Oldham claims to have read.[27] Oldham's partial transposition of Horace into modern terms reads very strangely:

> In my opinion 'tis absurd and odd,
> To make wild Satyrs, coming from the Wood,
> Speak the fine Language of the *Park* and *Mall*,
> As if they had their Training at *Whitehall*:

> Yet, tho I would not have their Words too quaint,
> Much less can I allow them impudent:
> For men of Breeding, and of Quality
> Must needs be shock'd with fulsom Ribaldry:
> Which, tho it pass the Footboy and the Cit,
> Is always nauseous to the Box, and Pit.
>
> (394-403; *SNP* 21)

Whether 'wild Satyrs, coming from the Wood' should 'Speak the fine Language of the *Park* and *Mall*' is no sort of question, but behind the words 'impudent', 'fulsome Ribaldry', 'nauseous' lurks an important unexamined issue. The imperfectly-realised contact between the ancient and modern worlds allows this question of the manner, function and effect of satire to slip past.

We have observed how Oldham gives this poem some contemporary purchase by intermittent modern reference and a strengthening of the social and moral satire. But this does not in itself amount to a modern stance securely in possession both of its classical inheritance and of its contemporary obligations, a position that would have the true independence defined by Jonson. For all Oldham's use of modern reference, he is still tied too closely to Horace; his version lies uneasily between the inert faithfulness of Roscommon and the radical faithfulness of Boileau; and with a poem as heterogeneous, idiosyncratic and occasional as this, a more drastic treatment than Oldham's was probably necessary if it was to come alive in more than patches.

Paradoxically, the very self-assurance of Restoration writers, their confidence in the seventeenth-century English achievement, was a hindrance to a modern stance that would exemplify a centrality of judgment. Sheffield in the *Essay upon Poetry* rewrites Horace's lines on studying the Greeks by night and day to refer to recent English literature:

> Yet to our selves we Justice must allow,
> *Shakespear* and *Fletcher* are the wonders now:
> Consider them, and read them o're and o're,
> Go see them play'd, then read them as before.[28]

It is similarly the trilogy of Shakespeare, Jonson and Fletcher that is credited with having achieved so much that they are almost a hindrance to the creativity of Dryden and his generation,[29] and the same three are invoked by Oldham:

Why should the pievish Cricks now forbid
To *Lee*, and *Dryden*, what was not deny'd
To *Shakespear, Ben*, and *Fletcher* heretofore,
For which they praise, and commendation bore?
If *Spencer*'s Muse be justly so ador'd
For that rich copiousness, wherewith he stor'd
Our Native Tongue; for Gods sake why should I ⎫
Straight be thought arrogant, if modestly ⎬
I claim and use the self-same liberty? ⎭
This the just Right of Poets ever was, ⎫
And will be still to coin what words they please, ⎬
Well fitted to the present Age, and Place. ⎭
                   (97-108; *SNP* 6)

The energy of this passage hardly seems justified by the ostensible subject, the coining of words. It probably derives from a conviction, though, of the worth of current attempts to create a literature to stand next to Spenser and Shakespeare. As early as 1668 we meet this claim in Dryden:

> I cannot think so contemptibly of the Age in which I live or so dishonourably of my own Countrey, as not to judge we equal the Ancients in most kinds of Poesie, and in some surpass them; neither know I any reason why I may not be as zealous for the Reputation of our Age, as we find the Ancients themselves were in reference to those who lived before them.[30]

This position is admirable as a manifesto, but has no foundation in any achievement. We have here in Eugenius, in parts of Oldham's *Horace His Art of Poetry*, and in much of Sheffield, Soames and Roscommon, a premature Augustanism. Inspired by the French, they often recognised ideals without possessing them, and their attempt to define classical values suffered a hardening of the critical vocabulary because it was made too early, with only aspirations and no achieved literature in English to support it.

If we look back on this period from the achievement of Pope, we might expect to find some preparatory awareness not only of the value but also of the difficulty of being a poet. This is registered in the present poem when Horace's remark that the athlete and singer only succeed by long practice and hard discipline, whereas everyone thinks himself capable of writing poetry, is rendered thus by Oldham:

> But each conceited Dunce, without pretence ⎫
> To the least grain of Learning, Parts or sence, ⎬
> Or any thing but harden'd impudence, ⎭

> Sets up for Poetry, and dares engage
> With all the topping Writers of the Age:
> '*Why should not he put in amongst the rest?*
> '*Damn him! he scorns to come behind the best:*
> '*Declares himself a Wit, and vows to draw*
> '*On the next man, who e're disowns him so.*
> (705-13; *SNP* 36)

The embryonic drama here is developed as Oldham turns to the adulation demanded by 'Scribblers of Quality' from their sycophants:

> All signs of being pleas'd the Rogues will feign, ⎫
> Wonder, and bless themselves at every line, ⎬
> Swearing, "*Tis soft! 'tis charming! 'tis Divine!* ⎭
> Here they'l look pale, as if surpriz'd, and there
> In a disguise of grief squeeze out a tear:
> Oft seem transported with a sudden joy,
> Stamp and lift up their hands in extasie:
> But, if by chance your back once turn'd appear, ⎫
> You'l have 'em strait put out their tongue in jeer, ⎬
> Or point, or gibe you with a scornful sneer. ⎭
> (726-35; *SNP* 37)[31]

The dramatic power of this may have helped Pope to the more regulated and economical achievement of the *Epistle to Arbuthnot*:

> View him with scornful, yet with jealous eyes,
> And hate for Arts that caus'd himself to rise;
> Damn with faint praise, assent with civil leer,
> And without sneering, teach the rest to sneer;
> Willing to wound, and yet afraid to strike,
> Just hint a fault, and hesitate dislike;
> Alike reserv'd to blame, or to commend,
> A tim'rous foe, and a suspicious friend,
> Dreading ev'n fools, by Flatterers besieg'd,
> And so obliging that he ne'er oblig'd;
> Like *Cato*, give his little Senate laws,
> And sit attentive to his own applause;
> While Wits and Templers ev'ry sentence raise,
> And wonder with a foolish face of praise.
> (199-212)

Pope has not only made the drama work on a smaller scale: he has made it carry a wider sense than Oldham managed of the general literary activity of his contemporaries, and the qualities and values engaged in the business of criticism. So whereas Soames and Sheffield tended to borrow their key words and did nothing to reinvigorate them, Pope now gives to 'spirit', 'taste', 'sense' and 'read' a clear meaning and value by deft incarnations of their opposites:

> Pains, reading, study, are their just pretence,
> And all they want is spirit, taste, and sense.
> Comma's and points they set exactly right,
> And 'twere a sin to rob them of their Mite.
> Yet ne'r one sprig of Laurel grac'd these ribalds,
> From slashing *Bentley* down to pidling *Tibalds*,
> Each Wight who reads not, and but scans and spells,
> Each Word-catcher that lives on syllables . . .
>
> (159-66)

The lines run on with a genuinely poetic energy. The confidence of Pope is that of a poet who, because he is also a critic, has made for himself a securely central modern stance, secure in his relation both to ancients and moderns. This is a personal achievement, but it would hardly have been possible without the preparatory work of Soames, Sheffield, Roscommon and Oldham, whose attempts at Arts of Poetry leave their traces in the Twickenham footnotes to Pope's *Essay on Criticism*. But among these efforts only the example of Oldham could have taught Pope that versified treatises were not good enough: that criticism had to be turned into poetry.

An Imitation of Horace Book I. Satyr IX

In making his translation of this satire, Oldham had several predecessors. The first version was by Thomas Drant in *A Medicinable Morall* (1566). Parts of it were adapted by Donne in his *Satyre IIII* (*c.* 1597), and the whole was dramatised by Jonson in Act III Scenes i-iii of *The Poetaster* (1602). John Smith translated the poem in his selection from Horace called *The Lyrick Poet* (1649) and it was rendered again anonymously in Brome's Horace of 1666. Yet another translation was published by Thomas Creech in his collected Horace (1684).

Of particular interest to us is the anonymous version in the composite Horace of 1666, which, along with the introduction to Cowley's fable of the town mouse and the country mouse, was made by Thomas Sprat. Sprat locates the poem in contemporary England, but he has not been able to rethink it as an English poem. He can certainly write fluent speech:

> You'l raise a mighty Fortune under him,
> But yet me thinks it would great wisdom seem,
> If you would take some course those to prefer
> About him, who might still possess his ear
> To your advantage, and if I were one
> You might be sure [to] govern him alone.[32]

But his touch is unsure. When he writes 'O no; pale Death did them long since devour' he is probably trying to give the fop an inflated turn of phrase, but it fails to be an appropriate phrase for a man of the Restoration. Sprat's narrative transitions are adequate, but compared with those of Oldham they appear awkward:

> Of late along the *streets* I musing walkt ... (Sprat)
> As I was walking in the Mall of late ... (Oldham)
>
> Then he begins ... (Sprat)
> Strait he begins again ... (Oldham)
>
> Over against *Guild-hall* at length we came ... (Sprat)
> By this time we were got to *Westminster* ... (Oldham)

Sprat lacks Oldham's ease. He produces very clumsy lines from time to time:

> But now at last by great good hap there was ...
>
> In thousand different postures did I go ...
>
> But you, nor I have now not much to do ...

These are poetic failings, in no way dependent upon Sprat's theory of translation or imitation, and it is for reasons such as these that although these pieces deserve a place in an outline history of 'imitation' they have no place in the poetry of the seventeenth century because they do not register any of the life of that age poetically.[33]

Thomas Creech rejected the principle of modernisation that Sprat and Oldham adopted:

> Some few advis'd me to turn the *Satyrs* to our own Times, they said that Rome was now rivall'd in her Vices, and Parallels for Hypocrisie, Profaneness, Avarice and the like were easie to be found; But those Crimes are much out of my acquaintance (Sig. A7*r-v*).

He thinks it better

> ... to convey down the Learning of the Ancients, than their
> empty sound suited to the present time, and show the Age their
> whole substance, rather than their thin Ghost imbody'd with
> some light Air of my own (Sig. A7r).

But the only way of showing their 'whole substance' is to present the
Latin originals: in a translation the 'Ghost' or spirit of Horace is inevitably
'imbody'd' in one man's English. In fact it is hard to meet Horace in
Creech. The narrative flow suffers because he tries to be too faithful to the
literal meaning and the laconic style. Creech has no controlling sense of
how the poems should read in English, probably because as a professional
classicist he is too close to the Latin, though he shows little sign of being
inward with the poems. As a result he has to borrow too many lively
touches from his predecessors. Here is the opening of I.ix, a fine chance,
one would have thought, for any translator to display himself and his
master to the best advantage. Italicised are borrowings from Sprat and
Oldham:

> *As I was walking* through the streets of Rome,
> *And musing on I know not what* nor whom,
> A *Fop* came up, by name scarce known to me,
> He *seiz'd* my hand, and cry'd, *Dear Sir how d'ye*:
> I thank you, pretty well *as times go now*;
> All happiness: *I wish the same to you*:
> But when He follow'd me, I *turn'd* and cry'd,
> What farther *business*, Sir? And He reply'd,
> *What dont you know me Sir*?
>
> (pp. 410-11)

Much of the idiomatic strength is in those italicised words.

The procedure that I have adopted in discussing Oldham's translation of
Serm. I.ix is to reprint the complete texts of the Latin and English poems
in short but integral sections linked by a commentary. I hope that this
method will allow the reader to enjoy two entertaining poems, and to
form his own opinion of the relation between the two texts at each stage
independently of my own account. The commentary is intended to
explain why Oldham made certain choices and how he arrived at particular
effects. The translations by Smith, Sprat and Creech are not good enough
to make continuous comparison profitable, but as a sample of their work
here is the opening of the Latin poem, followed by the four translations:

IBAM forte via Sacra, sicut meus est mos,
Nescio quid meditans nugarum, totus in illis.
Accurrit quidem, notus mihi nomine tantum;
Arreptaque manu, Quid agis dulcissime rerum?
5 Suaviter, ut nunc est, inquam: & cupio omnia, quae vis.
Quum assectaretur: Numquid vis? occupo. At ille,
Noris nos, inquit: docti sumus. Heic ego, Pluris
Hoc, inquam, mihi eris.

By chance I on the sacred way did walke
(As 'twas my use) what trifles I did talke,
Not knowing well, and whole in them: one came
To mee which was but only known by name,
And having catcht my hand hee thus did say,
How dost my sweete? as well as now I may
I answered him, I wish thee well (said hee)
In every thing; when still he followed mee,
I to prevent did ask what he would more
Thou know'st (saith hee) of learning I have store,
Then I repli'd, because thou learned art
I thee esteeme;

                           (Smith, pp. 150-1)

Of late along the *streets* I musing walkt,
And to my self some learned *whimsie* talkt,
When loe a wandring *Trifler* to me came,
Whom scarce I knew, save onely by his name;
And with familiar freedom took my hand,
Asking me, *How I did? At your command*
(Said I) *God keep you Sir.* He following still,
I turn'd about, and stopt to know his will.
What? dont you know me, man? (said he) *I too
A Virtuoso am as well as you.
The more I honour you, Sir* (I repli'd)
                           (Sprat, pp. 227-8)

As I was walking in the *Mall* of late,
Alone, and musing on I know not what;
Comes a familiar Fop, whom hardly I
Knew by his name, and rudely seizes me:
5 *Dear Sir, I'm mighty glad to meet with you:* ⎫
And pray, how have you done this Age, or two? ⎬
'Well I thank God (said I) *as times are now*: ⎭

'*I wish the same to you*. And so past on,
Hoping with this the Coxcomb would be gone.
10 But when I saw I could not thus get free;
I ask'd, what business else he had with me?
Sir (answer'd he) *if Learning, Parts, or Sence*
Merit your friendship; I have just pretence.
'*I honor you* (said I) *upon that score,*
15 '*And shall be glad to serve you to my power.*
(Oldham, *SNP* 45-6)

As I was walking through the streets of *Rome*,
And musing on I know not what nor whom,
A Fop came up, by name scarce known to me,
He seiz'd my hand, and cry'd *Dear Sir how d'ye*:
I thank you, pretty well as times go now;
All happiness: I wish the same to you:
But when He follow'd me, I turn'd and cry'd,
What further business, Sir? And He reply'd,
What don't you know me Sir? No faith: *What no?*
Come Horace *now you Jest, I'me sure you do*;
Why I'me a Scholar: Sir, I'me glad of that,
'Twill make me prize you at a higher rate.
(Creech, pp. 410-11)

To dispose first of all of the verbal debts to his predecessors, Oldham
has taken 'of late' and 'musing' from Sprat, whose 'with familiar freedom'
helped him to 'familiar Fop', and his 'The more I honour you' to '*I honor*
you ... upon that score.' In Rochester's *Timon*, the introductory passage is
clearly reminiscent of *Serm.* I.ix —

... a dull dining sot
Seized me i'th'Mall, who just my name had got.
He runs upon me, cries, 'Dear rogue I'm thine!'
(5-7)

— and this has contributed 'seized' and the setting of the Mall.

In Horace the emphasis is firmly on the poet from start to finish,[34] but
in Oldham's poem more attention is given to the fop and the milieu that
he springs from. Oldham is not as securely in possession of his social world
as Horace. For all the latter's occasional modesty he does have an assured
social position: strangers would have approached him in the street (cf.
Serm. II.vi) as they would not have approached Oldham. A few details

bear out this change of focus from the poet to the social world. Oldham has no equivalent for 'sicut meus est mos' or 'totus in illis', phrases that create Horace for us. He does not take up the commentators' suggestion that Horace was composing verses at the time, and whereas in the Latin 'quidam, notus mihi nomine tantum' is a complete definition of the man (all that matters is how he stands vis-à-vis Horace) Oldham uses two self-sufficient 'placing' words, 'Fop' and 'Coxcomb'. The fop simply 'comes', appears just as any other character would, without there being any sense of intrusion into the poet's private world such as is present in 'accurrit', where 'the very speed of the onrush, so different from Horace's leisurely pace, bodes ill'.[35]

Now we come to the first exchange. In the Latin, says Fraenkel, 'the first short sentences that pass between the bore and Horace (4-8) ... have the characteristic colour of the polite, if thoroughly conventional, phraseology favoured by the educated classes. Their shallowness and quick pace gives us the impression that we are catching snatches of a typical conversation in the street'.[36] There is something of this in Oldham too: his replies are comparatively laconic, and have a conventional turn to them:

> *'Well I thank God ... as times are now:*
> *'I wish the same to you.*

> *'I honor you ... upon that score,*
> *'And shall be glad to serve you to my power.*

The fop's language is formal, and somewhat affected:

> *Sir ... if Learning, Parts, or Sence*
> *Merit your friendship; I have just pretence.*

The flat rhythm of these exchanges contrasts with the next passage, which is aptly energetic in its rhythm. 'Wild to get loose' springs up from the line:

>   misere discedere quaerens,
>   Ire modo ocyus, interdum consistere; in aurem
> 10   Dicere nescio quid puero. quum sudor ad imos
>   Manaret talos; O te Bollane cerebri
>   Felicem, ajebam tacitus.

> Mean time, wild to get loose, I try all ways
> To shake him off: Sometimes I walk apace,
> Sometimes stand still: I frown, I chafe, I fret,
> Shrug, turn my back, as in the *Baigno*, sweat:

20 And shew all kind of signs to make him guess
     At my impatience, and uneasiness.
     'Happy the folk in Newgate! (whisper'd I)
     'Who, tho in Chains are from this torment free:
     'Wou'd I were like rough Manly *in the Play,*
25 *'To send Impertinents with kicks away!*

Possible sources

(16-17) And still all wayes to shake him off I tri'd (Sprat)

(17-18) Sometimes I went a pace sometimes stood still (Smith)
        Sometimes I walkt *apace* (Sprat)

(22) I *whisper'd* in my *Foot-boys* ear (Sprat)

(25) *an impertinent man* (Sprat)

Again, we see here the slight changes that shift the emphasis from a personal to a social world. Horace's graphic 'sudor ad imos / Manaret talos' is unfortunately replaced by a reference to the Bagnio, about which we may infer from the book published in 1680 that there was a general knowledge and interest.[37] Perhaps the adage *A capite usque ad calcem*[38] led Oldham to think that Horace's phrase was just a tag. Oldham does not have a servant, and without him the word 'whisper'd', which he has taken from Sprat, is not as good as Sprat's own 'muttered'. But if we agree with Dacier that 'ce passage est un de ceux qui marquent le naturel d'Horace' and look for similar strengths in Oldham, we may be pleased by the rhythmically restless 'I frown, I chafe, I fret, / Shrug, turn my back ...', where the words are strong native verbs of long standing in the language, 'shrug' meaning 'to move the body from side to side as with uneasiness' (*OED* 5).

Newgate, like the Bagnio, is part of that public world to which Oldham can easily make reference without trespassing on private worlds, either his own or his readers'. Both places would be known more by report than experience. Manly comes from a similar sphere of reference. Bolanus — whether fact or fiction — would presumably have been well known to the circle of Maecenas. To find a representative figure that works similarly for his wider audience, Oldham turns to the stage. But there were two opinions available as to what Horace intended by the allusion to Bolanus. Bond, knowing Horace's esteem for 'quiet of mind' explains that 'Bollanus nullo strepitu conturbatur, ergo foelicis erat cerebri' ('Bolanus was not disturbed by any noise, so he was of a happy mind'). In effect, this is the interpretation that Sprat follows, though he debases the idea:

> *Oh happy he*! (to mutter I began)
> *Who hugs himself at an Impertinent man*!
> Oh happy! who as well himself can feast
> On the most *foolish* talker as the best!
>
> (p. 228)

Other commentators incline to an opposite view, taking 'cerebrum' not as 'brain, understanding' but as 'anger':

> Ob cerebrum tuum hujusmodi garrulitatis & ineptiarum
> impatiens, qvi hujusmodi hominem garrulum statim
> reprehenderes, & a te abigeres[39] (Lubinus; Minellius-Rappoltus).

> Bene est, o Bollane, quod sis cerebrosus & iracundus, adeoque
> nullius molestias perfers: Horatius vero solebat se moribus
> hominum accommodare[40] (Mares).

Oldham's choice of interpretation was probably due to the accident of which commentator or teacher he had learnt from, but having made the choice, why include it in such forceful terms? I suggest that Oldham's mind was such that he instinctively thought of literary parallels. Theophrastus tells us how to deal with 'The Garrulous Man':

> παρασείσαντα δὴ δεῖ τοὺς τοιούτους τῶν ἀνθρώπων καὶ
> διαράμενον ἀπαλλάττεσθαι, ὅστις ἀπύρετος βούλεται εἶναι·
>
> (Ἀδολεσχία, 18-19)

> ('He who would not have a fever must shake off such persons,
> and thrust them aside, and make his escape' – trans. Jebb)

If Oldham did recall Theophrastus, it was a natural comparison to make: in his seminal edition of Theophrastus Casaubon notes against the line just quoted: 'Sic Horatius metuit ne a garrulo illo suo enecetur' ('Thus Horace feared that he would be killed off by his garrulous man').[41]

There is a temptation to label the change of Bolanus into Manly a 'modernisation' and to believe that to be an explanation. It is, of course, modernisation, but more importantly it is part of a general process of interpreting Horace to which Oldham is the latest heir and the latest contributor. To reconstruct as much as we can of the interpretative bridge by which Oldham moved from Bolanus to Manly is a fumbling attempt to follow how he re-felt the Latin.

But when he had decided on the sort of character he was looking for, why choose Manly? Professor Brooks says that the reference seems to be

to Act II Scene i of *The Plain Dealer*, where Manly, after threatening
Novel with kicking, puts him and Lord Plausible out of the room. That
explains the reference to kicks; and Act I Scene i offers another reason
for Oldham's choice:

> *L. Plaus.*   I wou'd not have my visits troublesom.
>
> *Man.*   The onely way to be sure not to have 'em troublesom,
> is to make 'em when people are not at home; for your
> visits, like other good turns, are most obliging, when
> made, or done to a man, in his absence. A pox why
> shou'd any one, because he has nothing to do, go and
> disturb another mans business?
>
> *L. Plaus.*   I beg your pardon, my dear Friend. What, you have
> business?
>
> *Man.*   If you have any, I wou'd not detain your Lordship.
>
> *L. Plaus.*   Detain me, dear Sir! I can never have enough of your
> company.
>
> *Man.*   I'm afraid I shou'd be tiresom: I know not what you
> think.
>
> *L. Plaus.*   Well, dear Sir, I see you wou'd have me gone.
>
> *Man.*   But I see you won't ... [*Aside.*
>
> *Man.*   I'de sooner be visited by the Plague; for that only wou'd
> keep a man from visits, and his doors shut.
>
> (I.i.57-88)

Wycherley has provided Oldham with an English dramatic counterpart to
Horace's scene.

The scholarly commentators on Horace are an important trigger of
recreative translation. They give the laconic Horace a lengthy paraphrase
that makes the syntactical and psychological connections explicit where
he had left them to be inferred by the reader. Thus on Horace's

> quum quidlibet ille
> Garriret; vicos, urbem laudaret
> (12-13)

Lubinus explains: 'modo *vicos*, per quos transiebamus, modo *urbem*
Romam garrulorum more ex quovis loco quacunque garriendi occasione
arrepta *laudaret*' ('Now he praised the streets through which we passed,
and now the city of Rome, seizing in his garrulous fashion upon whatever
opportunity for chatter each place afforded'). Oldham has a more fertile
imagination:

He all the while baits me with tedious chat,
Speaks much about the drought, and how the rate
Of Hay is rais'd, and what it now goes at:
Tells me of a new Comet at the *Hague*,
30 Portending God knows what, a Dearth or Plague:
Names every Wench, that passes through the Park,
How much she is allow'd, and who the Spark,
That keeps her: points, who lately got a Clap,
And who at the *Groom-Porters* had ill hap
35 Three nights ago in play with such a Lord:

Our immediate impression here is that we are in close touch with the life of Restoration London. If we turn up Professor Brooks's notes we are gratified to find that naming the wenches and losing money at the Groom-porter's were indeed occupations familiar to Etherege and Pepys, while the drought was also contemporary and can be documented from Evelyn. And yet, though the drought and hay-prices sound convincingly contemporary they can also be glossed from Theophrastus, who makes his 'Garrulous Man' remark on

... how cheap wheat has become in the market ... that, if Zeus would send more rain, the crops would be better (trans. Jebb).

καὶ ὡς ἄξιοι γεγόνασιν οἱ πυροὶ ἐν τῇ ἀγορᾷ· ... καὶ εἰ ποιήσειεν ὁ Ζεὺς ὕδωρ πλεῖον, τὰ ἐν τῇ γῇ βελτίω ἔσεσθαι.

('Αδολεσχία, 8-11)

We should not now be too surprised to read in Casaubon's edition at this point a cross-reference to the very line of Horace that Oldham is here embroidering: 'Eius generis illi sermones apud Horatium. – *cum quidlibet ille / Garriret, vicos, urbem, laudaret*' ('Conversations of this kind can be found in Horace: "he chattered on, praising the streets and the city"').[42] The point here is how naturally Oldham writes Theophrastus into his Horace, and his own character of the fop is closer in execution to the characters of Theophrastus – who allows them to emerge dramatically, by what they say and do – than it is to those of Hall, who relies more on his own general comments about their behaviour.

The next exchange of dialogue again strikes us as natural: the verse moves with the ease of conversation, but also registers the strains between the two men:

ut illi
Nil respondebam Misere, cupis, inquit, abire,

15 Jam dudum video: sed nil agis: usque tenebo.
Persequar. Hinc quo nunc iter est tibi? Nil opus est te
Circumagi: quemdam volo visere, non tibi notum:
Trans Tiberim longe cubat is, prope Caesaris hortos.
Nil habeo quod agam, & non sum piger. usque sequar te.
20 Demitto auriculas, ut iniquae mentis asellus,
Quum gravius dorso subiit onus.

When he observ'd, I minded not a word,
And did no answer to his trash afford;
Sir, I perceive you stand on Thorns (said he)
And fain would part: but, faith, it must not be:
40 *Come, let us take a Bottle.* (I cried) *'No*; ⎫
'Sir, I am in a Course, and dare not now. ⎬
Then tell me whether you design to go: ⎭
I'll wait upon you. 'Oh! Sir, 'tis too far:
'I visit cross the Water: therefore spare
45 *'Your needless trouble. Trouble! Sir, 'tis none*:
'Tis more by half to leave you here alone.
I have no present business to attend,
At least which I'll not quit for such a Friend:
Tell me not of the distance: for I vow,
50 *I'll cut the Line, double the Cape for you,*
Good faith, I will not leave you: make no words:
Go you to Lambeth? *Is it to my* Lords?
His Steward I most intimately know,
Have often drunk with his Comptroller too.
55 By this I found my wheadle would not pass,
But rather serv'd my suff'rings to increase:
And seeing 'twas in vain to vex, or fret,
I patiently submitted to my fate.

Possible sources
(36) I did nothing mind (Sprat)

(39) fain be rid of me (Sprat)

(45) trouble (Sprat)
needlesse (Smith)

(52) Tower (Sprat)

A sample of Sprat here illustrates just how natural and flexible Oldham's writing is:

> (He said) *you'd fain be rid of me, I find;*
> *But you, nor I have now not much to do,*
> *I'le therefore wait upon you where you go:*
> *Where lies your way? O Lord, pray Sir do not*
> *Your self for me to so much trouble put;*
> *My journey lies almost as far's the Tower,*
> *To visit one you never saw before.*
> *That's nothing sir, I'm perfectly at leisure,*
> *And a long walk with you I count a pleasure.*

Sprat has some neat touches (e.g. 'O Lord ...') but his staple verse is comparatively crude. Oldham's contrasting finesse appears in his selection of a turn of phrase which is lively and natural:

> *Sir, I perceive you stand on Thorns* (said he)
> *And fain would part* ...

and which also improves upon Sprat's blunt 'fain be rid of me' because it registers the bore's infuriating determination to keep up the polite forms. Similarly, he presents his imposition as a favour (lines 49-50). Horace maintained the polite forms in reply ('Nil opus est te / Circumagi') and while matching this Oldham also shows how the forms are under strain. Here a horrified exclamation is covered up by a hasty excuse:

> (I cried) '*No;*
> '*Sir, I am in a Course, and dare not now.*

Donne also uses the image of illness, but to very different effect:

> I belch, spue, spit,
> Looke pale, and sickly, like a Patient
> (*Satyre* IIII.109-10)

Donne's verse is self-regarding; Oldham's invites us to delight in finding the ebb and flow of the meeting registered in so responsive a medium. Delight surely continues to be our reaction as we read on:

> Incipit ille:
> Si bene me novi, non Viscum pluris amicum,
> Non Varium facies: nam quis me scribere plureis,
> Aut citius possit versus? quis membra movere
> 25 Mollius? invideat quod & Hermogenes, ego canto.

     Strait he begins again: *Sir, if you knew*
60 *My worth but half so throughly as I do;*
     I'm sure, you would not value any Friend,
     You have, like me: but that I won't commend
     My self, and my own Talents; I might tell
     How many ways to wonder I excel.
65 *None has a greater gift in Poetry,*
     Or writes more Verses with more ease than I:
     I'm grown the envy of the men of Wit,
     I kill'd ev'n Rochester *with grief, and spight*:
     Next for the Dancing part I all surpass,
70 St. Andrew *never mov'd with such a grace*:
     And 'tis well known, when e're I sing, or set,
     Humphreys, *nor* Blow *could ever match me yet.*

     Possible sources
(59-60) If once you knew me sir (Sprat)

(70) the mode of France (Sprat)

This does not really require commentary. Sprat's inspired mistranslation of 'novi' has aided the self-condemning monologue, which is one of Oldham's strengths.

The victim interrupts:

     Interpellandi locus heic erat, Est tibi mater,
     Cognati, queis te salvo est opus? Haud mihi quisquam:
     Omneis composui. Felices. Nunc ego resto.
     Confice. namque instat fatum mihi triste, Sabella
30 Quod puero cecinit, divina mota anus urna:
     Hunc neque dira venena, nec hosticus auferet ensis,
     Nec laterum dolor, aut tussis, nec tarda podagra;
     Garrulus hunc quando consumet cumque. loquaces,
     Si sapiat, vitet, simulatque adoleverit aetas.

          Here I got room to interrupt: '*Have you*
     '*A Mother, Sir, or Kindred living now?*
75 *Not one: they are all dead.* '*Troth, so I guest*:
     '*The happier they* (said I) *who are at rest.*
     '*Poor I am only left unmurder'd yet*:
     '*Hast, I beseech you, and dispatch me quite*:
     '*For I am well convinc'd, my time is come*:
80 '*When I was young, a Gypsie told my doom*:

> *This Lad* (said she, and look'd upon my hand)
> *Shall not by Sword, or Poison come to's end,*
> *Nor by the Fever, Dropsie, Gout or Stone,*
> *But he shall die by an eternal Tongue:*
> 85 *Therefore, when he's grown up, if he be wise,*
> *Let him avoid great Talkers, I advise.*

Possible sources

(73-4) Here it was time to interpose: Have you
       No mother Sir, nor other kindred (Sprat)

(76) The happier they (Sprat)

(79) My last hour's come (Sprat)

(84) fatal tongue (Sprat)

(86) Talkers (Sprat)
     strong tedious talker (Jonson)

Here we must admit that Oldham's passage is no more than adequate. His faithfulness to the Latin is always erratic because it is essentially an imaginative faithfulness, and his responsiveness to the texture of the Latin is also erratic because his commitment to the English poem is primary. But it is a clear loss not to match the force of the first-person singular in 'omneis composui' ('I've buried the lot'). 'They are all dead' is weak, while the compensating 'murder'd' is heavy-handed. The reader of Horace needs to decide whether 'Felices. Nunc ego resto. / Confice ...' is muttered or spoken aloud. Oldham has not made clear what he intends, and has thus left unclear his interpretation of whether the polite forms still hold between the pair or not. The line *'The happier they* (said I) *who are at rest'* could be a perfectly polite commonplace, spoken aloud to the fop, as consolation, but with a double meaning. However the next line, *'Poor I am only left unmurder'd yet:'* could only be grossly explicit if spoken aloud, which would spoil the subtlety of the previous line. It may simply be that Oldham has failed to ensure typographical clarity.

In Horace the soothsayer's speech is a fine parody of awe-inspiring language. We should not expect Oldham to see the same importance in the speech, but he ought to give it some significance: as it is, there is nothing distinctive in the verse of this passage to suggest its *raison d'être*, though the touch of doggerel in its last couplet is (one hopes) intentional parody.

The poem continues:

35 Ventum erat ad Vestae, quarta iam parte diei
Praeterita, & casu tunc respondere vadato
Debebat: quod ni fecisset, perdere litem.
Si me amas, inquit, paullum heic ades. Inteream, si
Aut valeo stare, aut novi civilia jura:
40 Et propero; quo scis. Dubius sum, quid faciam, inquit:
Tene relinquam, an rem. Me sodes. Non faciam, ille
Et praecedere coepit. ego, ut contendere durum est
Cum victore, sequor.

By this time we were got to *Westminster*,
Where he by chance a Trial had to hear,
And, if he were not there, his Cause must fall:
90 *Sir, if you love me, step into the Hall*
For one half hour. 'The Devil take me now, ⎫
'(Said I) if I know any thing of Law: ⎬
'Besides I told you whither I'm to go. ⎭
Hereat he made a stand, pull'd down his Hat
95 Over his eyes, and mus'd in deep debate:
I'm in a straight (he said) *what I shall do:*
Whether forsake my business, Sir, or you.
'Me by all means (say I) *No* (says my Sot)
I fear you'l take it ill, if I should do't:
100 *I'm sure, you will. 'Not I, by all that's good.*
But I've more breeding, than to be so rude.
'Pray, don't neglect your own concerns for me: ⎫
'Your Cause, good Sir! My Cause be damn'd (says he) ⎬
I value't less than your dear Company. ⎭
105 With this he came up to me, and would lead
The way; I sneaking after hung my head.

There are several borrowed phrases in this passage. Sprat's 'Guild-hall' anticipates 'Westminster'. The phrase 'his cause must fall' reads oddly: perhaps because Oldham had his eye not only on 'cause' in Sprat (and Drant) but also on 'causa cadere deberet' ('his cause must fall') — the gloss for 'perdere litem' ('lose his suit') offered by Minellius-Rappoltus and Lubinus. Lines 91-3 derive from Jonson's

> Now, let me dye, if I know your lawes;...
> Besides, you know, sir, where I am to goe.
>   (III.i.214, 217)

Sprat's 'Here he perplext stood still, and scratcht his head' is elaborated into lines 94-5. Two phrases gain by glosses. 'Make a stand' combines the senses of pausing in movement, pausing in speech, and being perplexed (*OED* 2, 2*b* and 6). 'In a straight' is illustrated in the *OED* by reference to Philippians i.22-4: 'yet what I shal chuse, I wote not. For I am in a strait betwixt two, hauing a desire to depart, & to bee with Christ, which is farre better. Nevertheless, to abide in the flesh, is more needfull for you.' Cumbersome glossing like this has to be resorted to now in order to recover the natural and apt force of these phrases in seventeenth-century use. Again we see Oldham expanding the terse Latin to reflect the psychological tussle between the pair in lines 97-101; in 101 the *gaucherie* of alluding so bluntly to one's 'breeding' deftly places the fop.[43] The graphic phrase 'I sneaking after hung my head' is a version not of 'Ego, ut contendere durum est / Cum victore, sequor' ('I follow, for it is hard to contend with a victor') but of 'Demitto auriculas, ut iniquae mentis asellus, / Quum gravius dorso subiit onus' (20-1) ('I hang down my ears, like a resentful donkey accepting a heavier load on his back'), which Oldham left untranslated earlier.

The next paragraph is Oldham's own addition, a rapid series of contemporary topics:

> Next he begins to plague me with the *Plot,*
> Asks, whether I were known to *Oats* or not?
> '*Not I, 'thank Heaven! I no Priest have been*:
> 110 '*Have never* Doway, *nor* St. Omers *seen.*
> *What think you, Sir? will they* Fitz-Harris *try?* ⎫
> *Will he die, think you? Yes, most certainly.* ⎬
> *I mean, be hang'd. 'Would thou wert so* (wish'd I) ⎭
> Religion came in next; tho he'd no more
> 115 Than the *French* King, his Punk, or Confessor.
> *Oh! the sad times, if once the King should die!* ⎫
> *Sir, are you not afraid of Popery?* ⎬
> '*No more than my Superiors: why should I?* ⎭
> '*I've no Estate in Abby-Lands to lose.*
> 120 *But Fire, and Faggot, Sir, how like you those?*
> '*Come* Inquisition, *any thing* (thought I)
> '*So Heav'n would bless me to get rid of thee:*
> '*But 'tis some comfort, that my Hell is here:*
> '*I need no punishment hereafter fear.*

We feel that there is here something of the texture of life in the 1680s,

but once more there is a literary source. In Donne's *Satyre IIII* the fop
'like to a high stretcht lute string squeakt, O Sir, / 'Tis sweet to talke of
Kings' (73-4), which may have contributed to the tone of line 116, while
the concluding lines 123-4 probably derive from the opening of Donne's
poem:[44]

> Well; I may now receive, and die; My sinne
> Indeed is great, but I have beene in
> A Purgatorie, such as fear'd hell is
> A recreation to, and scarse map of this.
>
> (1-4)

When the fop asks Horace for an introduction to Maecenas the Latin
poem moves into a more personal mode than heretofore:

> Maecenas quomodo tecum?
> Hinc repetit. paucorum hominum, & mentis bene sanae.
> 45 Nemo dexterius fortuna est usus. haberes
> Magnum adjutorem, posset qui ferre secundas;
> Hunc hominem velles si tradere. disperam, ni
> Summosses omneis. Non isto vivimus illic,
> Quo tu iere, modo. domus hac nec purior ulla est,
> 50 Nec magis his aliena malis. nil mi officit umquam,
> Ditior hic, aut est quia doctior: est locus uni-
> cuique suus. Magnum narras, vix credibile. Atqui
> Sic habet. Accendis, quare cupiam magis illi
> Proximus esse. Velis tantummodo: quae tua virtus,
> 55 Expugnabis: & est qui vinci possit. Eoque
> Difficiles aditus primos habet. haud mihi deero:
> Muneribus servos corrumpam. non, hodie si
> Exclusus fuero, desistam: tempora quaeram:
> Occurram in triviis: deducam. Nil sine magno
> 60 Vita labore dedit mortalibus.

Horace's personal engagement here is something that Oldham cannot match:

> 125   Scarce had I thought, but he falls on anew
> *How stands it, Sir, betwixt his Grace, and you?*
> *'Sir, he's a man of sense above the Crowd,*
> *'And shuns the Converse of a Multitude.*
> *Ay, Sir,* (says he) *you're happy, who are near*
> 130 *His Grace, and have the favour of his ear:*

> *But let me tell you, if you'l recommend*
> *This person here, your point will soon be gain'd.*
> *Gad, Sir, I'll die, if my own single Wit*
> *Don't Fob his Minions, and displace 'em quite,*
> 135 *And make your self his only Favourite.*
> *'No, you are out abundantly* (said I)
> *'We live not, as you think: no Family*
> *'Throughout the whole three Kingdoms is more free*
> *'From those ill Customs, which are us'd to swarm*
> 140 *'In great mens houses; none e're does me harm,*
> *'Because more Learned, or more rich, than I:*
> *'But each man keeps his Place, and his Degree.*
> *'Tis mighty strange,* (says he) *what you relate,*
> *'But nothing truer, take my word for that.*
> 145 *You make me long to be admitted too*
> *Amongst his Creatures: Sir, I beg, that you*
> *Will stand my Friend: Your Interest is such,*
> *You may prevail, I'm sure, you can do much.*
> *He's one, that may be won upon, I've heard,*
> 150 *Tho at the first approach access be hard.*
> *I'll spare no trouble of my own, or Friends,*
> *No cost in Fees, and Bribes to gain my ends:*
> *I'll seek all opportunities to meet*
> *With him, accost him in the very street:*
> 155 *Hang on his Coach, and wait upon him home,*
> *Fawn, Scrape and Cringe to him, nay to his Groom.*
> *Faith, Sir, this must be done, if we'll be great:*
> *Preferment comes not at a cheaper rate.*

'His grace' is generalised, no particular reference being intended. This in itself is no defect, but the lack of any particular pressure behind the lines makes for some weak stretches. *A Satyr Addressed to a Friend* shows that Oldham had strong feelings about the humiliation of patronage, which were capable of being turned into fine poetry, but he has nothing to say about such a happy and honourable arrangement as Horace describes. Oldham's lines are a dilution of Jonson's:

> Sir, your silkenesse
> Cleerely mistakes MECOENAS, and his house;
> To thinke, there breathes a spirit beneath his roofe,
> Subiect vnto those poore affections
> Of vnder-mining enuie, and detraction,

Moodes, onely proper to base groueling minds:
That place is not in *Rome*, I dare affirme,
More pure, or free, from such low common euils.
There's no man greeu'd, that this is thought more rich,
Or this more learned; each man hath his place,
And to his merit, his reward of grace:
Which with a mutuall loue they all embrace.
                                        (III.i.248-59)

But there is some vigour in Oldham's assertion that

> > no Family
> '*Throughout the whole three* ʸ*ingdoms is more free*
> '*From those ill Customs, which are us'd to swarm*
> '*In great mens houses.*

The verse pivots on the word 'swarm', which briefly creates the swirling crowd of parasites, and a notable feature of these lines is the free verse-movement, running straight on from the end of the triplet. Again, it is a general 'Family' — the poetry is engaged (where it is engaged at all) with Characters — great men, customs, creatures. In that last word, 'Creatures', the fop damns himself with a word loaded with opprobrium.

The poetry now gathers momentum, and becomes full of telling touches:

> *I'll spare no trouble of my own, or Friends,...*
> *Hang on his Coach, and wait upon him home,*
> *Fawn, Scrape and Cringe to him, nay to his Groom.*

That last line, with a final twist of which Pope might be proud, draws not on anything in Horace's 'Occurram in triviis: deducam', but recalls instead a traditional loathing, of which familiar examples might be:

> No, let the candied tongue licke absurd pompe,
> And crooke the pregnant hindges of the knee
> Where thrift may follow fauning;
>   (*Hamlet*, III.ii.60-2)

> Once fawn'd, and cring'd, and servilly ador'd
> Heav'ns awful Monarch?
>   (*PL* IV.959-60)

This language of fawning and cringing has been combined by Oldham with Jonson's version:

Nay, I'le bribe his porter, and the groomes of his chamber; make
his doores open to mee that way, first: and then, I'le obserue my
times. Say, he should extrude mee his house to day, shall I
therefore desist, or let fall my suite, to morrow? No: I'le attend
him, follow him, meet him i'the street the high waies, run by his
coach, never leave him (III.i.271-7).

In presenting a dramatic Character with these clear moral pointers Oldham
is at some distance from that Horatian irony (at least, as it is exemplified
in this poem) which Dacier admired:

C'est l'ironie de Socrate. Il me semble que je le vois & que je
l'entens. Quiconque ne connoistra point Socrate à ces manieres,
ne connoistra jamais bien Horace.

The animal language continues in the transition to the last episode:

60   Haec dum agit: ecce
Fuscus Aristius occurrit mihi carus, & illum
Qui pulcre nosset. consistimus. Unde venis, &
Quo tendis? rogat. & respondet: Vellere coepi,
Et prensare manu lentissima brachia; nutans,
65   Distorquens oculos, ut me eriperet. male salsus,
Ridens, dissimulare. meum jecur urere bilis.
Certe nescio quid secreto velle loqui te
Ajebas mecum. Memini bene: sed meliori
Tempore dicam: hodie tricesima sabbata. vin' tu
70   Curtis Judaeis oppedere? Nulla mihi, inquam,
Relligio est. At mi. sum paullo infirmior; unus
Multorum: ignosces: alias loquar. Hunccine Solem
Tam nigrum surrexe mihi? fugit improbus, ac me
Sub cultro linquit. Casu venit obvius illi
75   Adversarius: Et, quo tu turpissime? magna
Exclamat voce: & licet antestari? ego vero
Oppono auriculam. Rapit in jus: clamor utrimque:
Undique concursus. sic me servavit Apollo.

        While at this Savage rate he worried me;
160 By chance a Doctor, my dear Friend came by,
That knew the Fellow's humor passing well:
Glad of the sight, I joyn him; we stand still:
Whence came you, Sir? and whither go you now?
And such like questions past betwixt us two:

165   Strait I begin to pull him by the sleeve,
      Nod, wink upon him, touch my Nose, and give
      A thousand hints, to let him know, that I
      Needed his help for my delivery:
      He, naughty Wag, with an arch fleering smile
170   Seems ignorant of what I mean the while:
      I grow stark wild with rage. *'Sir, said not you,*
      'You'd somewhat to discourse, not long ago,
      'With me in private? I remember't well:
      Some other time, be sure, I will not fail:
175   *Now I am in great hast upon my word:*
      A Messenger came for me from a Lord,
      That's in a bad condition, like to die.
      'Oh! Sir, he can't be in a worse, than I:
      'Therefore for Gods sake do not stir from hence.
180   *Sweet Sir! your pardon: 'tis of consequence:*
      I hope you're kinder than to press my stay,
      'hich may be Heav'n knows what out of my way.
      This said, he left me to my murderer:
      Seeing no hopes of my relief appear;
185   *'Confounded be the Stars* (said I) *that sway'd*
      'This fatal day! would I had kept my Bed
      'With sickness, rather than been visited
      'With this worse Plague! what ill have I e're done
      'To pull this curse, this heavy Judgment down?
190   While I was thus lamenting my ill hap,
      Comes aid at length: a brace of Bailiffs clap
      The Rascal on the back: *'Here take your Fees,*
      'Kind Gentlemen (said I) *for my release.*
      He would have had me Bail. *'Excuse me, Sir,* ⎫
195   *'I've made a Vow ne're to be surety more:* ⎬
      'My Father was undone by't heretofore. ⎭
          Thus I got off, and blest the Fates that he
          Was Pris'ner made, I set at liberty.

Professor Brooks is probably right in supposing that Richard Lower is the doctor friend referred to. Oldham thus shares a private joke with Lower by writing him into the poem, as Horace did with Fuscus and Sprat with Cowley. But this is *only* a private joke: Fuscus and Cowley are identified, Lower is not. This is not because Oldham had no friends whose names were worth dropping (Lower was probably the most celebrated doctor of his day) but because it would be alien to the nature of his poem. The earlier allusion to Rochester was not a boast of friendship, simply part of the poem's public frame of reference. The introduction of a doctor also provides a neat way round the obscure reference to the Jews. The ending makes no attempt to match what Fraenkel sees as an epic strain in the Latin,[45] and reverses Horace's agreement to testify, drawing on an idea from an earlier part of Jonson's episode: 'Sir, I haue made a most solemne vow: I will neuer baile any man' (III.i.154-5), perhaps with a hint for 'My Father was undone by't heretofore' from Theophrastus:

καὶ δίκην ὠφληκότι ἐγγύης προσελθὼν κελεῦσαι αὐτὸν
ἀναδέξασθαι· ('Ακαιρία, 4-5)

('He will go up to one that has stood bail and lost it, and pray him to be his surety' — trans. Jebb.)

When Oldham first composed a satire upon the contemporary social world he based his poem on the most dramatic and least prescriptive of Horace's *Sermones*. By concentrating on the dramatic elements in his poem, and by using classical models, Oldham was giving his work authority and integrity through its apparent independence from its author. And if Oldham's handling of the social world lacks Rochester's epigrammatic pungency, and Pope's subtle enforcement of values, he has nevertheless achieved much. The *Satyrs upon the Jesuits* had shown his strong natural abilities and great learning; now both are being disciplined, as Rapin, Bouhours and Soames would wish, by steady attention to Horace.

Two paraphrases from Horace: *Carmina* I.xxxi and II.xiv

To attempt here any account of the many reasons why seventeenth-century readers enjoyed the odes of Horace would be far beyond the scope of our undertaking, and in so far as it relied upon English translations of Horace for clues to readers' interests it would probably be an inquiry neither enjoyable nor rewarding. Surveying English translations from Horace, Ezra Pound wrote that 'it is difficult to imagine anyone wanting to feel like Horace with sufficient force to produce the equivalent idiom'.[46] Without endorsing Pound's opinion of the small-mindedness of Horace, we can agree that translators face a peculiarly difficult problem if they are to attempt to match the play of wit and feeling that produces those odd transitions that, at best, strike us as right and inevitable. To adhere too closely to the surface of the *Carmina* may produce a translation that is merely quirky; on the other hand, one would have to be a Donne to produce equivalents to those movements from one's own resources. And for any lesser poet there is always the inherited pressure of the Horace *moralisé*, Horace reduced to a bloodless philosopher of moderation and retirement.

Some of Horace's love poems were much appreciated: III.ix was frequently translated, Jonson and Oldham being among the better poets to attempt it, though their results are not good. But it is the Horace who forms part of the Beatus Ille tradition who was probably most familiar to seventeenth-century readers. In the early 1680s a particular slant was perhaps given to this tradition. Dryden's translations of *Epode* II and *Carm*. III.xxix (which appeared in *Sylvae* in 1685) invite the reader to make himself free from the vagaries of Fortune and the wearying pursuit of wealth. Otway's version of *Carmen* II.xvi in the *Miscellany Poems* of 1684 states the idea quite clearly:

> Since wealth and power too weak we find
> To quell the tumults of the mind;
> Or from the Monarchs roofs of state
> Drive thence the cares that round him wait.
>
> Happy the man with little blest
> Of what his Father left possest;
> No base desires corrupt his head,
> No fears disturb him in his bed.
>
> What then in Life, which soon must end,
> Can all our vain designs intend?
> From shore to shore why should we run
> When none his tiresome self can shun?
> (pp. 321-2)

But in this form, the ideas are little more than commonplaces of didactic poetry; what happens in Dryden's versions of Horace, and, to a lesser degree, in Oldham's, is that the poet evokes the sensuous delights of life with a greater zest and discrimination because he is reappraising their value in a world menaced by Fortune and death.[47] It is a way of finding again a centre at a time in national or private life when — as Yeats has it —

> Things fall apart; the centre cannot hold;
> Mere anarchy is loosed upon the world,
> The blood-dimmed tide is loosed, and everywhere
> The ceremony of innocence is drowned;

> The best lack all conviction, while the worst
> Are full of passionate intensity.⁴⁸

Should we be justified in claiming that Oldham found a centre again in translating these two odes?⁴⁹ Here, first, is I.xxxi in Latin, followed by Oldham's adaptation:

ODE XXXI

Ad APOLLINEM

Non divitias petit ab Apolline, sed tranquillam
*   hilaremque vitam & ut sit mens sana in*
*   corpore sano.*

QUID dedicatum poscit Apollinem
Vates? quid orat, de patera novum
    Fundens liquorem? non opimas
        Sardiniae segetes feracis:
5 Non aestuosae grata Calabriae
Armenta: non aurum, aut ebur Indicum:
    Non rura, quae Lyris quieta
        Mordet aqua, taciturnus amnis.
Premant Calena falce, quibus dedit
10 Fortuna vitem: dives & aureis
    Mercator exsiccet culullis
        Vina Syra reparata merce.
Dis charus ipsis: quippe ter, & quater
Anno revisens aequor Atlanticum
15   Impune. me pascunt olivae,
        Me cichorea, levesque malvae.
Frui paratis & valido mihi
Latoë dones: at precor integra
    Cum mente, nec turpem senectam
20   Degere, nec cithara carentem.

Paraphrase upon HORACE

BOOK I.   ODE XXXI

1.

What does the Poet's modest Wish require?
What Boon does he of gracious Heav'n desire?
    Not the large Crops of *Esham*'s goodly Soil,
    Which tire the Mower's, and the Reaper's toil:

Not the soft Flocks, on hilly *Cotswold* fed,
Nor *Lemster* Fields with living Fleeces clad:
He does not ask the Grounds, where gentle *Thames*,
   Or *Seavern* spread their fat'ning Streams.
   Where they with wanton windings play,
And eat their widen'd Banks insensibly away:
He does not ask the Wealth of *Lombard-street*,
Which Consciences, and Souls are pawn'd to get.
   Nor those exhaustless Mines of Gold,
Which *Guinny* and *Peru* in their rich bosoms hold.

2.

Let those that live in the *Canary* Isles,
On which indulgent Nature ever smiles,
   Take pleasure in their plenteous Vintages,
And from the juicy Grape its racy Liquor press:
   Let wealthy Merchants, when they Dine,
   Run o're their costly names of Wine,
Their Chests of *Florence*, and their *Mont-Alchine*.
Their *Mants*, *Champagns*, *Chablees*, *Frontiniacks* tell,
   Their Aums of *Hock*, of *Backrag* and *Moselle*:
   He envies not their Luxury
Which they with so much pains, and danger buy:
For which so many Storms, and Wrecks they bear,
For which they pass the *Streights* so oft each year,
And scape so narrowly the Bondage of *Argier*.

3.

He wants no *Cyprus* Birds, nor *Ortolans*,
Nor Dainties fetch'd from far to please his Sense,
Cheap wholsom Herbs content his frugal Board,
   The Food of unfaln Innocence,
Which the mean'st Village Garden does afford:
Grant him, kind Heav'n, the sum of his desires,
What Nature, not what Luxury requires:
He only does a Competency claim,
And, when he has it, wit to use the same:
Grant him sound Health, impair'd by no Disease,
   Nor by his own Excess:
Let him in strength of Mind, and Body live,
But not his Reason, nor his Sense survive:

> His Age (if Age he e're must live to see)
> Let it from want, Contempt, and Care be free.
> But not from Mirth, and the delights of Poetry.
> Grant him but this, he's amply satisfied,
> And scorns whatever Fate can give beside.

Horace gives his *Carm.* I.xxxi a marked Roman setting, beginning with the dedication of a new temple, and passing on to evoke the fertile areas of Italy and the trade and agriculture that provided the wealthy Roman with the luxuries of life. The economy of Horace's final prayer for health and simple pleasures depends upon the contrast with the public world of ceremony and riches.

Oldham does not attempt to match the ritual opening: there was no hymnic tradition available to him comparable with that which Horace is using.[50] But where previous translators had contented themselves with something along the lines of, 'What does thy Poet aske ...' (Hawkins), Oldham begins by defining the thrust of his poem as the question 'What does any man need?', and taking a hint from Pseudo-Acro's note about 'modestiam uotorum suorum' starts thus: 'What does the poet's modest Wish require?'.

Horace now has a series of local references, to Sardinia, Calabria and Liris, for which Oldham has taken the trouble to find very appropriate English equivalents. In following the reasons for his choices we shall have to turn to written authorities, but Oldham himself was a Gloucestershire man who would have needed no such reminder of the agricultural riches around him. Just before he was born, a fine new hall for the wool trade was completed in Tetbury, where it still dominates the main street. His first equivalent is Evesham for Sardinia.[51] This was an apt choice, for Camden tells us that the Vale of Evesham 'for plentiful fertility hath well deserved to be called the Garnary of all these countries; so good and plentifull is the ground in yeelding the best corne abundantly'.[52] Horace's next reference is to Calabria and its 'armenta'. Modern scholars dispute the meaning of 'armenta': it probably refers to cattle. But the dispute has arisen because Calabria's chief claim to fame is its sheep. Certainly this was the interpretation that Lubinus gave to 'armenta' when he glossed it 'lanigera' (woolly), and Hawkins thought they were 'flocks'. Oldham follows this interpretation:

> Not the soft Flocks, on hilly *Cotswold* fed,
> Nor *Lemster* Fields with living Fleeces clad:

In the Cotswolds, says Camden, 'There feed in great numbers, flockes of sheepe, long necked and square of bulke and bone, by reason (as it is commonly thought) of the weally and hilly situation of their pasturage: whose wool being most fine and soft is had in passing great account among all nations' (p. 364). It was not only local pride in Oldham that dictated these choices: Camden also tells us of Leominster that 'the greatest name and fame that it hath at this day is of the wooll in the territories round about it, (*Lemster Ore* they call it) which setting aside that of *Apulia* and *Tarentum* all Europe counteth to be the very best' (p. 620). So the comparison between Leominster and Calabria had already been made. Horace's Sardinia, Calabria and Liris are all far apart, but Oldham has chosen an area of England where cornfields, flocks of sheep and fine rivers are all to be seen together:

> This Country [Herefordshire] besides that it is right pleasant, is for yeelding of Corne, and feeding of Cattaile, in all places most fruitfull, and therewith passing well furnished with all things necessary for mans life: In so much as it would scorne to come behinde any one Country throughout all England for fertility of Soile, and therefore say that for three w.w.w. wheat, wooll, and water it yeeldeth to no Shire in England.[53]

These, then, are

> the Grounds, where gentle *Thames*,
> Or *Seavern* spread their fat'ning Streams.
> Where they with wanton windings play,
> And eat their widen'd Banks insensibly away:

The vocabulary here seems carefully chosen. 'Grounds' and 'Streams' come from Hawkins's translation; 'spread' is used by Spenser and Milton of rivers passing through valleys;[54] and 'fatten' has the specific sense (*OED* 3) of enriching by irrigation, though the dictionary records no earlier use of the participle 'fat'ning'. Drayton — the expert on river-language — writes that the 'beautious *Severne* playes' and 'wantonly doth straine', and calls it 'winding',[55] which is literally true: '*Severn* ... with many windings and turnings in, and out, speedeth him unto the Ocean.'[56] And Oldham's last two lines have been shaped by these from Cowley:

> he now with wanton play,
> Kisses the smiling Banks, and glides away.
> (*Poems*, p. 245)

Yet the effect of Oldham's lines is not at all hackneyed. The verse moves slowly but not languidly. There is more activity than in the Latin, activity registered precisely by 'spread their fat'ning Streams', 'wanton windings', 'widen'd', 'insensibly', all of which briefly catch the slow but definite changes in nature, and they are all words that refresh one another by their use in new combinations.

Finally in this first stanza comes the translation of 'non aurum, aut ebur Indicum'. Oldham's emphasis on greed for money may have been prompted by Lubinus, who wrote in his commentary: 'Horum & consimilium cupiditate vel desiderio ego nihil sollicitor; & illa occupantibus nihil etiam invideo' ('I am not at all disturbed by greed or desire of these and similar things; and I do not in the least envy those who possess them'). Lombard Street was the resort of bankers and merchants, but since 'Lombard' was pronounced 'Lumber' (and 'Lumber' was a word for a pawnshop) the suggestion is made that these men are loading themselves with riches that are impediments to life, while at the same time pawning their souls and consciences by gaining money from usury. Guinea and Peru replace India as sources of gold, while Oldham adds the idea of the gold coming from 'exhaustless Mines'. 'Exhaustless' is perhaps a coinage, and like other words in '-less' of which Oldham was fond invites the reader to pause briefly on the root word, thus enhancing the force of its opposite.[57]

The second stanza is devoted to wines. The Canaries were a source of popular wine (especially sack) throughout the seventeenth century.[58] 'Press' may be an adaptation of 'premant', and 'Liquor' of 'Liquorem' from line 3, but we know from handbooks on viticulture that 'liquor' was actually the technical word for the juice squeezed out by the press.[59] 'Juicy' and 'racy', with the felicitous alliteration of 'pleasure' and 'plenteous', hint at the sensuous delight of wine-growing and wine-drinking. Horace now has a reference to wine brought from Syria – the trade with Syria being for exotic merchandise. Oldham's list of wines proves on inspection to be a very careful choice of exactly those wines which were most prized at the time. Florence wine was rare in Restoration London, but there are records of it being drunk by important government officials such as Sandwich, Conway and Williamson. It was only after the date of this poem that imports of Florence wine rose, until at the end of the century it was widely available in London taverns. 'Chests' is the technical term for the measure in which this wine was imported.[60] These uses of 'Florence' and 'Chest' antedate the first examples in the *OED*, which are from 1707 and 1708 respectively. 'Mont-Alchine' is not recorded in the *OED*, but John Evelyn wrote that travelling from Siena to Rome on 2 November 1644 he passed by 'Mount Alcini famous for the rare Muscatello'.[61]

The list of French wines – which does not include the commonly-drunk Bordeaux, now out of fashion in polite society – begins with 'Mants'. The editor of the 1697 reprint of Oldham displayed his lack of taste in emending to 'Nants', a brandy, but although Mants is not recorded in the *OED*, W. Hughes mentions 'your *Mant*-wine, a very good Claret' in his *Compleat Vineyard* (p. 65). A fine wine fits the context better than a common brandy: the playhouse prostitutes are drunk on Nants in Robert Gould's satire *The Playhouse* (1685). Champagne first became known in England in 1662, the king and his Court having acquired a taste for it during their exile in France. Saint-Évremond was particularly partial to champagne, and it was due to his enthusiasm that it became popular amongst the courtiers. André Simon says that

> ... Supplies, however, were difficult to obtain, as there existed
> no regular commercial relations between the Reims or Epernay
> wine growers and the London wine merchants. Rich and well-
> connected people used to buy their Champagne through some
> acquaintance residing in France, and they had it forwarded to
> England either direct or through the medium of some friendly
> ambassador, thus avoiding the duty.[62]

Oldham's use of Chablis is cited by the *OED*, which gives a quotation from Shadwell in 1668 as its first example. 'Frontiniak', a white wine from Languedoc was 'a very pretty pleasant wine', 'a luscious rich Wine', and appears to have been a favourite of the connoisseur, for Davenant writes: 'Nothing could please your haughty Pallat but The Muskatelli, and Frontiniak Grape!'[63]

'Aum' is another technical term, for the measure of Rhenish wine. Often the wine that was marketed as Rhenish was no such thing, supplies being scarce. André Simon tells us that

> towards the latter part of the seventeenth century, the German
> and Alsatian wines began to be known in England under more
> distinct appellations, some being the names of their growths,
> as Bacharach and Hockheim. Charles Bertie writing from London
> to his niece, the Countess of Rutland, at Belvoir, on September
> 8th, 1681, says: "I am glad your hogshead of Bacharach is
> arrived. Very little pure Rhenish is drunk in England. I will try
> to help you to another hogshead of Moselle or Pincair. I have
> written for a foudre of Hockheim." (III, 304).

It appears, then, that discriminating drinkers were by 1681 no longer satisfied with something just called 'Rhenish' but distinguished between the different areas, as Oldham does. Blount wrote that the Bacharach wines were called 'vulgarly, Rhenish wines'.[64] 'Moselle' is not noticed by the *OED* until 1687.

But while these names have been selected to make a precise impression upon contemporaries, the poem is not obtrusively topical. The import of French wines had been prohibited since 1679, so Oldham is not trying to make an immediate, satirical point. Indeed, there is a relish for this connoisseurship in the poem, and Oldham avoids opportunities for any crudely satirical strokes. There is no equivalent for 'Dis charus ipsis' (a phrase used by Horace with a touch of sarcasm) and Oldham does not share the condemnation of the merchants voiced by Lubinus: 'Imo vero maxime odiosus & invisus, quippe qui ... per summa vitae pericula ingentes opes sibi acquirat, & calamitosam maxime vitam vivat' ('He is indeed most odious and hateful who, at the greatest danger to his life, acquires huge wealth for himself, and leads a life fraught with great disasters'). The slow rhythm of Oldham's verse aids an almost objective statement:

> He envies not their Luxury
> Which they with so much pains, and danger buy:
> For which so many Storms, and Wrecks they bear,
> For which they pass the *Streights* so oft each year,
> And scape so narrowly the Bondage of *Argier*.[65]

In the third stanza Oldham works into Horace's ode a number of thoughts from *Epode* II and the Beatus Ille tradition. Despite the reference to 'Syra ... merce' Horace had not specified in I.xxxi any particular imported luxuries that he disdained, whereas Oldham writes:

> He wants no *Cyprus* Birds, nor *Ortolans*,
> Nor Dainties fetch'd from far to please his Sense ...

'*Cyprus* Birds' are Beccafigos, which are delightfully described by Willughby:

> *Beccafigo's* abound in ... the Island of *Cyprus*, where they are
> salted up in great numbers, and transported into other Countries.
> With us in *England* they are called by a general name, *Cyprus-birds*, and are in no less esteem with our Merchants for the
> delicacy of their taste, than they were of old with the *Italians*
> ... for feeding upon two of the choicest fruits, viz. Figs and
> Grapes, they must needs become a more wholsom food than
> other birds, yielding a better nourishment, and of more easie
> concoction.[66]

'*Ortolans*' are a delicacy introduced into the language by Cowley in his translation of Horace's *Epode* II:

> Nor *Ortalans* nor *Godwits* nor the rest
> Of costly names that glorify a Feast.
>
> (*Essays*, p. 413)

That these are 'fetch'd from far' is the burden of lines 49-55 of the Epode. 'Dainties' is another word from the Beatus Ille tradition: Spenser writes of 'the simple clowne, / That doth despise the dainties of the towne', (*FQ* VI.ix.7.4-5) and when Dryden translates *Epode* II he renders 'dapes inemptas' as 'unbought dainties of the poor'. It might have been a recollection of 'inemptas' in the Epode that prompted Lubinus's gloss on I.xxxi: 'frugalis victus non magno emtus' ('frugal victuals bought for very little'), which seems to have suggested 'Cheap' and 'frugal' in Oldham's next line:

> Cheap wholsom Herbs content his frugal Board,
>   The Food of unfaln Innocence,
> Which the mean'st Village Garden does afford:

where Oldham has also recalled Cowley's *The Garden*:

> Could nothing more delicious afford,
>   Then Natures Liberalitie,
> Helpt with a little Art and Industry,
> Allows the meanest Gard'ners board.
>
> (*Essays*, p. 425)

In place of Horace's specific 'me pascunt olivae, / Me cichorea, levesque malvae' Oldham keeps the thought general with his 'Herbs' (taken from the commentators), and the description of a vegetarian meal as 'The Food of unfaln Innocence' (an attractively cadenced phrase) may be a recollection of the meal prepared by Eve for Raphael in Book V of *Paradise Lost*. The phrase 'Village Garden' keeps the ideal a possibility in the ordinary world, and again recalls the celebration of the riches of poverty in *Epode* II.

Oldham's expansion of 'valido mihi / Latoë dones: at precor integra / Cum mente',[67] into:

> Grant him sound Health, impair'd by no Disease
>   Nor by his own Excess:
> Let him in strength of Mind, and Body live,
> But not his Reason, nor his Sense survive:

draws upon the general commonplace of 'sit mens sana in corpore sano', and probably specifically upon Lubinus's formulation 'bonam valetudinem animi & corporis' for 'strength of Mind, and Body'. We saw in the dis-' cussion of *Horace His Art of Poetry* that 'Reason' and 'Sense' are two of the period's key words, and in particular that Oldham uses 'Sense' to denominate those standards of behaviour and expression which cultivated men now demand. He may therefore expect the reader to register the two occurrences of the word 'Sense' in this stanza, and to ask himself how he values the senses that are pleased by dainties, as against the sense that values Nature, Innocence and Reason. It is remarkable that the care and relish with which material luxuries are evoked here invite us not to dismiss them but enjoy them, conscious all the time of a larger perspective, the values of Sense.

Finally, what would make old age a 'turpem senectam'? For Fanshawe it would be 'dotage', but for Oldham 'want, Contempt and Care'. These are indeed the concomitants not only of poverty but also of riches: the old man in *Horace His Art of Poetry* heaped up 'new cares' with his wealth. So Oldham wishes us to be free from the slavery to money that both poverty and wealth compel:

> Grant him, kind Heav'n, the sum of his desires,
> What Nature, not what Luxury requires:
> He only does a Competency claim,
> And, when he has it, wit to use the same.

Once again Oldham finds his note by adapting a phrase from one of Cowley's renderings of the corpus of poetry about the Happy Man; this time it is from *Georgics* II: 'on whom kind Heav'n bestows / At home all Riches that wise Nature needs' (*Essays*, p. 409). With this state of mind a man will, like Horace at the end of *Carm.* III.xxix be free from the vagaries of Fate and Fortune. But that was not how Horace ended the present poem. 'Nec cithara carentem' is not a limitingly personal wish, but it is more particular than Oldham wishes to be. He could have written enthusiastically about 'the delights of Poetry' but his purpose was not to write a private poem. Oldham therefore invokes values that all his readers could share, and yet keeps the expression of them free from banality by investing them with the rhythm of personal endorsement.

Although his translation of I.xxxi managed to renew many of the commonplaces of his subject by a careful choice of language and an expressive rhythm, II.xiv presents a much harder task, since countless poets had meditated upon death and the passing of the years. Oldham's version of II.xiv is less successful, chiefly because more of the traditional images remain mere commonplaces without being recharged. Here are the texts:

ODE XIV

Ad POSTHUMUM

Vita brevis, & mortem vitari non posse

EHEU fugaces, Posthume, Posthume,
Labuntur anni: nec pietas moram
   Rugis, & instanti senectae
     Afferet, indomitaeque morti.
5 Non si tricenis, quotquot eunt dies,
Amice, places illacrymabilem
   Plutona tauris: qui ter amplum
     Geryonen, Tityonque tristi
Compescit unda: SCILICET omnibus,
10 Quicunque terrae munere vescimur,
   Enaviganda, sive Reges,
     Sive inopes erimus coloni.
Frustra cruento Marte carebimus,
Fractisque rauci fluctibus Adriae:
15   Frustra per Autumnos nocentem
     Corporibus metuemus Austrum:
VISENDUS ater flumine languido
Cocytus errans, & Danaï genus
   Infame, damnatusque longi
20   Sisyphus Æolides laboris.
LINQUENDA tellus, & domus, & placens
Uxor: neque harum, quas colis, arborum,
   Te, praeter invisas cupressos,
     Ulla brevem dominum sequetur.
25 Absumet haeres Caecuba dignior,
Servata centum clavibus: & mero
   Tinget pavimentum superbum,
     Pontificum potiore coenis.

Paraphrase upon HORACE

BOOK II.   ODE XIV.

1.

Alas! dear Friend, alas! time hasts away,
Nor is it in our pow'r to bribe its stay:
The rolling years with constant motion run,
Lo! while I speak, the present minute's gone,
And following hours urge the foregoing on.
 'Tis not thy Wealth, 'tis not thy Power,
 'Tis not thy Piety can thee secure:
  They're all too feeble to withstand
Grey Hairs, approaching Age, and thy avoidless end.
  When once thy fatal Glass is run,
  When once thy utmost Thred is spun,
 'Twill then be fruitless to expect Reprieve:
  Could'st thou ten thousand Kingdoms give
In purchase for each hour of longer life,
  They would not buy one gasp of breath,
Not move one jot inexorable Death.

2.

All the vast stock of humane Progeny,
  Which now like swarms of Insects crawl
Upon the Surface of Earth's spacious Ball,
Must quit this Hillock of Mortality,
  And in its Bowels buried lie.
The mightiest King, and proudest Potentate,
 In spight of all his Pomp, and all his State,
Must pay this necessary Tribute unto Fate.
The busie, restless *Monarch* of the times, which now
  Keeps such a pother, and so much ado
    To fill Gazettes alive,
 And after in some lying Annal to survive;
 Ev'n He, ev'n that great mortal Man must die,
And stink, and rot as well as thou, and I,
As well as the poor tatter'd wretch, that begs his bread,
And is with Scraps out of the Common Basket fed.

3.

In vain from dangers of the bloody Field we keep,
        In vain we scape
    The sultry *Line,* and stormy *Cape,*
    And all the treacheries of the faithless Deep:
In vain for health to forein Countries we repair,
    And change our *English* for *Mompellier* Air,
    In hope to leave our fears of dying there:
    In vain with costly far-fetch'd Drugs we strive
    To keep the wasting vital Lamp alive:
    In vain on Doctors feeble Art rely;
Against resistless Death there is no remedy:
    Both we, and they for all their skill must die,
And fill alike the Bedrols of Mortality.

4.

    Thou must, thou must resign to Fate, my Friend,
And leave thy House, thy Wife, and Family behind:
    Thou must thy fair, and goodly Mannors leave,
    Of these thy Trees thou shalt not with thee take,
    Save just as much as will thy Coffin make:
Nor wilt thou be allow'd of all thy Land, to have,
    But the small pittance of a six-foot Grave.
        Then shall thy prodigal young Heir
    Lavish the Wealth, which thou for many a year
    Hast hoarded up with so much pains and care:
    Then shall he drain thy Cellars of their Stores,
Kept sacred now as Vaults of buried Ancestors:
    Shall set th'enlarged Butts at liberty,
    Which there close Pris'ners under durance lie,
    And wash these stately Floors with better Wine
Than that of consecrated Prelates when they dine.

Tempus fugit is just the first of the commonplaces that this poem
touches upon. The difficulty of writing yet again on this subject is one
of finding a freshness of language that also carries a freshness of thought,
and Oldham does in fact make some linguistic innovations that invite
the reader to see more in the old *topoi* than he had previously. 'Hasts
away, is more urgent than 'labuntur', a sense of urgency being continued
in 'bribe its stay', where 'bribe' is picked up from Horace's lines 5-7,

which Fanshawe translated as 'though thou bribe with daily Blood /
Sterne *Dis*', but Oldham gives to 'bribe' the meaning (apparently new
to the language[68]) of 'purchase or obtain by bribery'. When Oldham writes
about the years rolling on, his imagination seems to have been caught by
Ovid's account in *Metamorphoses* xv of the pattern of change in nature:

> Cuncta fluunt, omnisque vagans formatur imago.
> Ipsa quoque adsiduo labuntur tempora motu,
> Non secus ac flumen. neque enim consistere flumen
> Nec levis hora potest, sed ut unda inpellitur unda
> Urgeturque eadem veniens urgetque priorem,
> Tempora sic fugiunt pariter pariterque sequuntur
> Et nova sunt semper.[69]
>
> (178-84)

Oldham's line 'And following hours urge the foregoing on' has been
shaped by lines 181-2 in Ovid (prompted perhaps by 'urgentis' in
Lubinus's gloss on Horace) and his phrase 'with constant motion' may
therefore be a rendering of Ovid's 'adsiduo ... motu'. Oldham's line 'Lo!
while I speak, the present minute's gone' is also an addition to Horace,
perhaps from Boileau's 'Le moment où je parle est déjà loin de moi.'[70] The
sacrifice to Pluto is rendered by the empty phrase 'Couldst thou ten
thousand Kingdoms give', but the end of the stanza has an effective
addition to Horace; 'gasp' and 'jot' are strong, while 'inexorable' provides
a firm Latinate ending that is also rhythmically successful.

In the second stanza the commonplace of death the leveller is a difficult
one to renew. Oldham begins with the inflated language that is sometimes
the result of his attempts to be solemn, but quickly moves on to a miniature Homeric image of man as a swarm of insects.[71] When writing of the
fate of kings Oldham achieves an impersonal sympathy through the
measured repetition in 'all his Pomp, and all his State'. The 'inopes ...
coloni' whom Horace contrasts with the 'reges' are poor husbandmen;
Fanshawe writes of beggars, but this is too limiting for Oldham, who
wishes to make the point a general one, so that we cannot dissociate
ourselves so easily:

> As well as the poor tatter'd wretch, that begs his bread,
> And is with Scraps out of the Common Basket fed.

The point is tellingly made by plain language and appropriately abrupt
rhythms.

At the beginning of the final stanza the verse movement and the word
'resign' are dignified, while 'my Friend' softens the impersonality of the

gerundive 'LINQUENDA'. But Oldham omits 'placens', whereas Dryden, translating the parallel passage in Lucretius, will write warmly of

> thy Chast Wife, and thy dear prattling boys,
> Whose little arms about thy Legs are cast
> And climbing for a Kiss prevent their Mothers hast.[72]

Compared with this, Oldham's lines are austere, and the rhythm is awkward until the last line, where the stress on 'pittance' and 'six-foot Grave' is apt. The expression of the whole stanza is restrained. The words 'prodigal ... lavish ... hoarded' work well, but there is no attempt to make a moral point by translating 'dignior'; instead, just a brief reminder of the 'pains and care' that we met in I.xxxi. 'Wash' is a good word, but his predecessors have it too, and the ending is perhaps tame. We must presume that Oldham deliberately decided not to make an attack on overindulgent bishops: the implication of 'pontificum ... coenis' would have been clear to him from his textbook of Roman history, where Godwyn tells us that 'this word *Pontifex*, is commonly translated a Bishop or Prelate ... These Pontifies were wont to exceed in their diet, insomuch that when the Romans would shew the greatness of a feast, they would say it was *Pontifica coena*.'[73] But when a satirical manner is not appropriate, Oldham can eschew it.

No neat conclusion seems possible to this account of Oldham's work with Horace. It is not a neat subject. In some ways Horace's achievement is inimitable, and we should not expect many of his poems to be patient of translation. But Horace has set Oldham an important challenge, that of discovering decorum — a challenge which includes that of finding appropriate modern equivalents but goes far beyond it, in demanding renewed attention to his rhythms and vocabulary too as part of the act of rethinking and recreating Horace. Considering the difficulty of the task, Oldham has managed remarkably well in finding an appropriate tone and manner for the *Ars Poetica*, though he does not quite have the subtle control over verse argument that we meet in Horace or Dryden. In his version of *Serm.* I.ix Oldham has worked carefully at creating appropriate modes of speech that realise a social world. His translations of the two odes are not equally successful: I.xxxi has been made to address itself to questions about the choice of life that were close to Oldham's heart; II.xiv only rises intermittently above a list of forceful commonplaces. Yet all the time Oldham is discovering the range and temper of his talent through this recreative translation.

5

JUVENAL

Juvenal in the seventeenth century

Although some of Juvenal's admirers in the Renaissance, such as Scaliger and Lipsius, considered him to be a better poet than Horace, he had to wait until 1647 for a complete translation into English.[1] The fact that this work was being done in the midst of the civil war may be another illustration of the proposition that with the passing of Ben Jonson the impulse afforded by the Jacobean Renaissance was grasped at by men like Cowley who prized its achievement but who, under its very pressure, made mistaken choices in attempting to maintain its values. In the present instance a recognition of the value of Juvenal and a desire to improve the moral conduct of contemporary society issue in the presumption that the way to bring Juvenal into English culture is by a complete translation. This is an assumption that is so often misguided, since good translation has to be occasional.

In 1644 Sir Robert Stapylton published *The First Six Satyrs of Juvenal*, which was followed in 1647 by *Juvenal's Sixteen Satyrs*, a revised text of the earlier volume, adding translations of the remaining poems with marginal notes. This was again revised for the handsome folio *Mores Hominum* in 1660. All three versions are dedicated to his relative Henry Pierrepoint, Earl of Kingston and great-uncle of Oldham's patron. Stapylton recalls in his preface that it was Pierrepoint who urged him to begin the translation in 1638. He commends 'the usefulnesse of this Booke to all that study Men, to unlocke the secrets of whose brests he [Quintilian] knew no such key could be found in the larger fields of Rhetoricke'.[2] Addressing Pierrepoint, Stapylton hopes that

> ... after the learned *Authours* of *Sciences* and *Lawes* have taken up your *serious time*, ... the Authour I present, may entertaine your houres of recreation; which I would not promise to my selfe, but that he *delights* with *profit*; for your Lordships *recreations* are more *serious* then most men's *studies*, your very *mirth* being *observations* upon *men* and *businesse*.[3]

What sort of profit and delight did Stapylton believe that Juvenal offered?

First, he did not consider that English society was as corrupt as that of Rome under Domitian, and therefore when Juvenal lashes extraordinary vices modern readers would not feel outraged by receiving palpable hits as the 'Sect of *formall Stoicks*'[4] had felt in Juvenal's own day:

> For our Nation hath long since disclaimed the *Roman power* and *crimes* together: and sure no *Englishman* will now degenerate, after we have for so many ages bin delivered from their bondage, to confesse himself *slave* to their vices, with being troubled at any thing this book containes; And therefore I have made it plaine and easy; not doubting but the same sharpnesse of wit, that once displeased the vitious, will be now understood with pleasure, by the vertuous Readers.[5]

Indeed, Stapylton seems to have believed that although human nature was still the same, English society now possessed a higher degree of humane culture than Juvenal's Rome, and would therefore be more receptive to his satire:

> I am confident, his successe will be much better now, when he admonishes a *Kingdom* as eminent in knowledge as in *Luxury*, where he will from henceforth attend the Noble in their chambers, and the People at Church doores; that such as have scaped the *Preacher*, may fall vpon the *Satyrist*, and then, no doubt but they will reforme, if not for *Christian duty*, yet for shame to be thus *divinely* reproved by a *Heathen*.[6]

Much of Juvenal's teaching is positive, for 'scarce any Philosopher hath left so many excellent morall Precepts and incouragements to virtue, as this Poet',[7] and 'if we pay respect (and worthily) to *speculative Authors* that informe the *understanding*; how much more is due to *Juvenal*, for instructing us in point of *Manners*, teaching the world to *know* and *practise virtue*, and persecuting or (more properly) baiting *Vices* with his *Satyrs*?'[8]

Stapylton does not, however, ask whether some of Juvenal's satires are more valuable than others, whether they are all equal in their moral rectitude and contemporary relevance, or whether they are all delightful in the same ways. For delightful they certainly are: 'while he delights his *worst* and *guiltiest* Readers, like an excellent Phisitian, he does a cure upon them, by pleasure opening of the way to benefit'. How this connection between pleasure and profit works is not clear — both the idea and its nebulousness being an inheritance from Aristotle through Horace. But

Stapylton does venture a little further in his account of what it is that gives pleasure in a reading of Juvenal. His first point concerns the nature of the verse (it is worth noting in passing that Stapylton is already using the terminology of Denham's lines on style in *Cooper's Hill* (1642)):

> ... his Verse, flowing like a river when the wind breathes gently, *smooth* besides the bankes, *strong* in the current, and not inclining to *roughnesse* but (according to nature) at reaches, *windings* of designe.

His philosophy is enacted in his poetry: he is

> ... not one of those that *dispute* of Virtue and Vice, but that with inimitable *sweetnesse* of *Language*, and *Majesty* of *Sentences*, sets before our eyes the loveliness of the one, and the deformity and horour of the other; with all the skill and *perfection* of *Philosophy*.

Quoting Scaliger and Lipsius, Stapylton adds that Juvenal is 'furious':

> ... he assaults and kils. His stile is extremely handsome, in which together with the *Roman purity*, he hath the happines of excellent connexions. His *verse* is farre above *Horace*, his *sentences* sharper, and he speakes things more to the life ... He touches vice to the quicke, reproves, cries out upon it: now and then he makes us laugh, but very often mixes bitter stinging jests.[9]

The next translator, Barten Holyday, whose version appeared in 1673, agreed with these ideas about the poetic qualities of Juvenal. Again citing Scaliger's comparison of Juvenal with Horace he reports that Juvenal '*ardet, instat, aperte jugulat*'; his Purity is *Roman*, his Composure happy, his Verse better, his Sentences sharper, his Phrase more open, his Satyre more accurate'.[10] As befitted an archdeacon of Oxford, Holyday 'ventur'd on this work, not doubting but that a man may, not without success, though without custome, Preach in Verse'. As befitted a scholar and a friend of Ben Jonson, his translation is accompanied by many pages of notes and illustrations. But we must concur with Dryden's verdict that the 'Interpretation, and Illustrations of *Juvenal* are as Excellent as the Verse of his Translation and his *English* are lame and pitiful.'[11] Neither Stapylton nor Holyday were poets: Holyday, indeed, scarcely writes verse. The reader of these versions would at times have been hard put to work out a meaning from the crabbed and contorted English, and certainly would have derived from them little of that pleasure in stylistic brilliance for which the translators valued their original. If profit is really a concomitant of pleasure the flatness of these translations must have reduced their value as instruments of moral reform. Nevertheless, they would have provided a handy guide to Roman life, and in the case of Stapylton the verse does at least indicate topics of concern:

> For here to money's Majesty we yeeld
> Divine respect; though, fatall Gold, we build
> To thee no Temples yet: though Silver hath
> No Altars like to Victory, Peace, Faith,
> Virtue, and Concord . . .[12]

There may be a touch here of the verse-movement of Jonson's *Epigrammes*, but the enjambement is perhaps determined more by a lack of ease in handling the verse than by a thought that (as in Jonson) needs to find a knotty expression. Stapylton's command of his medium is erratic; this passage from *Satire* VI shows him at his best:

> Th' Imperiall Strumpet with one Maid, stole out
> In her Night-hoods, and having put about
> Her black hair a red Perriwig, she got
> Into the Stews, where th'old rugge still was hot:
> In a spare room, kept for her, there gold-chain'd,
> Bare breasted stood, her name LYCISCA fain'd:
> High-born BRITANNICUS thy womb display'd;
> Smil'd upon all that came, her bargain made;
> And when the Wenches were dismis'd, she last
> ('Twas all she could) sadly the dore made fast;
> And many thirsted-for encounters try'd,
> Departed tir'd with men, not satisfied:
> And foul'd with candle-smoak, her cheeks smear'd o're,
> The Brothel-steam to CAESAR's pillow bore.[13]

The passage is not an achieved whole. Stapylton has no sustained poetic impetus, though there are moments when the verse does work remarkably well — in the phrase 'sadly the dore made fast', and in the last four lines, which compare very favourably with Dryden's translation:

> All Filth without and all a Fire within,
> Tir'd with the Toyl, unsated with the Sin.
> Old *Caesar*'s Bed the modest Matron seeks;

> The steam of Lamps still hanging on her Cheeks
> In Ropy Smut; thus foul, and thus bedight,
> She brings him back the Product of the Night.
>
> (184-9)

Compared with the effective restraint and economy that Stapylton briefly achieves, Dryden's lines seem harsh and strident.

Satire VI seems to have been one of the *points de repère* of the sub-literature of the Restoration. Messalina is frequently referred to in satires against women;[14] Robert Gould has a quasi-Juvenalian orgy scene;[15] and both Oldham and Gould use the image of the bastard abandoned in a privy.[16] But VI was not the only satire to appeal to Oldham's contemporaries. In 1683 Thomas Wood published *Juvenalis Redivivus: Or, The First Satyr of Juvenal taught to speak plain English*, which works in references to contemporary poets (including Oldham) but which lacks the energy and point of Rochester's *An Allusion to Horace*. *Satire* X, of which we have the opening four lines of a translation by Oldham, (RMS 278) was the most frequently translated and probably the most highly regarded. Henry Higden introduces his *Modern Essay on the Tenth Satyr of Juvenal* (1687) by saying that *Satire* X is 'by All approved for the Gravest, and most *Phylosophical*, both for Argument and Matter, of all our Authors'.[17] Despite Dryden's claim, in his indifferent dedicatory poem,[18] that Higden has united the styles of Horace and Juvenal, the translation is no match at all for the original, partly because Higden's choice of octosyllabic verse imparts a throwaway quality:

> The greedy care of heaping Wealth
> Damns many a Soul and ruins Health,
> And in an Apoplectick Fitt
> Sinks them down right into the pitt.
> How many Upstarts crept from low
> Condition, vast possessions show?
> Whose Estate's audit so immense
> Exceeds all Prodigal Expence.
>
> (pp. 4-5)

In Higden's hands the accounts of old age (pp. 32-40) and of the sexual temptations of youth (pp. 47-56) appear merely unpleasant, as if he has failed to see what 'true wit' on these subjects might be like. Higden's version of *Satire* XIII, which came out in 1686, is heavily dependent upon Oldham's, in some places simply being a reworking of Oldham in octosyllabics.

Stapylton and Holyday fail to produce equivalents for Juvenal because they are crabbed and solemn; Wood and Higden because they are free and light. Wood, however, did recognise in part the crucial problem in translating Juvenal. He refers us to Rapin's discussion, which is worth quoting at length:

> Et cette delicatesse qui est proprement le ragoust de la Satyre, fut autrefois le caractere d'Horace: ce n'estoit qu'en badinant qu'il exerçoit la Censure. Car il sçavoit tres-bien que l'enjoüement d'esprit a plus d'effet que les raisons les plus fortes, & les discours les plus sententieux pour rendre le vice ridicule. En quoy Juvenal avec tout son serieux, a tant de peine à réüssir. Car enfin ces violentes manieres de declamation qu'il met par tout en usage, ont souvent tres-peu d'effet. Il ne persuade presque rien: parce qu'il est toujours en colere, et qu'il ne parle point de sangfroid. Il est vray qu'il a des lieux communs de morale qui sont capables d'éblouïr les petits esprits. Mais avec toutes ces expressions fortes, ces termes energiques, & ces grands traits d'éloquence, il fait peu d'impression: parce qu'il n'a rien de delicat, ny rien de naturel. Ce n'est point un veritable zele qui le fait parler contre les dereglements de son siecle, c'est un esprit de vanité et d'ostentation.[19]

To what extent will a translator wish to preserve the overheated and exaggerated manner in Juvenal? It is an element, as M. de Decker points out, that derives from Juvenal's immersion in the tradition of *declamatio*:

> Pendant de longues années, Juvénal a vécu dans cette atmosphère où la colère et l'indignation étaient de règle, où les moindres méfaits prenaient les proportions d'un parricide, où l'on s'excitait artificiellement afin de prendre le plus possible au tragique des situations qui n'avaient rien de réel.
>
> Faut-il s'étonner que le ton des Satires nous paraisse souvent forcé et que le style de notre poète soit emphatique à l'excès?[20]

But for the English poet this tradition of *declamatio* did not exist. The Roman reader whose taste was nurtured by the *declamationes* would be content with something 'finement présenté ou spirituellement écrit'; declamations in the English universities, however, though stylish, were abstracted debates over philosophical and theological points. The reader of Donne and Jonson would certainly have relished their wit: but in their satirical writing he is unlikely to have relished only that wit which is cleverness, and valued as nothing the wit which is moral intelligence. How could those two varieties of wit be brought to work together in a translation of Juvenal?

I shall suggest later that Oldham is not always in command of his material, and that he sometimes prefers a joke to the witty enforcement of a moral point. But I believe that his primary intention was that the poems should present a moral view of contemporary life. The wit that achieves this takes the form of a strong rhetorical verse whose vitality wins our assent to the justness of its presentation, and thus to the judgments that it evokes. Unbuttressed by notes, the poetry itself has to incorporate the cues as to its own significance: and the significance of Oldham's poetry lies in its criticism of its readers by the moral imperatives that they had inherited from Roman literature in general and from Juvenal in particular. What would Oldham and his readers have taken those imperatives to be?

The notes to Juvenal by Stapylton and Holyday give plenty of information about Roman antiquities, but few hints as to what Roman values were — what the essence of Roman culture might mean to the cultivated Englishman: or, perhaps more importantly, what it could be made to mean to the man who was drifting after 1642 or 1660 or 1678 with few certainties in his mind about moral, political and literary values. It is hard for us now to recover the imaginative intuitions about Roman civilisation that would have been the result of years spent reading, speaking and writing in Latin. Much of the classical teaching would have been austerely linguistic, leavened with antiquarian interests and precepts of virtue. Perhaps these precepts of virtue were more often precepts of prudence: the classical moralists such as Plutarch and Seneca were assimilable to the Beatus Ille tradition, which by Oldham's time was becoming stale and enfeebled. But one clue as to what Oldham may have been taught to see at the heart of Roman life comes in the textbook of Roman history that he owned. Thomas Godwyn illuminates briefly the quality and character of Roman life:

> Erasmus rather describing a *Romane*, then defining him, saith a *Roman* was grave in his conversation, severe in his judgment, constant in his purpose: Whence *Cicero* in his Epistles often useth this phrase, *more Romano*, for *ex animo, id est,* unfainedly.[21]

If Oldham's copy of Godwyn survived we would know whether he made any note on this passage, but it is very probable that he would at some stage have come across the adage to which Godwyn refers:

More Romano

In eadem epistola [i.e. 51.7] M. Tullius non sine proverbij specie
dixit, More Romano, pro eo quod est, simpliciter & absque fuco
potius quam erudite. Tales enim fuerunt illi Romani prisci,
Graecorum dissimiles. De quo, inquit, hominem tibi spondeo, non
illo uetere uerbo meo, quod quum ad te de Milone scripsissem,
iure lusisti, sed more Romano, quum homines non inepti
loquuntur, probiorem hominem, meliorem uirum, prudentiorem
esse neminem. Penes Romanos erat rusticana veritas . . .[22]

According to this adage the qualities at the heart of Roman civilisation are
simplicity, directness and honesty, both in speech and conduct. These
were essentially Republican virtues, maintained under the Principate by
those with a firm family sense of the old values. Perhaps they were
qualities that provincial families in seventeenth-century England would
also have prized (not always consciously or articulately) and have expected
their sons to imbibe from their education.

The demands of honesty and uprightness would have reached the
seventeenth-century reader of Roman literature in various guises. He would
be familiar from the Beatus Ille literature with the idea that honesty demanded a withdrawal from public life. He would have met the demands of
acting *more Romano* when he read of Aeneas leaving Dido with the words
'Italiam non sponte sequor'. And he would have found Erasmus's adage
illustrated most urgently in Tacitus, where the inscrutable oratory of
Tiberius and the specious prosecutions under Nero demonstrate the danger
of allowing men to lose the habit of honesty in their words and actions.
The ease with which men found themselves trapped by the lies of others is
a horrifying characteristic of the reign of Nero; but it is characteristic too
of the Popish Plot. Here was a subject of compelling urgency for Oldham.

The Thirteenth Satyr of Juvenal, Imitated

If these were some of the moral issues that a study of Roman literature
and society left working in Oldham's mind, and if he accepted the prevailing estimate of Juvenal as a moralist, then it is natural that *Satire* XIII
should have seemed a *locus classicus*.

What did Oldham inherit as received opinion about the poem? This is
the Argument that he prefixed to his translation:

> The POET comforts a Friend, that is overmuch concerned for
> the loss of a considerable Sum of Money, of which he has lately

been cheated by a person, to whom he intrusted the same. This he does by shewing, that nothing comes to pass in the world without Divine Providence, and that wicked Men (however they seem to escape its Punishment here) yet suffer abundantly in the torments of an evil Conscience. And by the way takes occasion to lash the Degeneracy, and Villany of the present Times (*PT* 25-6).

Apart from the last sentence, this translates the Argument in Farnaby's edition. Lubinus thought that XIII was by far the most outstanding of Juvenal's satires ('longe praeclarissima') — not, apparently, for any literary reasons but because it could be read as conforming to Christian notions about divine providence and the workings of conscience:

> Hac autem praeclara Satyra Dei prouidentia potissimum esse demonstratur, quae nihil impunitum nocentibus permittat, & quod nemo malus felix sit, neque suam vindictam effugiat. Imo vero quam secum in animo & conscientia quouis tortore truculentiorem semper circumgerat.[23]

Furthermore, when Holyday, who hoped that his translation would be a form of preaching in verse, draws out the congruence of Juvenal with Christianity (which, of course, Christians had been doing ever since the Church Fathers) he uses *Satire* XIII for several illustrations:

> But (if we set aside this Licence) and look upon the Invention of our Poet, though a Natural man, O how admirable are his Instructions? His Passions how Devout? What are his Satyres, but the Great Commentary of Nature upon the Law of Nature? The *Multitude of Gods* does he not count a Multitude, making them as destitute of Wisdom, as of Power? ... The *variety of their Oaths,* does he not describe and detest, as the variety of their Gods, shewing how they would excuse themselves out of one guilt by another? ... The very Purpose, nay the Deliberating *Desire of Sin,* (*Sat*. 13) before it is grown up to the Age of Act, does he not Condemn, and by endeavor Prevent? And like an exact *Casuist* (*Sat*. 13) does he not make Conscience Man's Keeper and *Judge*? (Sig. a2r-v)

It requires some thought to identify the parts of *Satire* XIII to which Holyday is referring, so distant are his extracted examples from the procedures of the poem itself. By contrast, Oldham's translation, while pointing to Christian ideas, allows these to find expression through the poetry, whereas Holyday, who keeps closely to the Latin, needs this introduction to spell out his ideas about how the poem matters.

In determining how seriously we can take Oldham's poem as a piece of moral thought we may do best to ask first whether Oldham made anything of the ideas that Godwyn and Erasmus associated with *more Romano*, and to begin with a passage in Juvenal that gave him the chance to be quite specific about the values that he was holding up for our attention and assent. The lines in question are 38-52, which describe life during the Golden Age under Saturn. Oldham has no use at this point for gods and goddesses, nor for the images of pastoral innocence, and instead invokes the myth of honest and heroic Anglo-Saxon England. (It is worth noting that, just as Juvenal does not put forward Republican Rome as an ideal, so too there is no recent period of English history to which Oldham wishes to refer.) Oldham's lines draw on the common seventeenth-century myth of Anglo-Saxon freedom and the Norman yoke, according to which the Normans were the creators of a legal system that left the common man frustrated and powerless. But Oldham does not rely on the myth, or upon his readers' predictable enjoyment of any satire directed against lawyers, but stresses the loss of honesty:

> Fair dealing then, and downright Honesty,
> And plighted Faith were good Security ...
> Each took the other's word, and that would go
> For currant then, and more than Oaths do now.
> (67-8; 74-5; *PT* 29-30)

The writing is clear and open — particularly to anyone who comes to the poem from the satires of Donne, Hall and Marston. The verse makes its points economically:

> Nor traps were yet set up for Perjurers,
> That catch men by the Heads, and whip off Ears.
> (78-9; *PT* 30)

The flick of the rhythm in that last phrase is chillingly appropriate. Oldham's concern at the inefficacy of the law reappears in the parenthetical remarks that he adds to Juvenal, such as:

> If he miraculously keep his Trust,
> And without force of Law deliver all
> (90-1; *PT* 30)

and, more tellingly, in the later passage translating Juvenal 135-9, where, inspired by Lubinus's quotation of Plautus's line 'Tamen inuenitur rhetor qui factum neget' ('however an advocate is found who will deny the deed'), he writes that

> *Temple-Walks*, and *Smithfield* never fail
> Of plying Rogues, that set their Souls to sale
> To the first Passenger, that bids a price,
> And make their livelihood of Perjuries.
>
> (221-4;*PT* 37)

Oldham exhibits these false witnesses because they exemplify a common human tendency in setting 'their Souls to sale'. This is an unexpectedly strong phrase, indicating that Oldham, like Holyday, saw Juvenal as 'an exact *Casuist*' who made 'Conscience Man's Keeper and *Judge*', and was determined to write an exacting account of this trade in truth.

Because Oldham has to make this area of moral awareness vibrant again, some of the old words that would most naturally be invoked cannot be set to work in the verse. Thus although conscience is a key idea, comparatively little use is made of the word. In rendering Juvenal's story of the Spartan who seeks the oracle's advice before cheating his friend, Oldham translates 'Reddidit ergo metu, non moribus' (204) by 'Hence Fear, not Honesty, made him refund' (337; *PT* 43), invoking 'Honesty' rather than Stapylton's 'conscience' or Holyday's 'Goodness', since both conscience and goodness are too nebulous (and too much private attributes) to work here as guardians of right conduct. Honesty, however, is a principle guiding relations with one's fellows (particularly commercial relations), a quality working *in foro externo*.

A more explicit indication of Oldham's conception of moral authority is afforded by his translation of this passage:

> MAGNA QVIDEM SACRIS quae dat praecepta libellis
> VICTRIX FORTVNAE Sapientia. DICIMVS AVTEM
> Hos quoque felices qui ferre incommoda vitae
> Nec iactare iugum vita didicere magistra.
>
> (19-22)

For 'Sapientia' Farnaby offers 'Philosophia moralis' as a gloss, and Lubinus has 'philosophia vel studium humanitatis', an idea which one regrets that Oldham found no use for. Stapylton likes the idea of 'Philosophy; especially in the Stoicks books, that bid every man look for all manner of evils and adversities' (1660, notes), but in his translation says instead:

> 'Tis true that *Science* makes the happy men
> That conquers Fortune with celestiall books.

Holyday offers:

> Wisdom, which does our Sacred Volums fill
> With Precepts, conquers Fortune with rare skill,

but it is not clear what either means. Oldham has no time for precepts, and is quite certain about in which 'sacris . . . libellis' truth is to be found:

> Almighty Wisdom gives in Holy Writ
> Wholsom Advice to all, that follow it:
> And those, that will not its great Counsels hear,
> May learn from meer experience how to bear
> (Without vain strugling) Fortune's yoke, and how
> They ought her rudest shocks to undergo.
>
> $(29-34;PT\ 27)$

The enjambement here (closer to that of Donne or Jonson than Oldham's contemporaries) helps to suggest that the lesson given by Wisdom is not easy but will produce a calm resolution. Oldham does not suggest that Fortune can be conquered: perhaps his reading of the *loci classici* in Horace and Milton had worked with his own experiences to convince him that no precepts but only a life lived within bounds could protect a man from dependence upon Fortune. Even that man would not be immune from Fortune's 'rudest shocks', but he would have taught himself how to bear them: how to live, and therefore how to die.

Such is the lesson of Socrates, for 'no change of fortune could make him change his countenance'.[24] Juvenal says little about him:

> dulcique senex vicinus Hymetto
> Qui partem acceptae saeua inter vincla cicutae
> Accusatori nolet dare.
>
> $(185-7)$

By Oldham's day Socrates had become an honorary Christian. He was, says Lubinus, 'animo patientissimo & vere Christiano' ('of a most patient and truly Christian spirit'), and in the preface to his copy of Plato's *Dialogi selecti* Oldham would have read John North's judgment that the dialogues were 'viri inter Gentiles praestantissimi divina quaedam monumenta' ('almost divine monuments of a man who was the most outstanding of the Gentiles').[25] This is the view that Oldham follows, but the language and movement of his lines surely indicate that he had made the thought his own:

> Not so of old, the mild good *Socrates*,
> (Who shew'd how high without the help of Grace,
> Well-cultivated Nature might be wrought)
> He a more noble way of suff'ring taught,
> And, tho he Guiltless drank the poisonous Dose,
> Ne'er wish'd a drop to his accusing Foes.
>
> (194-9; *PT* 41)

We touch here Oldham's fundamentally conservative nature, and his opinion of classical literature as being necessary for the achievement of humane living, but not sufficient. There now follows an addition to Juvenal that is not prompted by anything in the commentators:

> Not so our great good *Martyr'd King* of late
> (Could we his bless'd Example imitate)
> Who, tho the great'st of mortal sufferers,
> Yet kind to his rebellious Murderers,
> Forgave, and bless'd them with his dying Pray'rs.
>
> (300-4; *PT* 41-2)

The religious point of these lines is clear, but why pick Charles? If Oldham was sympathetic to Charles, as the references here and elsewhere suggest,[26] then it is likely that he had looked through the immensely popular Ἐικὼν Βασιλικὴ and one point that is insisted upon throughout the book is that Charles had always acted according to his conscience, or, if he had failed to, he deeply regretted it:

> I never met with a more unhappie conjuncture of affairs, then in the businesse of that unfortunate Earl [Strafford] : when between My owne unsatisfiednesse in Conscience, and a necessitie (as some told me) of satisfying the importunities of some people, I was perswaded by those, that I think wished me well, to chuse rather what was safe, then what seemed just; preferring the outward peace of My Kingdoms with men, before that inward exactnesse of Conscience before God ... I see it a bad exchange to wound a mans own Conscience, thereby to salve State sores; to calme the storms of popular discontents, by stirring up a tempest in a mans owne bosome.[27]

'Inward exactnesse of Conscience' is, I suggest, one of Oldham's chief concerns, both here and in the *Satyrs upon the Jesuits*.

Oldham now draws out the implications of his examples:

> Thus, we by sound Divinity, and Sense
> May purge our minds, and weed all Errors thence:
> These lead us into right, nor shall we need
> Other than them thro Life to be our Guide.
> Revenge is but a Frailty, incident
> To craz'd, and sickly minds, the poor Content
> Of little Souls, unable to surmount
> An Injury, too weak to bear Affront:
>
> (305-12; *PT* 42)

Juvenal's 'sapientia' has now been split into the two pillars of Christian Humanism. There was no compulsion upon Oldham to introduce 'Divinity' (he could have followed his predecessors and confined himself to secular philosophy), so this is all the clearer an indication of his priorities. But divinity still has to be 'sound': the aberrations of religious feeling that led to the execution of Charles I and the Popish Plot need to be restrained by the second guiding principle, which is 'Sense', a word that Oldham uses for many of the emerging norms in literature and society. The verse moves slowly through this expository passage, inviting us to pause over each phrase, so that even the traditional metaphors of 'purge' and 'weed' have a brief quiver of their original life. There is compassion in the lines on those who resort to vengeance (309-12). When this language first appeared in Oldham's poetry it was part of the invective of the rakes and the Jesuits against those who were too timid to break out of their enslavement to the traditional moral, religious and political values:

> Let rabble Souls, of narrow aim, and reach,
> Stoop their vile Necks, and dull Obedience preach: ...
> Dull creatures, whose nice bogling consciences
> Startle, or strain at such slight crimes as these;
> Such, whom fond inbred honesty befools,
> Or that old musty piece the *Bible* gulls:
>
> (*SJ* 9-10)

In the lines from the translation of Juvenal Oldham has discovered a new rhythm and rhetoric: the poetry is now unified, working with assurance in one direction, no longer subject to the heady inflated rhetoric and uncertain irony of the earlier poems.

Oldham also has the confidence now to expose the irresponsibly casual attitudes of the rakes whose language he once shared. The phrases from the *Satyrs upon the Jesuits* can be paralleled in one of Rochester's most thoughtful poems, 'After death nothing is', where we find reference to 'slavish souls', to the fires of hell as 'senseless stories', 'Devised by rogues, dreaded by fools'. In the rakes' own language, 'Trifles' were the sanctions of morality and religion heeded by the unthinking virtuous: Oldham now turns the tables:

> *But, Oh, Revenge more sweet than Life!* 'Tis true,
> So the unthinking say, and the mad Crew
> Of hect'ring Blades, who for slight cause, or none,
> At every turn are into Passion blown:
> Whom the least Trifles with Revenge inspire . . .
>   (284-8; *PT* 41)

The first line here may be Juvenalian hyperbole, but the following lines on the 'Blades' are a fairly accurate comment. Oldham shows up their lack — we might say — of Sense and Proportion. In seeking to activate a moral vocabulary that concerns not so much private qualities (e.g. 'goodness') as the quality of a man's relations with his fellows (e.g. 'honesty'), Oldham's poetry is moving away from dangerous ground. I have already suggested how deeply Oldham distrusted casuistry, which juggled with words and encouraged a divorce between belief, speech and action. Although this habit was represented for Oldham by the Jesuits, Hobbes too had made a nominalist attack upon the traditional language of moral imperatives, and had made a distinction between a man being bound *in foro interno* by the Law of Nature and *in foro externo* by the commands of the Sovereign, so that an action might be desirable *in foro interno* but impermissible *in foro externo*. These were two congruent contemporary incentives for Oldham to attempt to retrieve the moral vocabulary, and make the Aristotelian point that virtue does not just lie in a man's heart, but in all his actions. Furthermore, in choosing this field for his poetry, Oldham becomes less vulnerable to those private needs and impulses which in earlier days could not always be trusted not to disrupt the modes of publishable poetry. We cannot know whether Oldham would consciously have concurred in this judgment that he and his mentors were not always capable of translating private feeling into public forms. But Oldham's translations from Juvenal and from Boileau are developing a controlled public mode that is closer to Pope's *Imitations of Horace* and *Moral Essays* than is anything in Rochester.

Since Oldham shared some of the difficulties of Cowley and Rochester, since his earlier verse used moral terms equivocally, it would be surprising if *The Thirteenth Satyr of Juvenal* were entirely free from uncertainty. When Juvenal has exclaimed about the degeneracy of his times, he turns to Calvinus and asks:

> nescis
> Quem tua simplicitas risum vulgo moueat, cum
> Exigis a quoquam ne peieret, & putet vllis
> Esse aliquod numen templis, araeque rubenti?
>
> (34-7)

Oldham translates:

> For Gods sake don't you see ⎫
> How they all laugh at your simplicity, ⎬
> When gravely you forewarn of Perjury? ⎭
> Preach up a God, and Hell, vain empty names,
> Exploded now for idle thredbare shams,
> Devis'd by Priests, and by none else believ'd,
> E're since great *Hobbes* the world has undeceiv'd?
>
> (54-60; *PT* 29)

Holyday's note at this point says that Juvenal 'speaks not as his own belief, but by way of Satyre, to express the Common Atheisme of those Times'. But in Oldham's version, where do the scales come to rest in their oscillation between endorsement and dismissal? Much of his vocabulary here is re-used from the *Satyrs upon the Jesuits*, where it was part of an unstable ironic mode. On the other hand, we could cite Rochester's translation from Seneca's *Troades* ('After death nothing is'), which is apparently serious:

> For Hell and the foul fiend that rules
> God's everlasting fiery jails
> (Devised by rogues, dreaded by fools)
> With his grim, grisly dog that keeps the door,
> Are senseless stories, idle tales,
> Dreams, whimseys, and no more.

Clearly, Oldham's language is in some degree ironic at the expense of those who have swallowed the Hobbist line; but is there also a suggestion that we should treat Hobbes's philosophy seriously as an undeceiving? Has Oldham at last found an irony that is carefully ambiguous, and deliberately disquieting to the reader?

A further test for Oldham was Juvenal's passage on those who ascribe all changes to Fortune:

> SVNT QVI IN FORTVNAE iam casibus omnia ponunt
> Et nullo credunt mundum rectore moueri
> Natura voluente vices & lucis & anni . . .
>
> (86-8)

> There are, who disavow all Providence,
> And think the world is only steer'd by chance:
> Make God at best an idle looker on,
> A lazy Monarch lolling in his Throne.
> Who his Affairs does neither mind, or know,
> But leaves them all at random here below:
> (129-34;PT 32-3)

Lubinus thought that here Juvenal was getting to the root of the degeneracy of the Romans:

> Reddit iam rationem tantorum scelerum & periuriorum quam demonstrat esse impietatem qua homines omnia casu, nihil autem prouidentia Dei fieri censeant ... Iuxta Epicurum, qui Deum & prouidentiam sustulit.[28]

Once again Oldham has to face the subject of the beliefs that were current among 'the wits'. Keith Thomas found a letter from Oxford in 1660 that reported:

> ... as you know very well [it] is the way of Christ's Church, especially of those of that gange who stile themselves the wits, to carpe att and censure all people who will not follow that high degree of debauchery or rather Atheism they are now att, that they dare dispute it publicly whether there be any such thing as the providence of God.[29]

But we know from Rochester's conversations with Burnet that the doubting of providence was not just a pose; in his case at least it was a genuinely disquieting problem, and it was besides a subject of debate among the professional theologians.[30] Oldham's tactic at this point uses humour to define a middle ground. By adding to Juvenal the lines depicting a God who has a strong resemblance to Charles II, he gently suggests the ludicrous and self-indulgent side to this 'philosophy' without coming anywhere near the strident disapproval of more humourless conservatives.

He is also a good enough classicist not to saddle Epicurus and Lucretius with the distortions of their philosophy that abounded in the Restoration. He avoids mentioning Epicurus (who is cited here by Lubinus) and avoids him again at the point where Juvenal disclaims knowledge of the moral philosophers — Cynics, Stoics and Epicurus (120-3). Oldham says instead that he has

> never yet read *Plutarch*, hardly saw,
> And am but meanly vers'd in *Seneca*.

Oldham has chosen two safe, traditionally esteemed, classical moralists.

Given the difficulties that Oldham had in writing an assured public poetry, it is remarkable how successfully the moral imperatives have been enacted poetically, without recourse to didactic moralising. His observations of conduct are usually just:

> These are the thoughts which guilty wretches haunt,
> Yet enter'd, they still grow more impudent:
> After a Crime perhaps they now and then ⎫
> Feel pangs and strugglings of Remorse within, ⎬
> But straight return to their old course agen: ⎭
> They, who have once thrown Shame, and Conscience by,
> Ne'er after make a stop in Villany:
> Hurried along, down the vast steep they go,
> And find, 'tis all a Precipice below.
>
> (401-9; *PT* 47)

The last couplet offers a vividly arresting image of sudden disintegration. Oldham avoids the easy recourse to his old language about surpassing the bounds of iniquity, a temptation explicitly offered him in the Latin:

> NAM QVIS
> PECCANDI FINEM posuit sibi?
> (240-1)

('Car s'est on iamais prescript des bornes à ses pechez?'
— Marolles.)

The wit that informs this passage is a compassionate intelligence, an attribute that is distinctive of Oldham as he matures, and one that is capable of inspiring a controlled range of tone. This next quotation moves from an almost impersonal injunction to conversational sarcasm:

> Then cease for shame, immoderate regret,
> And don't your Manhood, and your Sense forget:
> 'Tis womanish, and silly to lay forth
> More cost in Grief than a Misfortune's worth.
> You scarce can bear a puny trifling ill,
> It goes so deep, pray Heav'n! it does not kill.
>
> (17-22; *PT* 27)

Sometimes the wit plays down the seriousness of the main propositions, so that what Lubinus called Juvenal's 'egregia sententia':

> TAM FACILE ET PRONVM est superos contemnere testes,
> Si mortalis idem nemo sciat.
>
> (75-6)

becomes:

> Little do folks the heav'nly Powers mind,
> If they but scape the knowledg of Mankind:
> (108-9; *PT* 31)

which does not have a comparable weightiness either in language or rhythm. Lubinus thought that in the subsequent passage Juvenal 'Accurate & Graphice depingit talium hominum constantem malitiam' ('accurately and graphically shows the constant evil of such men'), but this sees a moral purpose in the lines that may not have been much to the fore in Juvenal's own mind, since he seems to delight here chiefly in imagining the curses. Certainly the moral purpose carries little weight with Oldham, who takes the opportunity for a piece of dramatic writing in which the enjambement aids a movement that strongly invites the reader to invest the words with a tone of bogus aggrieved innocence:

> *As God shall pardon me, Sir, I am free*
> *Of what you charge me with: let me ne'er see*
> *His Face in Heaven else: may these hands rot,*
> *These eyes drop out; if I e're had a Groat*
> *Of yours, or if they ever touch't, or saw't.*
> (120-4; *PT* 32)

Similarly Oldham's sense of comic possibilities ignores Lubinus's solemn gloss on

> Pecudem spondere sacello
> Balantem, & laribus cristam promittere galli
> Non audent.
>
> (232-4)

> Non audent votum facere. Nam Deum sibi infestum credunt, & desperant de Dei misericordia, qua nihil esse potest miserius.[31]

The tentative comedy of:

> Nor dare they, tho in whisper, waft a Prayer,
> Lest it by chance should reach th'Almighty's ear,
> (397-8; *PT* 47)

is far removed from Lubinus's 'Dei misericordia'.

But this last example raises the doubt about whether the poem can be successful in its moral intentions if at some of the key points Oldham backs away from confrontations and prefers a joke. Yet is this not part of Juvenal's own procedure? His wit may surprise us into new perceptions that provoke thought about relative values, but it is also, perhaps primarily, the wit of the entertainer:[32]

> Tu miser exclamas, vt Stentora vincere possis,
> Vel potius quantum Gradiuus Homericus, audis
> IVPITER HAEC NEC labra moues, cum mittere vocem
> Debueras vel marmoreus, vel Aheneus? Aut cur
> In carbone tuo charta pia thura soluta
> Ponimus & sectum vituli iecur, albaque porci
> Omenta? VT VIDEO NVLLVM discrimen habendum est
> Effigies inter vestras statuamque Batilli.
>
> (112-19)

> Mean time, poor you at Heav'n exclaim, and rail,
> Louder than *J*— at the Bar does bawl:
> *Is there a Pow'r above? and does he hear?*
> *And can he tamely Thunderbolts forbear?*
> *To what vain end do we with Pray'rs adore?*
> *And on our bended knees his aid implore?*
> *Where is his Rule, if no respect be had,*
> *Of Innocence, or Guilt, of Good, or Bad?*
> *And who henceforth will any credit show*
> *To what his lying Priests teach here below?*
> *If this be Providence; for ought I see,*
> *Bless'd Saint,* Vaninus! *I shall follow thee:*
> *Little's the odds 'twixt such a God, and that,*
> *Which Atheist* Lewis *us'd to wear in's Hat.*
>
> (178-91; *PT* 35-6)

Reading the Oldham, our laughter becomes nervous. The examples are threatening, and unlike Juvenal Oldham cannot take Calvinus's exaggerated complaints and translate them zestfully into a literary realm where the pain is almost forgotten, and enjoyment takes over.

A Satyr, in Imitation of the Third of Juvenal

If one of the chief incentives that impels a reading of Oldham is to consider what Dryden might have meant when he wrote that

> our Souls were near ally'd; and thine
> Cast in the same Poetick mould with mine.

then we might well turn for some evidence on the matter to Oldham's *A Satyr, in Imitation of the Third of Juvenal*; and the poem may seem the more worthy our inspection if we also have in our minds the secondary question (vaguer, and harder to handle because fifty years of 'Augustan' culture separate them): What qualities in Oldham did Johnson value sufficiently for him to plan an edition? For Oldham, Dryden and Johnson have all left versions of the same Latin poem, and when we add to the pile the first and sixth *Satires* of Boileau — again imitated from Juvenal III — there seem to be ample resources for a spectacular critical juggling trick that could display the common and contrasting concerns of these four major translators. It is probably fortunate that the procedural complexity of such an attempt is enough to warn off the rash adventurer, for it would be hard to offer any satisfactory criticism with one's attention so divided. I shall therefore concentrate in this account upon Oldham's poem, contenting myself with occasional illustrations of the different tempers of the translations.

One question that would arise in the course of any discussion of the versions of *Satire* III is the nature of each poet's interest in the ostensible subject of the poem, the evils of life in the capital. The opening of Oldham's translation suggests that he wishes to keep the thought as general as possible:

> THO much concern'd to leave my dear old Friend,
> I must however his Design commend
> Of fixing in the Country: for were I
> As free to chuse my Residence, as he;
> The *Peake*, the *Fens*, the *Hundreds*, or *Lands-end*,
> I would prefer to *Fleetstreet*, or the *Strand*.
> What place so desart, and so wild is there,   ⎫
> Whose Inconveniencies one would not bear,   ⎬
> Rather than the Alarms of midnight Fire,   ⎭
> The falls of Houses, Knavery of Cits,
> The Plots of Factions, and the noise of Wits,
> And thousand other Plagues, which up and down
> Each day and hour infest the cursed Town?
>   (1-13; *PT* 180-1)

Our first reaction may be that this is modernisation — bringing the poem home to a contemporary audience by references from Restoration England

— but the observation would only be superficial. Oldham has added to the Latin the idea of what he would do 'were I / As free to chuse my Residence, as he', so that the possibility of free choice for a man to determine how he acts in the face of corruption is already clearly floated. In the glancing reference to '*Fleetstreet*, or the *Strand*' Oldham is turning down the opportunity to score an initial hit, for he would have read in Holyday's notes to Juvenal that 'Suburra was the Cheapside of *Rome* . . . perhaps not the Number only but the Quality of its Inhabitants, offended the good man: For a Multitude of Whores lived there.' The poem is introduced with an urbane language ('Design commend / Of fixing in the Country', 'to chuse my Residence', 'Inconveniencies one would not bear'), which is brought up against the 'desart' and 'wild' alternatives, again generalised, but almost elemental (contrast Juvenal's more personal 'miserum . . . solum'). 'Plagues' is given an almost personified force ('Plagues, which up and down . . . infest') and the language, typically, as we shall see, is generalised but not abstracted, carrying a strong though limited spark of realised life.

When the friend begins his speech Oldham seeks to give the indictment some objective force (the force of a considered judgment) by expanding 'Hic tunc Vmbricius' into:

> I ask'd what sudden causes made him flie
> The once-lov'd Town, and his dear Company:
> When, on the hated Prospect looking back,
> Thus with just rage the good old *Timon* spake.
>
> (20-3; *PT* 181)

We may feel that, by contrast, Boileau has overdone his sketch:

> Mais le jour qu'il partit plus defait & plus blême,
> Que n'est un Penitent sur la fin d'un Caresme,
> La colere dans l'ame, & le feu dans les yeux,
> Il distila sa rage en ces tristes adieux.
>
> (1.17-20; p. 18)[33]

and the impression of overstatement is confirmed as we read on:

> Puisqu'en ce lieu jadis aux Muses si commode,
> Le merite & l'esprit ne sont plus à la mode,
> Qu'un Poëte, dit-il, s'y voit maudit de Dieu,
> Et qu'ici la Vertu n'a plus ni feu ni lieu;
> Allons du moins chercher quelque antre ou quelque roche,
> D'où jamais ni l'Huissier, ni le Sergent n'approche,

>Et sans lasser le Ciel par des voeux impuissans,
>Mettons-nous à l'abri des injures du temps.
>   (1.21-8; p. 18)

Surely we have to make ourselves small to read this, to fit into 'commode
... à la mode ... à l'abri des injures'. The editors of Juvenal who printed
'artibus honestis nullus in urbe locus' in italics or small capitals felt that
this was a *sententia*, a general truth, and it is robbed of its laconic power
by the almost whining resentment of Boileau. Oldham's version avoids
this narrowing of the idea:

>   Since Virtue here in no repute is had,   ⎫
>   Since Worth is scorned, Learning and Sense unpaid, ⎬
>   And Knavery the only thriving Trade;   ⎭
>   Finding my slender Fortune every day
>   Dwindle, and wast insensibly away,
>   I, like a losing Gamester, thus retreat,
>   To manage wiselier my last stake of Fate:
>   (24-30; *PT* 182)

Here Oldham follows Boileau in specifying the qualities that are not
appreciated, but he achieves an objectivity missing in the French.
'Worth', 'Learning' and 'Sense' have a wider moral appeal than 'merite'
and 'esprit', and there is an embryonic drama in the words 'scorn'd',
'unpaid', 'thriving' missing from 'si commode' and 'à la mode', a
drama neatly created by the structure of Oldham's lines, where the
juxtaposition ('Worth is scorn'd ... Sense unpaid') briefly realises what
Pope called 'The strong Antipathy of Good to Bad'. We may note too the
apt rhythm of 'Dwindle, and wast insensibly away'. Part of the incentive
for Oldham to make that a telling line was his belief that 'res' could not
be given any narrow financial meaning. It was not merely fortune
but Fortune, not just money but the whole life of man that dwindled and
wasted away in the city. So resources have to be husbanded: in Dryden's
words,

>   To morrow and her works defie,
>   Lay hold upon the present hour,
>   And snatch the pleasures passing by,
>   To put them out of Fortunes pow'r: [34]

or in Oldham's image (adding here to Juvenal):

>   I, like a losing Gamester, thus retreat,
>   To manage wiselier my last stake of Fate:

The gambling image is not frivolous. Dryden adds it to Horace's *Carm.*
III.xxix ('Fortune ... makes a Lottery of life'), and Plutarch reminds us
that

> Plato ... compared life to a game of dice in which we must try,
> not only to throw what suits us best, but also, when we have
> thrown, to make good use of whatever turns up. But with circum-
> stances, though it is not in our power to throw what we please,
> yet it is our task, if we are wise, to accept in a suitable manner
> whatever accrues from Fortune (περὶ εὐθυμίας, 467 A-B).

While the stress on freedom from Fortune is not present in Juvenal at this
point, it is a note that he strikes elsewhere in his insistence that Fortune is
a goddess of our own creation (x.363-6; xIV.315-16).

As we read on through Oldham's account of those who are able to
flourish in London, we find again that the verse is partly realising the
activity:

> Let thriving *Morecraft* chuse his dwelling there,
> Rich with the Spoils of some young spend-thrift Heir:
> Let the Plot-mongers stay behind, whose Art
> Can Truth to Sham, and Sham to Truth convert:
> Who ever has an House to Build, or Set
> His Wife, his Conscience, or his Oath to let:
> (36-41; *PT* 182)

This is differently achieved from Boileau's

> On le verra bien-tost pompeux en cette Ville,
> Marcher encor chargé des dépoüilles d'autrui,
> (I.74-5; p. 20)

There is no one walking and being seen in Oldham: Morecraft is present
only as essential, relevant activity – 'thriving', 'chuse', 'Rich with the
Spoils' – as an exemplar he needs no more than this limited presence
in the verse. Yet he needs to be taken seriously, and if we recall that the
bishop's bed in *The Desk* was 'Rich with ye spoils of all ye feather'd
race' (RMS 127), we can see that Oldham has modified that 'heroic'
language (about the tone and purchase of which he was always uncertain)
into an emphatic, controlled language that can place its subject with just
the right degree of sparkle and weight.

This ability to 'place' the subject is not just a technical poetic facility.
The poetry's authority comes in part from the intelligence, maturity and
compassion with which the poet has considered his subject, and these

qualities (and their absence) will be manifest not only in the words but in the whole tone and movement of the verse. It is particularly important for a satirist to convey the moral norms with which his poetry operates without his implicit claim to be the steward of morality appearing glib or self-righteous. Oldham is able to inform his translation of 'Quid Romae faciam?' with an attractive uprightness: but to gauge the nature of this strength we may first need to recall what Boileau made of the passage:

> Mais moi, vivre à Paris! Eh, qu'y voudrois-je faire?
> Ie ne sçai ni tromper, ni feindre, ni mentir,
> Et quand je le pourrois, je n'y puis consentir.
> Ie ne sçai point en lâche essuyer les outrages
> D'un Faquin orgueilleux qui vous tient à ses gages:
> (1.42-6; p. 19)

There is a sullen tone to this:

> Ie suis rustique & fier, & j'ay l'ame grossiere.
> Ie ne puis rien nommer, si ce n'est par son nom:
> I'appelle un chat un chat, & Rôlet un frippon.
> (1.50-2; p. 19)

This sort of intransigent pride probably did justify the classic riposte from Cotin:

> J'appelle Horace Horace, et Boileau — traducteur.

for it seems that in translating Juvenal here Boileau has done little more than use the Latin as a crutch for his own self-conceit:

> De servir un Amant, je n'en ai pas l'adresse:
> I'ignore ce grand Art qui gagne une maîtresse,
> Et je suis à Paris, triste, pauvre & reclus,
> Ainsi qu'un corps sans ame, ou devenu perclus.
> (1.53-6; p. 19)

Now, Oldham needed the first line of Boileau's passage to help him to a necessary sense of actual speech, but his tone is very different:

> I live in *London?* What should I do there?
> I cannot lye, nor flatter, nor forswear:
> I can't commend a Book, or Piece of Wit,
> (Tho a Lord were the Author) dully writ:
> I'm no Sir *Sydrophel* to read the Stars,
> And cast Nativities for longing Heirs,

When Fathers shall drop off: no *Gadbury*
To tell the minute, when the King shall die,
And you know what — come in:
(54-62; *PT* 183-4)

Although we could inject scornful self-righteous vehemence into the
lines as we read them, that would not be appropriate, for they are
relaxed, with a lightness of touch through the reference to Butler's Sir
Sydrophel, deft comic strokes in 'longing Heirs' and 'drop off' (both
given apt rhythmic stresses), and through the wry coyness of 'And you
know what — come in', which mocks the awed secrecy of whispered
conversations during the Popish Plot. Then when we are given the under-
pinning conviction —

nor can I steer,   ⎫
And tack about my conscience, whensoe're,   ⎬
To a new Point, I see Religion veer.   ⎭
(62-4; *PT* 184)

— it employs a finely realised metaphor, combining the strong implicit
moral imperative of steering straight by one's conscience, with energetic
hints (they fall short of being encapsulations) of those who equivocate in
the shifting winds of religious politics. Once again Oldham gives us the
idea in a form midway between example and *sententia*. While the commentators who interpreted 'ranarum viscera numquam inspexi' to mean 'I have
never dabbled in poisons' suggested to Oldham the activities of the Jesuits,
the resulting point has become universal. Yet the passage is not completely
assured: these next two lines are adequate, and reflect the prevailing
exploitation of the city by the Court:

Let others pimp to Courtier's Lechery,
I'll draw no City Cuckold's Curse on me:
(65-6; *PT* 184)

but the price of pandering seems overstated, merely gestured towards, not
appropriately conceived:

Nor would I do it, tho to be made great,
And rais'd to the chief Minister of State.
(67-8; *PT* 184)

The problem for the translator of this section is not one of making the
thought relevant to modern times, but making the reader feel that the
thought has some currency, and is not just another obvious proposition to

which he can nod assent and pass on. Johnson's verse at this point is not compelling, merely allusive:

> For what but social Guilt the Friend endears?
> Who shares *Orgilio*'s Crimes, his Fortune shares.
>
> (83-4)

Dryden's lines are flat, with the thoughts completed and static:

> They get Reward alone who can Betray:
> For keeping honest Counsels none will pay.
> He who can *Verres*, when he will, accuse,
> The Purse of *Verres* may at Pleasure use.
>
> (93-6)

Oldham's lines are more active – the idea seems to be working with and impelling the construction of the verse:

> By none thou shalt preferr'd, or valued be,
> That trusts thee with an honest Secresie:
> He only may to great men's Friendship reach,
> Who Great Men, when he pleases, can impeach.
>
> (74-7; *PT* 184)

We note the work done by the verbs – 'preferr'd', 'valued', 'trusts' – each with an implicit vignette of Court life behind it – the striking rhythmic endorsement of 'honest Secresie' and 'reach', and the final clinching word 'impeach'. As so often in Oldham the local strength is a strength of movement, and the élan of 'reach' is repeated in 'Let others thus aspire to Dignity' (78; *PT* 185), where 'Dignity' (like 'Grandeur' in the next line) is a grand abstraction ironically contrasting with the active sound and stress of 'aspire'.

Next, in showing what has to be sacrificed to obtain this sort of greatness and renown, Oldham moves away from Juvenal's 'somno careas' and Lubinus's 'conscientia mala' to a larger proposition:

> What would it boot, if I, to gain my end, ⎫
> Forego my Quiet, and my ease of mind,   ⎬
> Still fear'd, at last betray'd by my great Friend. ⎭
>
> (82-4; *PT* 185)

The key phrase here is 'my Quiet, and my ease of mind'. 'Ease' is not 'ignoble ease, and peaceful sloath'[35] but the quality hinted at in 'One dieth in his full strength, being wholly at ease and quiet' (Job xxi.23). The biblical citation is not gratuitous, for 'What would it boot ...' has been shaped by Christ's question: 'For what shall it profit a man, if he shall gaine the whole world, and lose his own soule?' (Mark viii.36). Quiet of Mind is of course a central humanist ideal, manifest through the seventeenth century in the Beatus Ille tradition of rural retirement and rejection of life at Court:

> I kisse not where I wish to kill,
> I faine not loue where I most hate:
> I breake no sleepe to winne my will,
> I wayte not at the mighties gate:
> I skorne no poore, nor feare no ritch,
> I feele no want nor haue to much ...
>
> this is my choyse, for why I finde,
> no wealth is like the quiet minde.³⁶

This anonymous Elizabethan conveniently reminds us that an element in the Beatus Ille poetry insists that one cannot escape the demands of honest relations with one's fellows, and that this active honesty is a necessary condition of, and product of, the Quiet Mind. Johnson appears to have felt that Oldham's addition to Juvenal was just, for in *London* we read:

> Turn from the glitt'ring Bribe thy scornful Eye,
> Nor sell for Gold, what Gold could never buy,
> The peaceful Slumber, self-approving Day,
> Unsullied Fame, and Conscience ever gay.
>
> (87-90)

While 'gay' is not a word that Johnson would have picked up from the tone of Oldham, 'Conscience' does spring from Oldham's distinctive concern, not only in this poem but in the *Satyr addressed to a Friend*, where he speaks of being

> accountable to none,
> But to my Conscience, and my God alone.
>
> (*PT* 143)

Since those lines impressed Johnson sufficiently for him to quote them in his Dictionary to illustrate 'accountable', we may suppose that this strain was one of the attractions that Oldham's work as a whole had for him.

But if this is one point in Oldham's poem where the subject really mattered to him, and because it mattered issued in a poetry good enough to impress a poet and critic of Johnson's calibre, we are not able to claim the same note of authority for other passages where the verse appears to be adequate, or even characteristic.

There can be little doubt that Oldham worked hard on his character of the 'needy *Monsieur*'. He has used his predecessors extensively, and the passage has much rhythmic verve. But though the verse has a lively surface it makes few imaginative connections with real life. There is, for example, a neat point in 'Both the King's Player, and King's Evidence', and a deft fleeting image in 'the Cur will fetch and bring', but nowhere does Oldham quite manage to incarnate life for more than a few words at a time. The wit is rapid, and he sometimes touches on points without making them. We almost get a vivid sketch here of Restoration fashion, but the lines tail off:

> What would'st thou say, great *Harry*, should'st thou view
> Thy gawdy flutt'ring Race of *English* now,
> Their tawdry Cloaths, Pulvilio's, Essences,
> Their *Chedreux* Perruques, and those Vanities,
> Which thou, and they of old did so despise?
> (95-9; *PT* 185-6)

Oldham's eye for the passing detail is at work, but it is too schematic, and when he launches into the list of possible trades for the Frenchman —

> Groom, Page, Valet, Quack, Operator, Fencer,
> Perfumer, Pimp, Jack-pudding, Juggler, Dancer:
> (117-18; *PT* 187)

— the words exist only on the page: we have no sense that Oldham has come near to understanding — spiritually — a restless time-server, as we have with Dryden's lines on Zimri. Dryden's success with Zimri is partly due to his having first of all a character to render, and secondarily this literary source that helpfully corresponded. Oldham had the Latin to translate, but no other particular compulsion, and not being imaginatively inward with the character his writing at this point lacks any centre.

Yet when Oldham in his turn has a clear idea of what he is trying to do and then turns for help to literary sources, the result is much more convincing. The phrase 'And here's the mischief' buttonholes the reader and ushers in a dramatic passage, moving often with the freedom of blank verse:

> And here's the mischief, tho we say the same,
> He is believ'd, and we are thought to sham:

Do you but smile, immediately the Beast
Laughs out aloud, tho he ne'er heard the jest;
Pretend, you're sad, he's presently in Tears,
Yet grieves no more than Marble, when it wears
Sorrow in Metaphor: but speak of Heat;
O God! how sultry 'tis? he'l cry, and sweat
In depth of Winter: strait, if you complain
Of Cold; the Weather-glass is sunk again:
Then he'l call for his Frize-Campaign, and swear,
Tis beyond *Eighty*, he's in *Greenland* here,
(144-55; *PT* 188)

This reads as something more than an old *topos*: Oldham has reshaped it with a dramatic imagination.

Given Oldham's own social position, we may expect him to be deeply engaged when Juvenal writes about the plight of the poor. In particular we might look to the contrasting treatment meted out by society to the impoverished poet and the wealthy bachelor. First the poet:

The moveables of P—ge were a Bed
For him, and's Wife, a Piss-pot by its side,
A Looking-glass upon the Cupboards Head,
A Comb-case, Candlestick, and Pewter-spoon,
For want of Plate, with Desk to write upon:
A Box without a Lid serv'd to contain
Few Authors, which made up his *Vatican*:
And there his own immortal Works were laid,
On which the barbarous Mice for hunger prey'd:
P— had nothing, all the world does know;
And yet should he have lost this Nothing too,
No one the wretched Bard would have suppli'd
With Lodging, House-room, or a Crust of Bread.
(312-24; *PT* 197)

Recalling Boileau, our first reaction may be to wonder at the restraint. Oldham is not whining, bitter or resentful. He operates with a controlled wit: the decorous stock joke about the Vatican; the adjective 'immortal' without overloaded sarcasm or more than a wry smile; and then a small but telling touch points to how even the mice are starving. There is a plain strength in 'P— had nothing', and in the final couplet upon which the cumulative rhythm deposits us with such emphasis. The plainness of Oldham differs from the plainness of Dryden, whose

> Beg'd naked through the Streets of wealthy *Rome*;
> And found not one to feed, or take him home.
>
> (344-5)

has a more urbane shape, and the restrained image in the first line is particularly successful (apart from the weak insistence in 'wealthy'). Johnson may have drawn on Dryden for his lines:

> Then thro' the World a wretched Vagrant roam,
> For where can starving Merit find a Home?
>
> (190-1)

Oldham presents us more bluntly with the naked life; Dryden is rhythmically smoother, the music of the line carrying a tough pity; Johnson is strong and tragic.

When Oldham comes to describe the gifts offered to the rich man, he seems to delight in being specific about the luxury:

> Nay, while 'tis burning, some will send him in
> Timber, and Stone to build his House agen:
> Others choice Furniture: here some rare piece
> Of *Rubens*, or *Vandike* presented is:
> There a rich Suit of *Moreclack*-Tapestry,
> A Bed of Damask, or Embroidery:
> One gives a fine Scritore, or Cabinet,
> Another a huge massie Dish of Plate,
> Or Bag of Gold:
>
> (333-41; *PT* 198)

The poetic interest in the objects themselves brings to mind Ben Jonson, whose *Volpone* may lie behind these lines:

> Women, and men . . .
> That bring me presents, send me plate, coyne, iewels.
>
> A piece of plate, sir. — Of what bignesse? — Huge,
> Massie, and antique . . .
>
> Here, I have brought a bag of bright *cecchines*,
> Will quite weigh down his plate.[37]

It is remarkable how Jonson's poetry moves with Mosca and Volpone's delight in materials. Oldham's, by contrast, carries the objects as if foreign bodies in a stream; each is momentarily presented to our view.

Oldham's imagery and rhetoric is by now usually kept subordinate to his moral purposes:

> What living for an *English* man is there, ⎫
> Where such as these get head, and domineer, ⎬
> Whose use and custom 'tis, never to share ⎭
> A Friend, but love to reign without dispute,
> Without a Rival, full, and absolute?
> Soon as the Insect gets his *Honor's* ear,
> And fly-blows some of's pois'nous malice there,
> Strait I'm turn'd off, kick'd out of doors, discarded,
> And all my former Service dis-regarded.
>
> (173-81; *PT* 190)

We observe how the directness of statement is enforced by the modulation of speech in the opening line; the active verbs 'get head' and 'domineer'; the surprising enjambement at the end of the triplet throwing extra weight on 'share'; and if we hold in our minds first Dryden's *Mac Flecknoe* and then Pope's Sporus we can more easily see how these lines are pregnant with implicit drama, a drama that is not indulged, but held into the prose sense; for the real drama comes in the last couplet. This has some of the precision and 'minimal' quality that Eliot valued in Johnson,[38] but without Johnson's controlling stasis; and indeed, without the universality (grounded in an essentially tragic perception) that Leavis described as Johnson's 'irresistible weight of experience — of representative human experience', which is used to 'invest his generalities with substance'.[39]

I have claimed that one of Oldham's strengths is his ability to actualise Restoration life without losing hold of the moral direction of his poem, and one passage that does seem remarkably assured is the account of 'the drunken Scowrers of the Street':

> If this you scape, twenty to one, you meet
> Some of the drunken Scowrers of the Street,
> 407 Flush'd with success of warlike Deeds perform'd,
> 408 Of Constables subdu'd, and Brothels storm'd:
> These, if a Quarrel, or a Fray be mist,
> Are ill at ease a nights, and want their Rest.
> For mischief is a Lechery to some,
> And serves to make them sleep like *Laudanum.*
> Yet heated, as they are, with Youth, and Wine,
> If they discern a train of Flamboes shine,
> If a Great Man with his gilt Coach appear, ⎫
> And a strong Guard of Foot-boys in the rere, ⎬
> The Rascals sneak, and shrink their Heads for fear. ⎭
> Poor me, who use no Light to walk about,

> Save what the Parish, or the Skies hang out,
> They value not: 'tis worth your while to hear ⎫
> The scuffle, if that be a scuffle, where   ⎬
> Another gives the Blows, I only bear: ⎭
> He bids me stand: of force I must give way,
> For 'twere a sensless thing to disobey,
> And struggle here, where I'd as good oppose
> My self to *P*– and his Mastiffs loose.

427 *Who's there?* he cries, and takes you by the Throat,
    Dog! are you dumb? Speak quickly, else my Foot
    Shall march about your Buttocks: whence d'ye come,
430 *From what Bulk-ridden Strumpet reeking home?*
    Saving your reverend Pimpship, where d'ye ply?
    How may one have a Job of Lechery?
    If you say anything, or hold your peace,
    And silently go off; 'tis all a case:
    Still he lays on: nay well, if you scape so:
    Perhaps he'l clap an Action on you too
    Of Battery: nor need he fear to meet
    A Jury to his turn, shall do him right,
439 And bring him in large Damage for a Shooe
440 Worn out, besides the pains, in kicking you.
    A Poor Man must expect nought of redress,
    But Patience: his best in such a case
    Is to be thankful for the Drubs, and beg
    That they would mercifully spare one leg,
    Or Arm unbroke, and let him go away
    With Teeth enough to eat his Meat next day.
                (405-46; *PT* 202-4)

We note the tang of real speech in the idiom 'twenty to one' and the sour 'drunken Scowrers' (rhythmically emphatic), which goes along with a mature ironic tone in 407-8, where the wit is under perfect serious control (how inadequate the phrase 'mock-heroic' would be to describe the tone).[40] The drunkard's self-conscious, insistent, mocking wit has a ring of truth (427-30). Oldham has made Juvenal's 'vadimonia deinde Irati faciunt' a more sombre indictment by attributing to the jury that logic characteristic of a bully (439-40). The subdued irony of 'A Poor Man must expect nought of redress, / But Patience' works with 'mercifully' to remind us of serious Christian values, and the witty turn of the ending in no way conceals the ugliness of the reality.

If we look ahead to Pope's account of Timon's villa, we may see how Oldham does not have the same delight in using the material of life to create a poetic image that has its own independence. Oldham never allows his fancy to take flight into this kind of autonomous world, and compared with the anarchic results when Butler gave himself a similar freedom in *Hudibras*, Oldham's is a disciplined art. Compared with Pope, there is a lack in Oldham's verse of a subtle music, a flexible movement and intonation, but this goes along with a reticence of fancy and a plainness of statement to create a mode that concentrates on getting the moral imperatives right, the values clear, the *exempla* actual; and the whole is given an individual thrust by an uncompromising manly stress of phrase, and a continual controlled energy as of present speech. It was perhaps exactly the preparatory work that was necessary for Pope's later achievement: a revival of comprehensive moral satire in a verse that had shed the crabbed and heated obscurity of much of the satire from Donne to Cleveland.

6

BOILEAU

The influence of Boileau upon the course of English satire is a question too large to admit of adequate treatment here. His significance for Oldham, Dryden and Pope is sufficiently evident to be of central interest for any historian of satire between Ben Jonson and Samuel Johnson; but such an historian, besides charting the connections – such as they are – between Donne, Hall, Marston and Cleveland on the one hand, and Oldham, Rochester, Dryden and Pope on the other, would have to reconsider A.F.B. Clark's account of the influence of Boileau and his colleagues in England, before he could say whether we were justified in separating that first group of names from the second, and in implying that there was in the later 1670s a new impetus as a result of Englishmen coming to appreciate something in the new French writers that was not available to them from their English predecessors. Yet even such an ambitious inquiry would fail to satisfy (fail to be more than a skeletal form of literary history) unless it wrestled with the nature of English culture in the period, and the changes it underwent. In giving an account of the procedures of satire, we could not omit some discussion of changes in religious belief, in political theory and practice, in morals and manners; of the pulpit and the stage as guides and arbiters of these values; of the cultured circles and the coterie cliques; of the ways in which individuals used some of these varied social arrangements to help them understand, order and perhaps change their own mysterious and unruly selves. And if we were really concerned to establish the importance of Boileau, we should demand of such an historian that he should perform this social investigation for France as well, so that we might have some idea of what attracted these Englishmen to French culture, and of which elements in it proved unassimilable to English tempers.

Such an undertaking could only be the fruit of mature reading and reflection, and of a sensitive and somewhat speculative sympathy, since in the cases of Dryden and Pope the French influences are not always easy to locate with precision. One might, for example, win assent for the proposition that *Mac Flecknoe* is clearly endebted to *Le Lutrin* without being able to carry conviction with any more detailed account.

The aim of this present chapter is to improve the preparatory documentation for such a study by examining the influence of Boileau at some of its more tangible moments, in Oldham's versions of Boileau's fifth and eighth satires and in two poems that illustrate in contrasting ways the stance that Boileau helped Oldham to achieve: the *Satyr Dissuading from Poetry* and the *Satyr addressed to a Friend*. Some occasional reference will be made to how Dryden and Pope relate to this material, but the chief intention is to complete the account of Oldham's uses of Boileau that was begun in Chapter 3.

To begin with, however, it may be convenient to review briefly Boileau's appearances in English before Oldham, and the clearest way of doing so will be in the form of a table:[1]

1668   Boileau publishes *Satires* I-IX.

1673   Boileau reads out *Le Lutrin* and *Art Poétique*.
         May: Dryden writes to Rochester about Etherege's version of *Satire* I.

1674   Boileau publishes *Le Lutrin*, *Art Poétique*, and *Traité du Sublime*.
         Rochester writes *Timon* (using *Satire* III).
         Rochester writes *Satyr against Reason and Mankind* (using *Satire* VIII), which is at some unknown date transcribed by Oldham into RMS.

1676   Between mid-1676 and mid-1678 Dryden writes *Mac Flecknoe* (using *Le Lutrin*).

1677   Dryden refers to Boileau in the Preface to *The State of Innocence*.

1678   Oldham uses *Satire* II and *Art Poétique* in *A Letter from the Country*.
         October: Oldham translates parts of *Le Lutrin*.

1679   Anon., *Satyr against Man* (from *Satire* VIII) published in *A Ternary of Satyrs*.
         Rochester's *Satyr against Reason and Mankind* printed.

1680   Pulteney's translation of the *Traité du Sublime* published.
         Butler, who died this year, had translated *Satire* II.

1681   Anon., *Utile Dulci*, from *Satire* VII.

1682   *October*: Oldham translates *Satire* VIII, and probably around the same time translates *Satire* V.
         N.O.'s translation of *Le Lutrin* published.

1683   Publication of Oldham's versions of *Satires* V and VIII in *PT*.
         Soames-Dryden translation of *Art Poétique* published.

Of all these, only Oldham shows any sustained attempt to come to terms with Boileau.

But why this interest? There had been strong connections with French life and letters for many years, particularly via the Stuart Court. Denham, Cowley and Marvell may have profited from their time in France during the Commonwealth, though French influence is not very apparent in their work. Besides, Oldham is interested in the new French writers – Boileau, Rapin, Pascal: from Voiture he takes only a poem that had already been translated once.[2] But as de la Valterie said, 'There are very few true Models ... *Voiture* is not one; and much less *Balzac*. *Voiture*'s Pretty-nesses and *Balzac*'s Flights have an Affectation naturally displeasing.'[3] Saint-Évremond, whose favourite reading was from earlier generations – Montaigne, Malherbe, Corneille, Voiture – and who was no friend of Boileau, recognised nevertheless something very special in this new poetry:

> In many places it contains the finest lines I have ever seen. It is
> evident throughout that the author has discovered the art of
> composing and arranging them as well as any one of the Age;
> his style, though beneath that of Horace, is very fine all the
> same, and his translation of *Longinus* is extremely pleasing to
> my mind. In short, I think the public is much obliged to him,
> and I have a share in this obligation for the pleasure he gives
> me and the profit I derive from it ... It seems to me that
> Monsieur *Despréaux* wanted to appropriate the style of *Horace*,
> and has turned out to be a very exact and elegant *Juvenal*,
> doubtless the best of the kind we have.[4]

Still, it is not clear why a young Englishman should be similarly attracted and it is therefore interesting to have the reactions of a cultivated man of twenty-one, a student at the Inns of Court, who, although this was in 1715 when the ground had to some extent been prepared for him, was coming to Boileau quite fresh, and with the sense of making a new discovery:

> I think I cannot too often read his works: they are the most
> proper to form one into a polite and natural way of thinking
> and writing of any modern writings whatsoever. I should be glad
> if I could get the habit of thinking in his way and manner.

> Read some of Boileau. I am more and more pleased with him the
> more I read him. I find his poetry has a very different air and
> manner from the usual poetry. It is very much in the style and
> manner of Juvenal and Horace. His talent lies in a certain familiar

way of thinking that makes whatever he says come into the mind
with a peculiar kind of delight and pleasure. He does, as it were
give you your own thoughts and reflects the image of your own
mind; whatever he says you have it as if it were your own and
though you could not express it in so agreeable a manner as he
has done, yet now he has once done it for you, you are apt to
think you could have done it easily too.[5]

Perhaps something similar possessed Oldham as he read Boileau for the
first time — a feeling that this poetry challenged him to make his own work
wider in scope, more urbane in tone, more subtle in execution.

The Eighth Satyr of Monsieur Boileau, Imitated

With two versions of *Satire* VIII already in existence, there must have been
good reasons why Oldham felt that the poem needed to be translated
again. The anonymous version in *A Ternary of Satyrs* (1679) keeps very
close to the French, and has no poetic merit, though in its own terms it
successfully provides a verse crib for anyone who wanted the bones of
Boilcau's poem in English.

Rochester's *Satyr against Reason and Mankind* is based only loosely
on Boileau, and is in essence a very different poem.[6] Partly it is an attack
upon the speculative intellect that leads man astray, and Rochester is
able to imagine this in a dramatic image that has a strong universality:

> Then old age and experience, hand in hand,
> Lead him to death, and make him understand,
> After a search so painful and so long,
> That all his life he has been in the wrong.
> Huddled in dirt the reasoning engine lies,
> Who was so proud, so witty, and so wise.
> (25-30)

Then immediately, though without any indication of a deliberate change,
the poem moves into a series of disjointed couplets that seem to be
primarily autobiographical in reference:

> Pride drew him in, as cheats their bubbles catch,
> And made him venture to be made a wretch.
> His wisdom did his happiness destroy,
> Aiming to know that world he should enjoy.
> And wit was his vain, frivolous pretense
> Of pleasing others at his own expense.
> (31-6)

Rochester returns later to the question of the Reason that leads men astray by dissociating their intellect and feeling, instead of concentrating and intensifying their unity (94-109), and then takes from Boileau the disparaging references to man vis-à-vis animals. Man's behaviour to his fellow-men Rochester attributes to fear:

> Whilst wretched man is still in arms for fear.
> For fear he arms, and is of arms afraid,
> By fear to fear successively betrayed;
> Base fear, the source whence his best passions came:
> His boasted honor, and his dear-bought fame ...
> Look to the bottom of his vast design,
> Wherein man's wisdom, power, and glory join:
> The good he acts, the ill he does endure,
> 'Tis all from fear, to make himself secure.
> Merely for safety, after fame we thirst,
> For all men would be cowards if they durst.
>   (140-4; 153-8)

There may be a Hobbesian element here, but Hobbes did not insist on fear as the sole root of human motivation. Nor, in spite of the bravura of the final paradox, is Rochester's assertion sufficiently true to win our assent without further explanation. As with the cryptic references to fear in the passage cited earlier —

> The pleasure past, a threatening doubt remains
> That frights th'enjoyer with succeeding pains: ...
> 'Tis not that they're belov'd, but fortunate,
> And therefore what they fear at heart, they hate.
>   (39-40; 44-5)

— the attempt to understand some of his own motives impedes Rochester's presentation of supra-personal truths about man.

It was, in any case, a different form of public poetry to which Oldham aspired. By following the structure of Boileau's poem he points up the futility of many activities — political and religious strife, military glory, scientific inquiry, academic debate, scholarly travail — with a brief account of the pettiness of each. His poem has greater coherence than Rochester's, though without the other's underlying quality, which, had it been sustained (and the result of sustained contemplation) we might have been tempted to call a tragic perception of life.

One of the most remarkable features of *The Eighth Satyr of Monsieur Boileau, Imitated* is the way Oldham handles the exchanges between the

'Poet' and the 'Doctor of the University', not only so as to create interest through the variety of tone, but through that variety to suggest something of the complexities of the subject, and to indicate where he is offering us a zestful exaggeration of the case, and where he is presenting a deeply-held conviction for our consideration.

At the beginning of the poem it is the bravura display which catches our attention:

> Of all the Creatures in the world that be,
> Beast, Fish, or Fowl, that go, or swim, or fly
> Throughout the Globe from *London* to *Japan*,
> The arrant'st Fool in my opinion's Man.
>   *What*? (strait I'm taken up) *an Ant, a Fly,*
> *A tiny Mite, which we can hardly see*
> *Without a Perspective, a silly Ass,*
> *Or freakish Ape?*
>   (1-8; *PT* 1-2)

The rhythm of line 2 and the phrase 'arrant'st Fool' are more aggressive than Boileau's opening:

> De tous les Animaux qui s'élevent dans l'air,
> Qui marchent sur la Terre, ou nagent dans la Mer,
> De Paris au Perou, du Iapon jusqu'à Rome,
> Le plus sot animal, à mon avis, c'est l'Homme.
>   (1-4; p. 66)

and Oldham's last four lines state the preliminary case with great rhythmical panache. Then there is a more conventional rhythm in the reply:

> *This idle talk,* (you say) *and rambling stuff*
> *May pass in Satyr, and take well enough*
> *With Sceptick Fools, who are dispos'd to jeer*
> *At serious things: but you must make't appear*
> *By solid proof.*
>   (18-22; *PT* 2)

The Doctor's definition of wisdom is quite appealing:

> *'Tis an evenness of Soul,*
> *A steddy temper, which no cares controul,*
> *No passions ruffle, nor desires inflame,*
> *Still constant to its self, and still the same,*

> *That does in all its slow Resolves advance,*
> *With graver steps, than Benchers, when they dance.*
>
>   (26-31; *PT* 3)[7]

but the attractive cadence of the first four lines gives way to the blander movement of the last two, whose cautious gravity places the Doctor's definition (it is a movement that takes no account of the various energies that we are to meet later). The Poet's reply maintains a considered rhythm:

> The wiser Emmet, quoted just before, ⎫
> In Summer time ranges the Fallows o're ⎬
> With pains, and labour, to lay in his store: ⎭
> But when the blust'ring North with ruffling blasts
> Saddens the year, and Nature overcasts;
> The prudent Insect, hid in privacy,
> Enjoys the fruits of his past industry.
> No Ant of sense was e're so awkard seen,
> To drudg in Winter, loiter in the Spring.
> But sillier Man, in his mistaken way,
> By Reason, his false guide, is led astray:
> Tost by a thousand gusts of wavering doubt,
> His restless mind still rolls from thought to thought:
> In each resolve unsteddy, and unfixt,
> And what he one day loaths, desires the next.
>
>   (34-48; *PT* 3-4)[8]

The tone of the second paragraph is surely *compassion*: 'Reason' is an addition due to Rochester, and the line 'His restless mind still rolls from thought to thought' echoes his epigram on Charles II, 'Restless he rolls about from whore to whore', but the more thoughtful phrasing of Oldham's lines indicates that while he understands the manifold restlessness of Rochester and his fellows he is trying to place it philosophically, to point up the general truth contained in the particular example.

The next summary by the Poet has more rhythmic verve:

> This is our image just: such is that vain,
> That foolish, fickle, motly Creature, Man:
> More changing than a Weathercock, his Head
> Ne'er wakes with the same thoughts, he went to bed,
> Irksome to all beside, and ill at ease,
> He neither others, nor himself can please:

> Each minute round his whirling humors run, ⎫
> Now he's a Trooper, and a Priest anon,   ⎬
> To day in Buff, to morrow in a Gown.   ⎭
>
> (61-9; *PT* 4-5)

The livelier imagery here contrasts with Boileau's more sententious phrasing:

> Voilà l'Homme en effet: il va du blanc au noir;
> Il condamne au matin ses sentimens du soir;
> Importun à tout autre, à soi-mesme incommode,
> Il change à tous momens d'esprit comme de mode;
> Il tourne au moindre vent, il tombe au moindre choc:
> Aujourd'hui dans un casque & demain dans un froc.
>
> (49-54; p. 68)

To English ears 'Irksome' and 'ill at ease' say much more than 'Importun' and 'incommode'. After a sarcastic passage —

> Yet, pleas'd with idle whimsies of his brain,
> And puft with pride, this haughty thing would fain
> Be thought himself the only stay, and prop,
> That holds the mighty frame of Nature up:
> The Skies and Stars his properties must seem,
> And turn-spit Angels tread the spheres for him:
>
> (70-5; *PT* 5)[9]

— there come some lines in Oldham that are worth comparing both with Boileau and with the *Ternary*:

> Ce Maistre pretendu qui leur donne des lois,
> Ce Roi des animaux, combien a-t-il de Rois?
> L'Ambition, l'Amour, l'Avarice, ou la Haine
> Tiennent comme un Forçat son esprit à la chaîne.
>
> (65-8; p.69)

> This titular Lord who gives them Laws, even he,
> This King of Beasts, how many Kings has he?
> Ambition, Love, Avarice, Hate, we find
> With slavish fetters do enchain his mind.
>
> (*Ternary*, p. 4)

> This boasted Monarch of the world, that aws
> The Creatures here, and with his beck gives laws;
> This titular King, who thus pretends to be

> The Lord of all, how many Lords has he?
> The lust of Mony, and the lust of Power, ⎫
> With Love, and Hate, and twenty passions more, ⎬
> Hold him their slave, and chain him to the Oar. ⎭
>
> (87-93; *PT* 6)

Oldham takes over 'titular' to good effect, and the *Ternary*'s line is modified to become 'The Lord of all, how many Lords has he?', which has a much greater, saddened strength. Then by using a triplet Oldham avoids the crowded third line of Boileau and the *Ternary*, and gives us a final line whose imagery and rhythm have become fiercer and more desperate.

The Doctor tries the argument that only man is civilised:

> Lui seul vivant, dit-on, dans l'enceinte des villes
> Fait voir d'honnestes moeurs, des coustumes civiles,
> Se fait des Gouverneurs, des Magistrats, des Rois,
> Observe une police, obeït à des lois.
>
> (119-22; p. 71)

> *'Tis he alone* (you'l say) *'tis happy he,*
> *That's fram'd by Nature for Society*:
> *He only dwells in Towns, is only seen*
> *With Manners and Civility to shine*;
> *Does only Magistrates, and Rulers choose,*
> *And live secur'd by Government, and Laws.*
>
> (162-7; *PT* 10)

Oldham makes explicit the idea that man is '*fram'd by Nature for Society*', perhaps because, although it is an old and respectable idea,[10] the recent work of Hobbes and Cowley had pointed out how violent were the passions that led men into civil association. The *cognoscenti* might therefore be expected by Oldham to question the Doctor's traditional assumption, and to pick up the hint in '*shine*' that '*Manners and Civility*' are but superficial glosses on a turbulent human nature.

In the following passage comparing men's actions with beasts' Boileau's eye seems to be more on the animals:

> Void-on les Loups brigans, comme nous inhumains,
> Pour détrousser les Loups, courir les grands chemins?
> Iamais pour s'agrandir, vid-on dans sa manie,
> Vn Tigre en factions partager l'Hyrcanie?
> L'Ours a-t'il dans les bois la guerre avec les Ours?
> Le Vautour dans les airs fond-il sur les Vautours?

A-t-on veu quelquefois dans les plaines d'Afrique,
Déchirant à l'envi leur propre Republique,
Lions contre Lions, Parens contre Parens,
Combatre follement pour le choix des Tyrans?
(125-34; pp. 71-2)

whereas Oldham sees the opportunity for embryonic beast-fables, and brings out the animal characteristics of the men who engage in these activities (we momentarily see the politician as a tiger):

Who ever saw the Wolves, that he can say, ⎫
Like more inhuman Us, so bent on prey, ⎬
To rob their fellow Wolves upon the way? ⎭
Who ever saw *Church* and *Fanatick* Bear,
Like savage Mankind one another tear?
What Tyger e're, aspiring to be great,
In Plots and Factions did embroil the State?
Or when was't heard upon the *Libyan* Plains,
Where the stern Monarch of the Desert reigns,
That *Whig* and *Tory* Lions in wild jars
Madly engag'd for choice of Shrieves and May'rs?
(171-81; *PT* 10-11)

The Doctor's reasonable tone returns when we have:

Gently, good Sir! (cry you) why all this rant?
Man has his freaks, and passions; that we grant:
He has his frailties, and blind sides; who doubts?
But his least Virtues balance all his Faults.
Pray, was it not this bold, this thinking Man,
That measur'd Heav'n, and taught the Stars to scan,
Whose boundless wit, with soaring wings durst fly,
Beyond the flaming borders of the sky;
Turn'd Nature o're, and with a piercing view
Each cranny search'd, and lookt her through and through:
(212-21; *PT* 12-13)[11]

There is a suggestion of hubris here; and the implications of the last two lines are obvious.

In a different mode is the mercenary father's advice to his son, a speech that gathers momentum until in the second paragraph the voice of the satirist is more in evidence than the voice of the persona:

When shoals of Poets, Pedants, Orators,
Doctors, Divines, Astrologers, and Lawyers,

> *Authors of every sort, and every size.*
> *To thee their Works, and Labors shall address,*
> *With pompous Lines their Dedications fill,*
> *And learnedly in* Greek *and* Latin *tell*
> *Lies to thy face, that thou hast deep insight,*
> *And art a mighty judg of what they write.*
> *He, that is rich, is every thing, that is,* ⎫
> *Without one grain of Wisdom he is wise,* ⎬
> *And knowing nought, knows all the Sciences:* ⎭
> *He's witty, gallant, virtuous, generous, stout,*
> *Well-born, well-bred, well-shap'd, well-drest, what not?*
> *Lov'd by the Great, and courted by the Fair,*
> *For none that e're had Riches, found despair:*
> *Gold to the loathsom'st object gives a grace,*
> *And sets it off, and makes ev'n* Bovey *please:*
> *But tatter'd Poverty they all despise,*
> *Love stands aloof, and from the Scare-crow flies.*
> (267-85; *PT* 15-16)

There is a fine control of rhythm here — in, for example, '*tell | Lies to thy face*', and the final line is a strongly-felt clinching statement that bears a personal impress unlike Boileau's sententious 'Mais tout devient affreux avec la Pauvreté' (210; p. 75).

After the passage detailing the wasted labours of biblical expositors and religious controversialists (which is phrased with far greater sympathy than the earlier passage against the scientific virtuosi) the Doctor is goaded into a reply in which Oldham deftly catches the tone of the blustering outraged don:

> A Doctor is no better than an Ass.
> *A Doctor, Sir? your self: Pray have a care,*
> *This is to push your Raillery too far.*
> (315-17; *PT* 18)

But the tone immediately moderates:

> *But not to lose the time in trifling thus,*
> *Beside the point, come now more home and close:*
> *That Man has Reason is beyond debate,*
> *Nor will your self, I think, deny me that:*
> *And was not this fair Pilot giv'n to steer,*
> *His tott'ring Bark through Life's rough Ocean here?*
> *All this I grant: But if in spite of it*

The wretch on every Rock he sees will split,
To what great purpose does his Reason serve,
But to mis-guide his course, and make him swerve?
(318-27; PT 18)

The tone of the rejoinder here is surely — unlike the tone in Rochester — one of compassion; and compassionate general statement is one of the poem's hallmarks:

While Man, who does to that false light pretend,
Wildly gropes on, and in broad day is blind.
By whimsie led he does all things by chance,
And acts in each against all common sense.
With every thing pleas'd, and displeas'd at once,
He knows not what he seeks, nor what he shuns:
(346-51; PT 19-20)

Groups of lines with this tone and movement recur like refrains between the more spirited satirical passages and the cautious sense of the Doctor, and while they indicate the poem's sad and puzzled central judgment, this whole patchwork of tones enacts the poem's recognition of the complexity of life. When Oldham writes:

Did we, like him, e're see the Dog, or Bear,
Chimera's of their own devising fear?
Frame needless doubts, and for those doubts forego
The Joys which prompting Nature calls them to?
And with their Pleasures awkardly at strife,
With scaring Fantoms pall the sweets of Life?
(356-61; PT 20)

he may be echoing Rochester's thoughts, but there is now a balance in the expression: both a warmth *for* the joys of 'prompting Nature' and a recognition — sad, but not angry — that this awkward strife is a characteristic of the human lot.

A Satyr Touching Nobility: out of Monsieur Boileau

Oldham's version of Boileau's *Satire* v takes the opportunity, in distinguishing between true and false nobility, of elucidating that conduct which was to be thought of as virtue, as true nobility. Throughout the poem the verse is sprightly, and presents the argument with some vigour, but the best poetry is often to be found making points that are not specifically connected with the subject of nobility. Here, for example, is the man whose behaviour belies his noble ancestry:

> Si tout sorti qu'il est d'une source divine,
> Son coeur dément en lui sa superbe origine:
> Et n'ayant rien de grand qu'une sotte fierté,
> S'endort dans une lâche & molle oisivité?
>
> (17-20; p. 49)

> If sprung, as he pretends, of noble Race,
> He does his own Original disgrace,
> And, swoln with selfish Vanity and Pride,
> To greatness has no other claim beside,
> But squanders life, and sleeps away his days,
> Dissolv'd in Sloth, and steep'd in sensual ease?
>
> (23-8; *PT* 128-9)

In that last couplet Oldham has emancipated himself from the drift of Boileau's argument, and has introduced a larger thought about how life is squandered by those who do not know how to live. So too where Boileau gives just a summary line to the fate of the worthless horse of noble stock, Oldham works the example up into a couplet that enacts the laborious misery of bondage:

> Et va porter la malle, ou tirer la charuë
>
> (34; p. 49)

> Condemn'd for Life to ply the dirty Road,
> To drag some Cart, or bear some Carrier's Load.
>
> (49-50; *PT* 130)

Oldham also modifies Boileau to stress his own concerns at points where Boileau is handling values that mean little to Oldham. One example is the passage on martial glory that Boileau added to his source in Juvenal VIII:

> Si vous estes sorti de ces Heros fameux;
> Montrez-nous cette ardeur qu'on vit briller en eux,
> Ce zele pour l'honneur, cette horreur pour le vice.
> Respectez-vous les loix? Fuiez-vous l'injustice?
> Sçavez-vous sur un mur repousser des assauts,
> Et dormir en plein champ le harnois sur le dos?
>
> (39-44; p. 50)

If you from such illustrious Worthies came,
By copying them your high Extract proclaim:
Shew us those generous Heats of Gallantry,
Which Ages past did in those Worthies see,
That zeal for Honor, and that brave Disdain,
Which scorn'd to do an Action base, or mean:
Do you apply your Interest aright,
Not to oppress the Poor with wrongful Might?
Would you make Conscience to pervert the Laws,
Tho brib'd to do't, or urg'd by your own Cause?
Dare you, when justly call'd, expend your Blood
In service for your King's and Countries good?
Can you in open Field in Armour sleep,
And there meet danger in the ghastliest shape?
(59-72; *PT* 130-1)

Though Oldham uses 'hero' elsewhere in this poem, he cannot use it to introduce a passage describing noble conduct: the 'heroic' is not something that means enough to him for him to be able to incarnate it in his poetry. Thus instead of 'Heros' we have the English word 'Worthies', which can be used as easily for people of learning and virtue as for the heroes of antiquity. Boileau's summary phrases — 'Respectez-vous les loix? Fuiez-vous l'injustice?' — assume a firm consensus about legal and just behaviour: Oldham's lines have to define what he considers honourable behaviour to be. Similarly 'la gloire' means nothing by itself: it has to be translated into 'service for your King's and Countries good'. The phrase 'danger in the ghastliest shape' suggests by its vagueness that Oldham has no clear conception of 'heroic' behaviour in war. In translating the whole passage Oldham substitutes for the Frenchman's implicit reliance on a socially-accepted martial and patriotic glory an English account of the varieties of a man's responsibility to serve his fellows.

A Satyr Dissuading from Poetry

In discussing Oldham's translation of Juvenal III we noted that he was at pains to achieve an objective stance, whereas Boileau used the poem to air his private grouses, writing into it the miserable treatment meted out to poets. This part of Boileau's adaptation of Juvenal Oldham kept for use in a separate poem, *A Satyr Dissuading from Poetry*, which draws on Boileau's *Satires* I and IX, and Juvenal VIII.[12]

When compared with Boileau's poems it is again the attempt at objectivity that impresses. The poem begins with the appearance of Spenser, who is asked by Oldham:

> *Teach me to tread the glorious paths of Fame.*
> *Teach me (for none does better know than thou)*
> *How, like thy self, I may immortal grow.*
>
> (22-5; *PT* 165)

The subsequent account of the sorry state of poetry comes from Spenser's ghost, not directly from the poet, so that we are not disturbed by the solipsism that we sometimes meet in Boileau. But the rhythm in Oldham's poem is for the most part the headlong movement, rapidly accumulating its charges, that we have observed Oldham modifying since 1678. There is a throwaway quality about the disillusionment, which is sometimes an almost bravura cynicism, facile in its reductiveness:

> He, who sung on *Phrygia*'s shore,
> The *Grecian* Bullies fighting for a Whore.
>
> (48-9; *PT* 167)

Much of the matter of the poem is restated from his earlier pieces. Yet one passage is worth quoting as an example of the strong, controlled rhetoric of which Oldham is capable:

> My own hard Usage here I need not press,
> Where you have every day before your face
> Plenty of fresh resembling Instances:
> Great *Cowley*'s Muse the same ill Treatment had,
> Whose Verse shall live for ever to upbraid
> Th' ungrateful World, that left such Worth unpaid.
> *Waller* himself may thank Inheritance
> For what he else had never got by Sense.
> On *Butler* who can think without just Rage,
> The Glory, and the Scandal of the Age?
> Fair stood his hopes, when first he came to Town,
> Met every where with welcomes of Renown,
> Courted, and lov'd by all, with wonder read,
> And promises of Princely Favour fed:
> But what Reward for all had he at last,
> After a Life in dull expectance pass'd?
> The Wretch at summing up his mis-spent days
> Found nothing left, but Poverty, and Praise:
> Of all his Gains by Verse he could not save

Enough to purchase Flannel, and a Grave:
Reduc'd to want, he in due time fell sick,
Was fain to die, and be interr'd on tick:
And well might bless the Fever that was sent,
To rid him hence, and his worse Fate prevent.

(167-90; *PT* 173-4)

While these lines carry the stamp of personal concern, they express not an individual's grudge, but a public scandal. Lines like

The Glory, and the Scandal of the Age ...[13]

And promises of Princely Favour fed ...

Found nothing left, but Poverty, and Praise ...

make their points with an effective but unobtrusive use of rhythm and alliteration. The rhythm can also be varied thus:

Bless me! how great Genius! how each Line ⎫
Is big with Sense! how glorious a Design ⎬
Does thro the whole, and each Proportion shine! ⎭
How lofty all his Thoughts, and how inspir'd!
Pity, such wond'rous Parts are not preferr'd:
Cries a gay wealthy Sot, who would not bail
For bare five Pounds the Author out of Jail,
Should he starve there, and rot;

(129-36; *PT* 171)

But such use of speech to define these social and literary values is limited. There is not the command of the social milieu, the assumption of an authority to be the arbiter of literary values, such as we find in the more mature Boileau:

Il a tort, dira l'un, *Pourquoi faut-il qu'il nomme?*
Attaquer P***! ah! c'est un si bon homme:
Balzac en fait l'Eloge en cent endroits divers.
Il est vrai, s'il m'eust creu, qu'il n'eust point fait de vers.
Il se tuë à rimer. Que n'écrit-il en prose?
Voilà ce que l'on dit: & que dis-je autre chose?
En blâmant les Escrits, ai-je d'un stile affreux,
Distilé sur sa vie un venin dangereux?
Ma Muse, en l'attaquant, charitable & discrete,
Sçait de l'homme d'honneur distinguer le Poëte.
Qu'on vante en lui la foi, l'honneur, la probité:

> Qu'on prise sa candeur & sa civilité:
> Qu'il soit doux, complaisant, officieux, sincere,
> On le veut, j'y souscris, & suis prest de me taire;
> Mais que pour un modele on montre ses Escrits,
> Qu'il soit le mieux renté de tous les beaux Esprits:
> Comme Roi des Auteurs, qu'on l'éleve à l'Empire;
> Ma bile alors s'échauffe, & je brûle d'écrire.
>
> > (*Satire* IX.203-20; pp. 88-9)

This was an authoritative command of the literary world not to be seen in England until the *Essay on Criticism* and *Epistle to Arbuthnot.*

A Satyr addressed to a Friend

In *A Satyr addressed to a Friend, that is about to leave the University, and come abroad in the World*, Oldham returns to the question of the choice of life, and to man's struggle to attain independence:

> How many men of choice, and noted parts,
> Well fraught with Learning, Languages, and Arts,
> Designing high Preferment in their mind,
> And little doubting good success to find,
> With vast and tow'ring thoughts have flock'd to Town,
> But to their cost soon found themselves undone,
> Now to repent, and starve at leisure left,
> Of miseries last Comfort, Hope, bereft?
>
> > (11-18; *PT* 138)

'Vast and tow'ring' has a satirical edge, but is not contemptuous of the young man's aspirations, and the last couplet has a tragic concision that anticipates Johnson. The responsibility for their failure is placed at first with the individuals who have these lofty expectations, not with the society that ignores them. Their fundamental life-choices are mistaken. The echo of *Paradise Lost*:[14]

> The world lies now before you, let me hear,
> What course your Judgment counsels you to steer:
>
> > (23-4; *PT* 138)

is not flippant or gratuitous: it is a clear reminder of the seriousness of the choice that has to be made, as well as another indication that Oldham valued *Paradise Lost* for dramatising and challenging life-choices.

In the Beatus Ille tradition the Happy Man had his farm or country house, usually inherited, and the poets who wrote this sort of poetry (Jonson, Marvell, Cowley) owned or had the use of such retreats. But Oldham now poses the question, How is a man to be happy when he doesn't have even the basic material blessings of the 'Happy Man'?

> Were you the Son of some rich Usurer, ...
> Left nought to do, but to interr the Sot,
> And spend with ease what he with pains had got;
> 'Twere easie to advise how you might live,
> (27-31; PT 138-9)

but instead Oldham is addressing one who can

> boast of no Inheritance,
> Save that small stock, which lies within your Brains.
> (33-4; PT 139)

The poetry of retreat and retirement is passing away: what now needs to be written in the dawn of the age of Pope is the poetry of honesty and integrity in the world. It is certainly right to say that Oldham sometimes anticipates the world of Grub Street,[15] but in this poem there is none of the resentful sarcasm of the *Satyr Dissuading from Poetry*. Oldham's account of the lot of the domestic chaplain is incisive, but achieves an impersonality too:

> Who tho in silken Skarf, and Cassock drest,
> Wears but a gayer Livery at best:
> When Dinner calls the Implement must wait
> With holy Words to consecrate the Meat:
> But hold it for a Favour seldom known,
> If he be deign'd the Honor to sit down.
> Soon as the Tarts appear, Sir *Crape*, withdraw!
> Those Dainties are not for a spiritual Maw:
> Observe your distance, and be sure to stand
> Hard by the Cistern with your Cap in hand:
> There for diversion you may pick your Teeth,
> Till the kind Voider comes for your Relief:
> For meer Board-wages such their Freedom sell,
> Slaves to an Hour, and Vassals to a Bell ...
>
> The menial thing perhaps for a Reward
> Is to some slender Benefice preferr'd,

> With this Proviso bound, that he must wed ⎫
> My Ladies antiquated Waiting-maid,   ⎬
> In Dressing only skill'd, and Marmalade. ⎭
> (78-102; PT 141-2)

The extended scene is not something we could match from Boileau, nor from English poetry before Oldham.[16] The line 'Slaves to an Hour, and Vassals to a Bell' has been adapted from Cowley's 'Unhappy Slave, and Pupil to a Bell' in his *Ode: Upon Liberty*: but what was sententious there has become dramatically cogent in Oldham's hands. In registering the social world with this ease and effective precision, in verse that judges both the chaplain and his employer, Oldham is preparing the way for Pope, and complementing the wider social analysis that he gives in his translations of Juvenal III and Boileau VIII. In all three poems he is covering ground not touched by Dryden.

The summary statements about freedom are clearly Oldham's own, but are not merely his. The couplet

> Let others who such meannesses can brook,
> Strike Countenance to every Great man's Look:
> (103-4; PT 142)

invites a general acceptance both by the classical echo in 'let others ...' and the finely dramatic image of 'Strike Countenance'. And when he makes the claim:

> I rate my Freedom higher, nor will I
> For Food and Rayment truck my Liberty.
> (107-8; PT 143)

the 'I' is not only the poet, but — because of the biblical echo — anyone who accepts that

> No man can serue two masters: for either he will hate the one and loue the other, or else hee will holde to the one, and despise the other. Ye cannot serue God and Mammon. Therfore I say vnto you, Take no thought for your life, what yee shall eate, or what ye shall drinke, nor yet for your body, what yee shall put on: Is not the life more then meate? and the body then raiment? (Matthew vi.24-5).

So too, when Oldham writes of his own real aspirations he does so in a way that makes a broad appeal:

> 'T has ever been the top of my Desires,
> The utmost height to which my wish aspires,

> That Heav'n would bless me with a small Estate,
> Where I might find a close obscure retreat;
> There, free from Noise, and all ambitious ends,
> Enjoy a few choice Books, and fewer Friends,
> Lord of my self, accountable to none,
> But to my Conscience, and my God alone:
> There live unthought of, and unheard of, die,
> And grudg Mankind my very memory.
> But since the Blessing is (I find) too great
> For me to wish for, or expect of Fate:
> Yet maugre all the spight of Destiny,
> My Thoughts, and Actions are, and shall be free.
>
> (115-28; *PT* 143-4)

Even here, the real aspiration is to freedom, not to retirement: Oldham sees that material comfort is not a condition of 'Quiet of Mind'. The first lines recall Cowley in his Essay *The Garden*:

> I Never had any other desire so strong, and so like to Covetous-
> ness as that one which I have had always, that I might be master
> at last of a small house and large garden ... But several accidents
> of my ill fortune have disappointed me hitherto, and so still, of
> that felicity ... I have made the first and hardest step to it, by
> abandoning all ambitions (*Essays*, pp. 420-1).

'Obscure retreat' is used by Cowley of the Country Mouse's 'seat', but is also an echo of Seneca's celebrated chorus in *Thyestes*:

> Stet quicumque volet potens
> aulae culmine lubrico;
> me dulcis saturet quies;
> obscuro positus loco ...   (391-4)

Cowley's rendering of this chorus may have suggested some of Oldham's phrases. The opening two lines of Oldham's passage are a reply to:

> Upon the slippery tops of humane State,
>   The guilded Pinnacles of Fate,
> Let others proudly stand
>   (*Essays*, pp. 399-400)

while

> There live unthought of, and unheard of, die,
> And grudg Mankind my very memory

may be drawing on Cowley's elaboration of Seneca:

> Nor let the Breath of Infamy or Fame,
> From town to town Eccho about my Name.
> Nor let my homely Death embroidered be
>   With Scutcheon or with Elegie.
> (p. 400)

Another key document in the seventeenth-century humanist account of 'How to Live' was Sir Henry Wotton's poem *The Character of a Happy Life*, of which the following lines may also have shaped Oldham's passage:

> H ow *happy* is he born and taught,
> That serveth not an others *will*? ...
>
> Who hath his *life* from *rumors freed*,
> Whose *Conscience* is his strong *retreat*: ...
>
> And entertaines the harmless day
> With a *Religious Book*, or Friend ...
>
> *Lord* of himselfe, though not of *Lands*,
> And having *nothing*: yet hath *all*.[17]

The concluding section of the poem is the fable of the wolf and the dog. Professor Brooks points out that the tale appears in Phaedrus (III.7) and La Fontaine (I.5), but these were not the only versions of the story that Oldham was using. Phaedrus's *Lupus ad Canem* was repeated by many of his imitators, chief of whom was Romulus, whose *Canis et Lupus* reworks the fable in the form that Oldham chiefly followed.[18]

Oldham begins with the contrast between the two animals (given by Phaedrus and La Fontaine, omitted by Romulus): the dog is fat, the wolf famished. The wolf asks:

> *Whence comes it, that you look so sleek, and gay?*
> *While I, who do as well (I'm sure) deserve,*
> *For want of Livelihood am like to starve?*
> (140-2; *PT* 144)

> Unde sic, quaeso, nites?
> Aut quo cibo fecisti tantum corporis?
> Ego, qui sum longe fortior, pereo fame.
> (Phaedrus)

('Whence is it (I pray) that you shine so? On what food have you built up such a great body? I, who am much stronger, am perishing with hunger.')

Unde, frater, sic nitidus et pinguis es? (Romulus).

('Whence is it, brother, that you are so sleek and fat?')

In Phaedrus the dog tells the wolf:

> Eadem est conditio tibi,
> Praestare domino si par officium potes.

('The same condition is yours — if you can perform the same duty for my master.')

and describes his duties as a guard dog, which the wolf expresses his willingness to share. La Fontaine for the most part follows this order, but Oldham prefers the construction of Romulus's tale, where the dog first details the delights of living in that household:

> Quia domi custos sum contra latrones. Affertur michi panis, dat dominus ossa, amat me tota familia. quisque michi cibum porrigit, aqua non deest, sub tectis cubo, et sic otiosus vitam gero.

('Because I guard his house against robbers. Bread is brought to me, my master gives me bones, the whole family loves me. Everybody offers me food, there is no shortage of water, I sleep under shelter, and thus I lead a life of ease.')

Romulus's 'amat me tota familia' is used by Oldham in '*I'm the Delight of the whole Family*' (155; *PT* 145), and his 'sic otiosus vitam gero' becomes: '*All this I get by idleness, and ease*' (170; *PT* 146). The phrasing of the wolf's interest and the dog's reply also draws upon Romulus rather than Phaedrus:

> *I envy your Estate*
> *Would to the Gods it were but my good Fate,*
> > (171-2; *PT* 146)

Bene, ... vellem michi ista contingerent (Romulus).

('Good, ... I wish these things would extend to me.')

> Ego vero sum paratus
> > (Phaedrus)

('Truly I am ready.')

> > *you need not doubt ...*
> *Only rely on me, and rest secure.*
> > (179-81; *PT* 146)

... noli timere (Romulus). (' ... do not fear')

The moment when the wolf sees the mark made by the collar is handled similarly by both fabulists, but Oldham is paraphrasing Romulus in the wolf's reaction:

> Not one step farther: Sir, excuse me now.
> Much joy t'ye of your envied, bless'd Estate:
> I will not buy Preferment at that rate:
> A Gods name, take your golden Chains for me:
>   (213-16; PT 148)

Non est, ait, opus michi istis frui quae laudasti; vivere volo liber, quodcumque venerit michi; liber ubi volo peragro. In eo quod placet nulla cathena me tenet, nulla me impedit causa (Romulus).

(I do not need, he said, to enjoy what you praise; I wish to live free, whatever happens to me; I wander freely where I wish. In what pleases me no chain holds me, nothing hinders me.')

Non plane est, inquit. Fruere quae laudas, Canis:
                              (Phaedrus)

('That is just not so, he said. Enjoy what you praise, dog.')

Phaedrus's blunt 'Canis' there may have suggested to Oldham his 'Sir Dog' and Oldham certainly returns to Phaedrus to adapt his splendid clinching line 'Regnare nolo, liber ut non sim mihi' ('I should not wish to rule, if not free to be myself') (which is omitted by Romulus) into: 'Faith, I'd not be a King, not to be free' (217; PT 148).

But as well as using the Latin texts, Oldham seems to have consulted other versions of the tale, which likewise use Romulus's structure. One was La Fontaine's in the Fables, which had first been published in 1668. Another French version was that in Baudoin's Les Fables D'Esope, Phrygien, Traduction nouuelle. Illustree de Discours Moraux, Philosophiques & Politiques published in 1631 and frequently reprinted.[19] These contribute several ideas and phrases that are not supplied by the Latin texts.[20]

Oldham turns to his French versions chiefly when they can contribute to his thinking on the subject of dependency. The dog advises the wolf:

> That you'd a little lay your Roughness by,
> And learn to practice Complaisance, like me.
>   (185-6; PT 146)

Oldham's last line is probably drawing upon La Fontaine's 'à son Maitre complaire', but the phrasing 'learn to practice Complaisance' alludes to the manuals that were popular in England at the time: books such as Antoine de Courtin's *Nouveau Traité de la Civilité qui se pratique en France parmi les honnestes gens,* which was translated in 1678 as *The Rules of Civility,* or the treatise by Eustache du Refuge, *The Art of Complaisance or the Means to oblige in Conversation* (1677). These may appear to be harmless courtesy books, but the epigraph of *The Art of Complaisance,* 'Qui nescit dissimulare, nescit vivere' ('he who does not know how to dissemble, does not know how to live'), alerts us to the way in which they advocate forms of servility and deviousness that Oldham had ever found repugnant. The second chapter of du Refuge, for example, treats 'Of Reservation or dissimulation': the arts of the courtier and the arts of the Jesuit are based on similar betrayals of truth.

Oldham's account of how the dog has betrayed his true nature and become 'complaisant' draws upon Baudoin:

> *— Sir, you must know,*
> *That I at first was rough, and fierce, like you,*
> *Of Nature curs'd, and often apt to bite*
> *Strangers, and else, who ever came in sight:*
> *For this I was tied up, and underwent*
> *The Whip sometimes, and such light Chastisement:*
> *Till I at length by Discipline grew tame,*
> *Gentle, and tractable, as now I am:*
> *'Twas by this short, and slight severity*
> *I gain'd these Marks and Badges, which you see:*
> *But what are they?* Allons Monsieur! *let's go.*
> (202-12; *PT* 147-8)

Tu dois sçauoir, luy respondit le Chien, qu'au commencement ie soulois aboyer aux Estrangers, & mesme à ceux de cognoissance, sans que ma dent espargnast non plus les vns que les autres. Mais d'autant que cela ne plaisoit pas à mon Maistre, il joüa si bien du bâton sur moy, qu'il me fit perdre ceste coûtume, me commandant sur toutes choses, de n'attaquer jamais que les voleurs, & les Loups. Ie me suis corrigé par ce moyen, & suis devenu plus doux que de coûtume, à force d'estre battu; neantmoins ceste cicatrice que tu me vois au col, m'est toûjours depuis restée, pour vne marque de ce que ie suis hargneux naturellement.

Oldham's wolf also disdains the dog's 'golden Chains' — an idea that, though it has precedents in, for example, *Utopia*, may in this instance come from Baudoin:

> Que si lon m'objecte à ceste raison, qu'il n'est point de seruiteur qui ne doiue aymer ses chaisnes, pourueu qu'elles soient dorées; Ie responds à cela, qu'vn homme libre, qui a les choses necessaires, se fait tort de se rendre esclaue, pour auoir les superflues, & concluds auec Esope; qu'il vaut beaucoup mieux s'en passer, que les achepter à si haut prix.

These sentiments from Baudoin's *Discours* on this fable are congruent with the ideas that Oldham has been outlining in his translation from Horace's *Carm*. I.xxxi.

I believe that one of the reasons why Oldham responded to Baudoin here was that these ideas were also amenable to the Cowleian way in which he was reading the fable. In Chapter 2 I pointed to *The Country Mouse* as a unique poem in which Cowley was celebrating the humble pleasures of the poor with a genial wit that was not repeatable:

> At the large foot of a fair hollow tree,
> Close to plow'd ground, seated commodiously,
> His antient and Hereditary House,
> There dwelt a good substantial Country-Mouse ...
>   (*Essays*, p. 414)

Apart from the occasional detail, what Oldham has chiefly responded to in Cowley's poem is the genial delight in sensuous ease: Cowley's city mouse lives

> Where all the Mice of quality resort;
> Where thousand beauteous shees about you move,
> And by high fare, are plyant made to love.
>   (*Essays*, p. 415)

and Oldham's dog boasts:

> *All the proud shees are soft to my Embrace*
> *From Bitch of Quality down to Turn-spit Race:*
> *Each day I try new Mistresses and Loves.*
> *Nor envy Sovereign Dogs in their Alcoves.*
>   (163-6; *PT* 145)

which has no equivalent in the Latin. But there is a difference of tone between the two — a difference evident again in the use of Cowley's

> And thus at ease on beds of straw they lay,
> And to their Genius sacrific'd the day.

in Oldham's

> *There on fresh Bed of Straw, with Canopy*
> *Of Hutch above, like Dog of State I lie.*
>
> (159-60; *PT* 145)

Oldham is drawing upon a different area of Cowley, his attachment to freedom manifested in the essay *Of Liberty*. But when Oldham evokes life at Court in a series of passing phrases ('*As I'm a Dog of Honour, Sir*', 'Allons, Monsieur', '*nor envy Sovereign Dogs*') and suggests its combination of dissipation and servility, he is performing a firm but economical act of moral definition that neither Cowley nor Boileau really wanted or dared to make. He has achieved an assured moral wit; he has, indeed, found his centre.

EPILOGUE

When Oldham died in December 1683 he was only thirty. Yet this brief career was productive, and not without influence on his contemporaries. His popularity is attested by the many editions of his work printed in the twenty years after his death,[1] and the judgment of his fellow-poets is recorded in the memorial poems that preface his *Remains* of 1684. The contributors were led by Dryden, and comprised Thomas Flatman, Nahum Tate, Thomas Durfey, Thomas Andrews, Thomas Wood and two anonymous writers. In 1685 Tonson published his own memorial poem to Oldham anonymously in *Sylvae*, and this, along with another tribute by Robert Gould, was added to the 1687 edition of the *Remains*. For the most part these pieces are unremarkable, but a few interesting points do emerge. Durfey and Andrews both stress Oldham's learning, the former listing his reading in Homer, Virgil, Lucretius, Ovid, Horace and Juvenal, and referring to his 'rare Garden of Philosophy'. Both these writers point to another quality in Oldham, his spiritual serenity: Andrews speaks of 'so serene a Mind'; Durfey says 'A Calm of Nature still possest his Soul'. I hope that this essay has provided some evidence for thinking that maturity of this kind is something to which he was attaining after the earlier uncertainties. The range of Oldham's talent also attracts comment; Andrews exclaims:

> *Horace* in Sweetness, *Juvenal* in Rage,
> And even *Biblis* must each Heart engage!
> (*R* Sig. A4*v*)[2]

Yet there were doubts about his harshness; from Dryden, of course, and from an anonymous writer:

> His early Wit how vig'rous and how gay
> (The fruits of Autumn with the bloom of May)
> How sharp his Satire soft his amorous Vein
> How strong yett easy is his lofty Strain!

Ah! could returning Time the Means dispence
To smooth his Numbers and refine his Sence
He of each Sex the praise and Love should share
Could he his vain presumptuous Rants forbear
Check his inveterate Spleen and helpless Woman spare.[3]

It is indeed Oldham's rant that is the most noticeable feature of his influence, at least upon the poetasters. His *Satyrs upon the Jesuits* were plundered in 1683 for passages in *Sylla's Ghost: A Satyr against Ambition, and the Last Horrid Plot*:

Go on, *Great Patriots*, with your *worthy Cause*,
Contemn all *Monarchs*, and confront their *Laws*;
Go on, in your *religious Villany*;
And be as fam'd for horrid deeds as I: ...
What glorious and unheard of Deeds I'd do,
Death should be tir'd, and I would still pursue
New horror, till no horror could be new.
No Sex, nor Age should 'scape my Cruelty,
Nor Infants in the Porch of Life be free.

(pp. 4-5)

Ferguson's Remonstrance (1684) combines this mode with that of the *Satyr against Vertue*:

Ten thousand *Curses* on that *Tim'rous* Sot,
    That Bankrupt *Ideot!*
Who had not *Soul* enough, to Act his *part* o' th' *Plot*;
    Had he not been of all that's good Bereft,
    Had he but had one thought of *Glory* left:
His *Coward* heart, cou'd ne're have stoopt so low ...

(p. 2)

Tom Brown borrowed the manner of the same *Satyr* for his poem 'The Extravagant':

Bravely *begun!* Oh had it *mounted* higher
Fed still with vig'rous thought, and *fresh* desire,
    Were I but Jove my *boundless* reign should prove
        But one continued *Scene* of Love:
        In *Extasies* wou'd I *dissolving* lye,
As long as all the *mighty* round of *vast* Eternity.[4]

And even if we turn to a poem that makes use of one of Oldham's more

mature achievements, his translation of Juvenal III, we find that his poise
has been ruined and his purposes perverted:

> Oh *Oldham, Oldham,* wonder of our Age,
> Had Death but spar'd thy true Poetick Rage,
> What biting Satyrs had thy Pen produc'd,
> Which in the *English* Minds might have infus'd
> A just true value for their Native Soil,
> And not to Mud and Slime have ow'd a smile?
> Which warm'd by Favour, instantly there springs
> Insects of various Sorts, with Claws and Wings;
> Who buzzing on all Parts about our Shore,
> As th'Plague of Flies in *Aegypt* heretofore;
> Wriggle in great Mens Ears, and hunt about
> To find a merited Preferment out:
> While needy Worth, and bashful Merit starves;
> And he's alone unhappy that deserves
> A better Usage from the Hand of Fate ...
> Thy Satyr, *Oldham,* would have scar'd 'em more
> Than did our Arms their Fathers heretofore.[5]

We could trace Oldham's influence further in the sub-literature of the
period, but to confirm the positive valuations in the previous chapters
we need to turn to his great successors, Dryden and Pope, to ask what
they appear to have seen in his work.

We are fortunate in having Pope's copy of Oldham,[6] which he bought
for 4s. in 1700, when he was twelve. In a note on the back endpaper
he lists 'The most Remarkable Works of this Author' as the fourth of
the *Satyrs upon the Jesuits,* the *Satyr against Vertue,* the translations
of Horace's *Ars Poetica* and *Serm.* I.ix, and *To the Memory of Mr.
Charles Morwent.* The second of these is perhaps the most surprising
choice, but the pages that cóntain this poem are well-thumbed, and
a number of passages are marked with marginal commas, which was
Pope's method of noting lines that he particularly admired. Although
Pope is recorded by Spence as having thought that 'Oldham is too
rough and coarse ... a very undelicate writer',[7] he made use of two of
Oldham's smoothest poems, *Bion* and *Adonis* in his *Pastorals.*[8] But
Pope also seems to have appreciated Oldham's recurring stress upon freedom.
From the translation of Horace's *Carm.* I.xxxi he echoes Oldham's Ortolans,
Esham, Cotswold, brandies and wines,[9] and he appears to have linked
Oldham's thinking on this point with Dryden's, for his lines:

> Cramm'd to the throat with Ortolans:
> Extremely ready to resign
> All that may make me none of mine.[10]

also echo Dryden's translation from Lucretius III:

> Why dost thou not give thanks as at a plenteous feast
> Cram'd to the throat with life, and rise and take thy rest?
>
> (130-1)

Pope also adapts some of the formulations of Oldham's *Satyr addressed to a Friend*. Oldham's line 'Slaves to an Hour, and Vassals to a Bell' receives a double metamorphosis in Pope:

> Slave to a Wife or Vassal to a Punk

> First slave to Words, then vassal to a Name.[11]

Oldham's couplet:

> Who tho in silken Skarf, and Cassock drest,
> Wears but a gayer Livery at best:

may have shaped Pope's:

> they beg but better drest,
> And all is *splendid Poverty* at best.[12]

But there is another part of Oldham's work that appealed to Pope. In *A Letter from the Country* Oldham described how his mind created poetry; he did so by re-imagining the scenes of chaos in the *Davideis* and *Paradise Lost*. When Pope in the *Dunciad* describes the chaotic creation of bad poetry he draws upon this passage:

> Here she beholds the Chaos dark and deep,
> Where nameless somethings in their causes sleep,
> 'Till genial Jacob, or a warm Third-day
> Call forth each mass, a poem or a play.
> How Hints, like spawn, scarce quick in embryo lie,
> How new-born Nonsense first is taught to cry,
> Maggots half-formed, in rhyme exactly meet,
> And learn to crawl upon poetic feet.   (*Dunciad* A, I.53-60)

Pope is also recalling Cowley,[13] but it is Oldham who made the crucial transposition of the extended image of chaos into the realm of literary creation. Not that Pope thought Oldham's poem suitable only for inverted uses: patches of *An Essay on Criticism* draw upon it too.[14]

But we must conclude with Dryden. It should be no surprise to find the apparent impact of Oldham on Dryden's work rather slight: if Dryden really did believe that 'One common Note on either Lyre did strike' there was no need for him to attempt to repeat Oldham's achievement. Yet it may be that the life and death of Oldham had a profound significance for Dryden; what follows is but a hypothesis.

We do not know what Dryden meant when he wrote of Oldham as 'too little and too lately known': he may have been speaking of their friendship, or he may have known Oldham only through his poetry. That he had recently been reading Oldham's work when writing the memorial poem is evident from his echoes of two passages in Oldham's *David's Lamentation for the Death of Saul and Jonathan*:

> Both excellent they were, both equally alli'd
> On Nature, and on Valour's side ...
> Together they did both the paths to Glory trace,
> Together hunted in the noble Chace,
> Together finish'd their united Race: ...
>
> Oh, dearer than my Soul! if I can call it mine,
> For sure we had the same, 'twas very thine.
> (*PT* 57, 62)

As well as using a poem in which Oldham celebrated a remarkable friendship, Dryden turns to Oldham's tribute to a great transmitter of the classical heritage, for part of his tribute to Oldham is adapted from Oldham's homage to Ben Jonson:

> Rich in thy self, to whose unbounded store
> Exhausted Nature could vouchsafe no more.
> (*PT* 79)

But we should also set Dryden's poem in the context of his other work during 1684, for this was the year in which he composed his contributions to *Sylvae*. Taken together, these pieces reveal Dryden exploring a crisis that was both professional and private.[15]

Sylvae opens with three translations from Virgil, of which the first two rehearse the story of Nisus and Euryalus, to which Dryden refers in the memorial poem. The first is from *Aeneid* V, the race in which Nisus and Euryalus compete; the second is the death of the two friends from Book IX; and the third is the death of Mezentius and Lausus from Book X. There are a number of details that suggest that Oldham's death was in Dryden's mind as he wrote these episodes. In the passage from Book IX Ascanius says to the younger man, Euryalus:

> But thou, whose years are more to mine ally'd,
> No fate my vow'd affection shall divide
> From thee O wondrous Youth: be ever mine,
> Take full possession, all my Soul is thine:
> My lifes Companion, and my bosom Friend;
> One faith, one fame, one fate shall both attend.
> *(Sylvae,* p. 17)

The language here has clear links with the poem on Oldham; it is also more emotive than the Latin warrants:

> te vero, mea quem spatiis propioribus aetas
> insequitur, venerande puer, iam pectore toto
> accipio et comitem casus complector in omnis
> nulla meis sine te quaeretur gloria rebus;
> (IX.275-8)

Nisus later watches the death of Euryalus, is even to some extent responsible; he feels guilty, rushes into the battle and dies too.

In that episode the young man's death is watched and then shared by his older friend. As a companion piece to that story Dryden chose from Book X the death of Lausus, at which his father Mezentius feels guilt and shame, and, joining the fight, dies too. In this there are some interesting words from Aeneas as he stands gazing at the dead Lausus:

> Poor hapless youth, what praises can be paid
> To love so great; to such transcendent store
> Of early worth, and sure presage of more!
> *(Sylvae,* pp. 38-9)

Again there is an echo of Dryden's poem on Oldham; and the last line and a half correspond to nothing in Virgil:

> quid tibi nunc, miserande puer, pro laudibus istis,
> quid pius Aeneas tanta dabit indole dignum?
> (X. 825-6)

Mezentius's emotion at the death of the boy is stronger in Dryden than Virgil:

> Love, anguish, wrath, and grief to madness wrought,
> Despair, and secret shame, and conscious thought
> Of inborn Worth, his lab'ring Soul opprest; (p. 43)

aestuat ingens
uno in corde pudor mixtoque insania luctu.
(x.870-1)

and the striking line 'When Lausus fell, I was already slain' (p. 46) has no equivalent in Virgil; later, Dryden decided that it was out of place.[16]

It seems possible that Dryden was using these two episodes — which are otherwise strange choices — to dramatise his feelings about the death of Oldham and about his own mortality. While the evidence suggests an affection for Oldham the man, it does not, I believe, allow us to speculate about Dryden's personal relations with Oldham. The strength of feeling most probably derives from Dryden undergoing a spiritual and poetic crisis. We may recall that in recent years all the major English poets of Dryden's age had died: Cowley in 1667; Milton in 1674; Marvell in 1678; Butler and Rochester in 1680; Oldham in 1683. Dryden himself was fifty-three in 1684. My suggestion is that the death of Oldham, coming after those translations from Horace and Juvenal, and the *Satyr addressed to a Friend*, poems in which Oldham tried to answer the questions, How should a man live? How can he face his death? How can he enjoy the material blessings of this world without being a slave to Fortune? — that the achievement and death of Oldham was the final stimulus that made Dryden reconsider his past career, and confront his life afresh.

In part, Dryden's debt to Oldham is to the man who first published heroic satire;[17] yet I cannot believe that this was the only debt. For it was Oldham who in that age first made serious use of recreative translation from the classics, and from this very year of 1684 until the end of his life Dryden was to make this his own chief work. Although Dryden had always used the classics, the year 1684 marks a turning-point, for it is in the pieces contributed to *Sylvae* that he first opens himself seriously to their challenge. Dryden says nothing about this explicitly in his memorial poem; perhaps he could not foresee how his own work would change. But the poem's radically classical poise is itself an indication of the way in which Dryden valued Oldham.

We may hazard one further conjecture. In the metaphor of the race there are implications that Oldham has 'run with patience the race that is set before us';[18] that his life had integrity. Did Dryden feel that he himself lacked such integrity? Our own life can often seem messy and poor in comparison with the apparent poise and wholeness of those whom we admire; yet perhaps Dryden did have some reason to feel that in a career devoted so far chiefly to plays and political poems he had come near to prostituting himself. Perhaps Oldham's stress upon independence convicted him of this. Why does Dryden say in the memorial poem that he himself has fallen 'upon the slippery place'? It is an odd detail to have taken over from Virgil unless he was guided by the connotations that 'slippery' had acquired from its use to translate the famous lines in Seneca:

> stet quicumque volet potens
> aulae culmine *lubrico* ...

> Upon the slippery tops of humane State ...
> Let others proudly stand.[19]

Was Dryden meditating on Seneca's grim warning?

> illi mors gravis incubat,
> qui notus nimis omnibus
> ignotus moritur sibi.

> For hym death greep'the right hard by the croppe
> That is moche knowen of other; and of him self alas,
> Doth dye vnknowen, dazed with dreadfull face.
> (Wyatt)

But Dryden was not to perish unknown to himself — without having contemplated poetically those things in life which meant most to him.

For Dryden was to set a new course for both his life and his poetry, not only through his conversion to Rome, but also by wrestling with Oldham's questions in the marvellous translations in *Sylvae*, which display both a resolute acceptance of mortality and a renewed relish for life — his *Lucretius Concerning the Nature of Love* and *Against the Fear of Death*; Horace's *Epode* II, which celebrates the riches of humble poverty; and the fine version of Horace's *Carm.* III.xxix, which he wanted to make his masterpiece:[20]

> Happy the Man, and happy he alone.
> He, who can call to day his own:
> He, who secure within, can say
> To morrow do thy worst, for I have liv'd to day.
> Be fair, or foul, or rain, or shine,
> The joys I have possest, in spight of fate are mine.
> Not Heav'n it self upon the past has pow'r;
> But what has been, has been, and I have had my hour.

And so let the last word on Oldham come from Dryden: for to his poem this book is but a footnote.

To the Memory of Mr. Oldham

Farewel, too little and too lately known,
Whom I began to think and call my own;
For sure our Souls were near ally'd; and thine
Cast in the same Poetick mould with mine.
One common Note on either Lyre did strike,
And Knaves and Fools we both abhorr'd alike:
To the same Goal did both our Studies drive,
The last set out the soonest did arrive.
Thus *Nisus* fell upon the slippery place,
While his young Friend perform'd and won the Race.
O early ripe! to thy abundant store
What could advancing Age have added more?
It might (what Nature never gives the young)
Have taught the numbers of thy native Tongue.
But Satyr needs not those, and Wit will shine
Through the harsh cadence of a rugged line.
A noble Error, and but seldom made,
When Poets are by too much force betray'd.
Thy generous fruits, though gather'd ere their prime ⎫
Still shew'd a quickness; and maturing time   ⎬
But mellows what we write to the dull sweets of Rime. ⎭
Once more, hail and farewel; farewel thou young,
But ah too short, *Marcellus* of our Tongue;
Thy Brows with Ivy, and with Laurels bound;
But Fate and gloomy Night encompass thee around.

CHRONOLOGICAL TABLE

An asterisk indicates unpublished material.

1653   Born 9 August at Shipton Moyne.

1670   Matriculated 17 June at Oxford.

1673   John Freind dies 20 March; Oldham writes memorial verses.*

1674   Returns from Oxford to Shipton Moyne.
(?) *To Madam L.E.*

1675   *To the Memory of Mr. Charles Morwent.*
On the Death of Mrs. Katharine Kingscourt.

1676   Becomes an usher at Whitgift School, Croydon; his acquaintance with Rochester probably follows MS circulation of the *Satyr against Vertue.*
15 May: *A Rant to his Mistress.**
July: *A Satyr against Vertue.*
September: *Presenting a Book to Cosmelia.*
(?) September: *The Parting; Complaining of Absence; Promising a Visit.*
22 December: *Paraphrase upon the 137. Psalm.*

1677   (?) *Upon a Lady.*
(?) February: *To the Memory of Mr. Harman Atwood.*
(?) Spring: *Character of a Certain Ugly Old P——.*
10 March: *The Dream.*
7 May: *In Aloisiae Sigeae Toletanae Satyram Sotadicam.**
5 August: *A Dithyrambick.*
September: *David's Lamentation for the Death of Saul and Jonathan.*
5 November: *Upon the Marriage of the Prince of Orange.*
(?) November: *Upon the Author of a Play called 'Sodom'.*

1678   Transcribes Dryden's *Mac Flecknoe.*
Between 1 January and 24 March: *Upon the Works of Ben. Johnson.*
18 March: John Spencer's verse letter to Oldham.*
Whitsuntide: *Upon a Woman.*
July: *A Letter from the Country.*
October: begins *The Desk.**
November: drafts *The Vision.**
December: begins *Garnet's Ghost.*

1679   January-February: GARNET'S GHOST and then SATYR
AGAINST VERTUE published in pirated editions.
March: leaves Croydon for a tutorship in the house of Sir Edward
Thurland at Reigate.
Spring: *Prologue* to the *Satyrs upon the Jesuits*.
(?) June: *Satyr II*.
After 16 July: *Satyr III: Loyola's Will*.
After 17 November: *Satyr IV: S. Ignatius' Image*.

1680   (?) *Horace His Art of Poetry* (after November 1679, when
Roscommon's version was published).
(?) *A Paraphrase upon Horace. Book I Ode XXXI*.
(?) *A Paraphrase upon Horace. Book II Ode XIV*.
February: *Paraphrase upon the Hymn of S. Ambrose*.
9 March: *The Careless Good Fellow*.
Spring: *The Passion of Byblis* (following OVID'S EPISTLES of
c. February 1680).
26 July: death of Rochester is followed by *Bion*.
c. November: SATYRS UPON THE JESUITS (1681) published.
December: *Upon a Printer*.

1681   2 June: *The Lamentation for Adonis* fair copy; an imitation of
Mimnermus* is on the other side of the sheet.
June: *An Imitation of Horace. Book I. Satyr IX*.
Autumn: SOME NEW PIECES published.
It is probably in this year that Oldham tries a period of indepen-
dence in London; this is followed by a tutorship in the house of
Sir William Hicks.

1682   (?) *A Satyr ... Dissuading from Poetry*.
(?) *A Satyr Touching Nobility* from Boileau's *Satire V*.
(?) *A Satyr addressed to a Friend*.
April: *The Thirteenth Satyr of Juvenal, Imitated*.
May: *A Satyr, In Imitation of the Third of Juvenal*.
c. May: SATYRS UPON THE JESUITS, second edition,
published.
Summer: drafts *Satyr upon the Town and Times*.*
October: *The Eighth Satyr of Monsieur Boileau, Imitated*.

1683   July: POEMS, AND TRANSLATIONS published.
(?) November: *Ode for St Cecilia's Day*.
7 December: Oldham buried at Holme Pierrepoint, having died in
the house of his new patron the Earl of Kingston.

1684   November: REMAINS published.

NOTES

Prologue

1 H.A. Mason, 'Hommage à M. Despréaux', *Cambridge Quarterly*, 3 (1967), 51-71, p. 51.
2 Matthew Arnold, *Lectures and Essays in Criticism*, ed. R.H. Super (Ann Arbor, 1962), p. 260.
3 *Ibid.* p. 262.

1. Origins

1 Sybil Rosenfeld, 'The Family of John Oldham', *NQ*, 164 (1933), 112-13; Harold F. Brooks, 'The Family of John Oldham', *NQ*, 167 (1934), 30-1; C.R. Elrington, 'The Survey of Church Livings in Gloucestershire, 1650', *Transactions of the Bristol and Gloucestershire Archaeological Society*, 83 (1964), 85-98, p. 92. Professor Brooks is preparing a separate biography of Oldham.
2 Anthony à Wood, *Athenae Oxonienses* (4 vols., London, 1813-20), IV, 119-20.
3 The most relevant works are: T.W. Baldwin, *William Shakspere's Small Latine and Lesse Greeke* (2 vols., Urbana, 1944); D.L. Clark, *John Milton at St. Paul's School* (New York, 1948); Foster Watson, *The English Grammar Schools to 1660* (Cambridge, 1908); Foster Watson, *The Beginnings of the Teaching of Modern Subjects in England* (London, 1909).
4 The statutes of Tetbury School prescribed Lily: see A.T. Lee, *The History of the Town and Parish of Tetbury* (London, 1857), p. 180.
5 Charles Hoole, *A New Discovery of the Old Art of Teaching Schoole* (London, 1660), pp. 300-2; cf. Clark, *Milton at St. Paul's*, pp. 110-13.
6 Lee, *History of Tetbury*, p. 180.
7 Sig. A4r. All quotations in this paragraph are my translations from the Latin.
8 *Poems of John Dryden*, p. 758.
9 RMS 255, 264.
10 Watson, *Modern Subjects*, pp. 441-2.
11 Mark H. Curtis, *Oxford and Cambridge in Transition, 1558-1642* (Oxford, 1959), pp. 137-9. On the wrapper of a letter from his

father addressed to him at Oxford, Oldham has written 'Jean de Vieilbourg' (RMS 180). As Professor Brooks suggests to me, this kind of play with a language usually appeals chiefly to a beginner.

12   M.L. Clarke, *Classical Education in Britain 1500-1900* (Cambridge, 1959), pp. 61-2.

13   Curtis warns against placing too much reliance upon the statutes, and his book is a useful demonstration of the extent and variety of extra-statutory learning.

14   Wood, *Athenae Oxonienses*, IV, 120. Wood says that Oldham was 'under the tuition of Will. Stephens bach. of div. where he was observed to be a good Latinist, and chiefly to addict himself to poetry', but (as T.W. Baldwin points out à propos of Massinger (*Shakspere's Small Latine*, I, 31)), this seems to have been Wood's standard formula for a poet's education. Stephens became prominent in the 1690s with a number of sermons, and a book, *The Growth of Deism*. Though these, and the replies that they evoked, are interesting in their own right, there is nothing in them that allows us to make inferences about the Stephens of the 1670s.

15   *VCH Oxfordshire*, III, 328-9.

16   Bodley MS Top. Oxon.f.31, pp. 157, 162, 174, 245, 165, 88, 83, 174-5. Some of the quotations are from Nathaniel's translation.

17   *Ibid*. pp. 56, 23-4, 45.

18   *Ibid*. p. 21; my translation from the Latin.

19   Trinity College Cambridge MS O.10a.33.

20   Bodley MS Top. Oxon.f.31, pp. 37-8.

21   *The Flemings in Oxford*, ed. J.R. Magrath (3 vols., Oxford, 1904-24), I, 262, 289-90, 304, 320; for his brother George at St Edmund Hall in 1689 see II, 251-2.

22   Trinity College Cambridge MS O.10a.33, p. 9.

23   *PT* 36.

24   *The Flemings in Oxford*, II, 212.

25   Oldham's copy now Cambridge University Library Cam.d.673.4.

26   Sig. A3r-v.

27   This paragraph is based upon William T. Costello, *The Scholastic Curriculum at early Seventeenth-Century Cambridge* (Cambridge, Mass., 1958), pp. 61-2.

28   'Vitanda est improba Siren desidia'; 'Quj ante non cavit post dolebit'; there is also a 'Descriptio Autumni': Bodley MS Top. Oxon.f.31, pp. 305f.

29   *Ibid*. p. 51. George Stanhope while at Cambridge wrote verses to members of his family (see Cambridge University Library MS Add 6339). Some of Oldham's earliest poems are addressed to Gloucestershire neighbours.

30   'Quaeritus An benefecit Nero quj inter Romae incendis Citheram pulsavit': Bodley MS Top. Oxon. f.31, p. 315.

31   Lewis and Short report that *Risus* (as a personification) and *dissitus* occur only in Appuleius.

32   Cf. Erasmus, *Modus Conscribendi Epistolas*, quoted by Baldwin,

Shakspere's Small Latine, II, 244; and see Clark, *Milton at St. Paul's*, pp. 186-98.

33 John Potenger, *Private Memoirs* (London, 1841), p. 4.
34 Duport (see n. 19), *passim*; Potenger, *Private Memoirs*, p. 2.
35 *The Flemings in Oxford*, II, 161.
36 *Adagiorum D. Erasmi Roterodami Epitome* (Oxford, 1666), pp. 106, 125.
37 *Ibid*. p. 2. *'Stem and Stern*: we use the phrase, "stem and stern" to indicate the whole of our design. For example, Godliness should be the stem and stern of our studies. There are some for whom money is the stem and stern of their thinking. It is similar to the image in Revelation: I am the Alpha and Omega, the sum of all things.'
38 *Ibid*. p. 42.
39 *Ibid*. pp. 330-1. *'Sardanapalus*: This name has become proverbial on account of the man's notorious effeminacy. For Sardanapalus was so unmanly in his pleasures that he used to put on woman's clothing and keep company with eunuchs and girls.'
40 Cf. White Kennett: 'Instances of y[e] unbecoming recreations of princes are Sardanapalus a spinning ...' (BL MS Lansdowne 937, fol. 26r).
41 *Adagiorum Epitome*, p. 334. *'A Dog has many kennels*: This is properly applied to men who are over-fond of women, particularly to those who, not content with the marriage-bed, take their pleasure promiscuously in one house after another.'
42 *Ibid*. p. 208. *'There is no greater plague than a woman*. Homer passes on this saying: There is nothing so vile, nothing worse than a woman.'
43 *Adagiorum Chiliades Des. Erasmi Roterodami* (Basle, 1559), p. 833: 'Bad things are frequently said about women in the ancient poets. And indeed, poets in our own day take great pains to ensure that their predecessors don't appear to have been talking nonsense.' Cf. *Mulieri ne Credas* (*Adagiorum Epitome*, pp. 208-9, and *Adagiorum Chiliades*, p. 611).
44 *The Flemings in Oxford*, I, 262; I, 290; II, 257.
45 Henry Fleming had bought a copy by 1680 (*ibid*. I, 323). Holdsworth recommended Godwyn at Cambridge (Curtis, *Oxford and Cambridge in Transition*, p. 113).
46 Harold F. Brooks, 'A Bibliography of John Oldham the Restoration Satirist', *Oxford Bibliographical Society Proceedings & Papers*, 5 (1936-9) (Oxford, 1940), p. 10.
47 Potenger, *Private Memoirs*, p. 25n.
48 One such is Victoria and Albert Museum MS Dyce 43, pp. 333f.
49 *The Diary of Samuel Pepys*, ed. Robert Latham and William Matthews (11 vols., London, 1970-   ), I, 28; V, 198; IV, 202; III, 107; IV, 190; I, 243 and note. Ovid would probably have been in Sandys's translation, a copy of which is in the Pepys library.
50 Other volumes in the Pepys library that confirm this interest in

the classics as mediated by the French are *L' Ovide Bouffon, ou Cabinet Satyrique* (2 vols., 1666) and Boileau's *Oeuvres Diverses* (1675).

51   *Letters of Sir George Etherege*, ed. Frederick Bracher (Berkeley, 1974), pp. 286-7.
52   See John C. Hodges, *The Library of William Congreve* (New York, 1955).
53   *Sale Catalogues of Libraries of Eminent Persons*, ed. A.N.L. Munby (12 vols., London, 1971-5), I, 9-38; IV, 1-43.
54   See J. McG. Bottkol, 'Dryden's Latin Scholarship', *MP*, 40 (1943), 241-54; T.A. Birrell, 'John Dryden's Purchases at Two Book Auctions', *English Studies*, 42 (1961), 193-217.
55   Michael Hunter, *John Aubrey and the Realm of Learning* (London, 1975), p. 40.
56   Potenger says: 'My tutor ... was so pleased with several of my performances in latin, and english verse, that he gave me several books for encouragement' (*Private Memoirs*, p. 29). The translation of Horace's *Carm.* II.xiv in *Sylvae* was later attributed to him (*ibid.* p. 73).
57   Curtis, *Oxford and Cambridge in Transition*, pp. 132-3.
58   Cambridge University Library MS Add. 6339. Stanhope was at King's from 1677 to 1688; Duke was a BA at Trinity when he wrote his poem on Oates, which was published as a broadside in 1679.
59   Bodley MS Don. f.29.
60   Potenger, *Private Memoirs*, pp. 30-2.
61   BL MS Lansdowne 937, fols. 8*v*, 14*r-v*.
62   *Ibid.* fols. 23*r*-24*v*.
63   From the library's borrowing book, BL MS Lansdowne 697, fols. 9*r*-10*v*. The contents of the library at this date may be ascertained by studying the arrangement of books (which is roughly chronological by accession) and the register of donations (Bodley MS Rawlinson D 398 fols. 44*r* f.).
64   *The Flemings in Oxford*, II, 84.
65   T.H. Mayo, *Epicurus in England* (Dallas, 1934), p. 1.
66   See D.G. Vaisey, 'Anthony Stephens: the rise and fall of an Oxford bookseller', *Studies in the Book Trade in Honour of Graham Pollard*, Oxford Bibliographical Society Publications, n.s. 18 (Oxford, 1975), pp. 91-117. Stephens was the Oxford agent for Oldham's works: he advertised *PT* in his catalogue at the back of *Witt against Wisdom*, which was published by October 1683, and in his shop he had '9 Oldham's poems' bound and '18 Oldham's in 3 pts' amongst the unbound sheets.
67   Thomas Creech, *Titus Lucretius Carus His Six Books of Epicurean Philosophy Done into English Verse ...* , 3rd ed. (London, 1683), Sig. B*r*.
68   BL MS Lansdowne 937, fols. 38*v*-44*r*.
69   *Witt against Wisdom*, Sig. c4*v*.
70   *CSPD 1671-2*, pp. 63-4, 72, 146. Actually, Rapin's treatises were

originally published anonymously in France, so readers such
as Oldham and Dryden who praise him as an eminent modern
critic were well informed.

71 *The Works of Mr. John Oldham, together with his Remains* (2
vols., London, 1722), p. xv.

72 This was not the family's first venture into literary patronage.
Besides five STC books dedicated to earlier Pierrepoints, Robert
Stapylton's translation of Juvenal was dedicated to Henry, the
second earl, as was Thomas Shipman's play *Henry the Third of
France, Stabb'd by a Fryer* (1678), which at the last minute was
provided with an additional topical dedication to Monmouth
(November 1678). On the other hand, there is also a Tory
pamphlet dedicated to the Earl of Kingston (whether the third
earl or the fourth is unclear): *Amoret, or, Policy Defeated*
(London, 1682). The literary and scientific interests of the
second earl (d. 1680) are celebrated by John Crouch in his *Elegy
upon the Marquess of Dorchester* (London, [1680]). They apparently included law, optics, mathematics, astronomy and
medicine. For the literary tastes of some of the family see P.F.
Hammond, 'A Commonplace Book owned by John Oldham',
NQ, 224 (1979), 515-18.

2. Indirections

1 Giles Jacob, quoted in *Rochester: The Critical Heritage*, ed.
David Farley-Hills (London, 1972), p. 190.

2 Abraham Cowley, *Poems*, ed. A.R. Waller (Cambridge, 1905),
p. 7.

3 Though Oldham uses *Ionsonus Virbius* in composing his own
poem on Jonson.

4 *Works of John Dryden*, XVII, 73.

5 The end of Satan's speech also finds its way into *The Desk*;
with Cowley's:

> Did I lose Heav'en for this?
> With that, with his long tail he lasht his breast,
> And horribly spoke out in *Looks* the rest.
> *(Poems*, p. 245)

compare Oldham:

> Did I ere think? — & more he would exprest,
> But left his looks & sighs to say ye rest.
> (RMS 131)

6 H.A. Mason, 'Hommage à M. Despréaux', *Cambridge Quarterly*,
3 (1967), 51.

7 See Maren-Sofie Røstvig, *The Happy Man: studies in the metamorphoses of a classical ideal*, 2nd ed., vol. 1 (Oslo, 1962).

8 Abraham Cowley, *Essays, Plays and Sundry Verses*, ed. A.R.
Waller (Cambridge, 1906), p. 388.

9   Harold F. Brooks, 'The Poems of John Oldham' in *Restoration Literature: Critical Approaches*, ed. Harold Love (London, 1972), p. 178.

10   See David M. Vieth, 'John Oldham, the Wits, and *A Satyr against Vertue*', *PQ*, 32 (1953), 90-3. Professor Brooks believes, however, that the meeting is more likely to have taken place at Beddington, the house of Sir Nicholas Carew. In RMS there are copies in Oldham's hand of the *Satire against Reason and Mankind* and *Artemisa to Chloe*.

11   Pope's copy is BL C.45.a.1. The passages that he admired are, as usual, marked with marginal commas. He did not mark the two lines beginning at 'Thus the lewd Gods'. It is possible that the opening lines of this quotation lodged in Pope's memory to shape a couplet in *An Essay on Criticism*: 'A Perfect Judge will read each work of Wit / With the same spirit that its author writ' (233-4).

12   Cf. Cowley's *The Prophet*:

> 'Tis I who *Love's Columbus* am; 'tis I,
> Who must new *Worlds* in it descry:
> Rich *Worlds*, that yield of *Treasure* more,
> Than all that has bin known before.
> *(Poems*, p. 102)

13   Cowley, *Poems*, p. 11.

14   Earl Miner, *The Restoration Mode from Milton to Dryden* (Princeton, 1974), pp. 423-4.

15   It is not uncommon for a spurious moral purpose to be used as a cover for pornography; see Roger Thompson, *Unfit for Modest Ears* (London, 1979), p. 65 etc.

16   See H.K. Miller, 'The Paradoxical Encomium, with special reference to its vogue in England, 1600-1800', *MP*, 53 (1956), 145-78.

17   This line may be an allusion to Rochester's 'I have blasphemed my God, and libelled Kings' in *To the Postboy*.

18   *Poems on Several Occasions*, by the Right Honourable, the E. of R— ('Antwerp', [1680]), pp. 129-31. Drafts for this poem survive in RMS.

19   I quote from BL MS Harley 7319, fols. 128*r*-132*v*. Some manuscripts date this poem 1683, which is improbably late, both because of the development of Oldham's work, and because of Soames's epigram (*ibid*. fol. 133*r*), which would be redundant if written after *SNP* appeared in 1681.

20   As has also been argued by John H. O'Neill, 'Oldham's "Sardanapalus": A Restoration Mock-Encomium and its Topical Implications', *Clio*, 5 (1976), 193-210, though O'Neill overestimates the degree to which Charles II is a subject of the poem.

21   Gilbert Burnet, *History of my own Time*, Part I: 'the reign of Charles II', ed. Osmund Airy (2 vols., Oxford, 1897), I, 448. The clause about Sardanapalus is crossed out in the manuscript. O'Neill

cites allusions to Sardanapalus in several contemporary satires.

22 A partial translation of Chorier's work, dated 1676, survives in a commonplace book that also contains two versions of *Sodom* and a text of *Sardanapalus*. See A.S.G. Edwards, 'Libertine Literature in Restoration England: Princeton MS AM 14401', *Book Collector*, 25 (1976), 354-68; also David Foxon, 'Libertine Literature in England, 1660-1745', *Book Collector*, 12 (1963), 21-36, 159-77, 294-307, and Thompson, *Unfit for Modest Ears*, pp. 28-33.

23 As far as Sandys is concerned, this is rather disingenuous, for a comparison of the two translations makes it clear that Oldham used Sandys. There were three editions of his *Metamorphoses*: the first in 1626, the second in 1632 with a commentary and some revisions to the text, and the third in 1638 with the 1632 text but no commentary. Oldham used the 1632 text, but not the commentary (which is fairly brief in the case of *Byblis*). Quotations are from *Ovid's Metamorphosis Englished* ... By G.S. (Oxford, 1632).

24 *The Passion of Byblis*, Made English ... By Mr Dennis (London, 1692), Sig. A2*r*.

25 Cf. Rochester, *A Satire against Reason and Mankind*, esp. 34-5.

26 A.S.F. Gow's *The Greek Bucolic Poets* (Cambridge, 1953) is a useful introduction to this material. English interest during the seventeenth century is exemplified by David Whitford's Latin translation of 1659 and Thomas Stanley's English translation of 1651. Because of the freedom with which Oldham translates, it is hard to determine which texts he was using. A few resemblances to the versions by Stanley and Ronsard are inconclusive. In *SNP* (Sig. A3*r*) Oldham mentions that he has used the Latin version of the *Epitaphios Adonidos* by Tanaquil Faber, as comparison of the two confirms.

27 See Wilfred P. Mustard, 'Later Echoes of the Greek Bucolic Poets', *American Journal of Philology*, 30 (1909), 245-83, and J.H. Hanford, 'The Pastoral Elegy and Milton's *Lycidas*', *PMLA*, 25 (1910), 403-47.

28 An abridged translation was appended by Creech to his translation of Theocritus in 1684.

29 My translation from *Renati Rapini Societatis Iesu Eclogae Cum Dissertatione De Carmine Pastorali* (Paris, 1659), Sig. i.iij*v* and p. 171; cf. also pp. 83-4.

30 Ezra Pound, *ABC of Reading* (London, 1961), p. 151.

31 P.F. Hammond, 'A Commonplace Book owned by John Oldham', *NQ*, 224 (1979), 515-18.

32 It is possible that Oldham's line 'They cull out thee, and let dull *Maevius* go' is a covert reference to Shadwell, since 'dull' is the epithet that *Mac Flecknoe* had branded him with, and in 1682 Richard Duke — an associate of Dryden — joked:

> Had Providence e'er meant that, in despight
> Of Art and Nature, such dull Clods should write,

> *Bavius* and *Maevius* had been sav'd by Fate
> For *Seitle* and for *Shadwell* to Translate.
> (*Poems by the Earl of Roscommon* (London, 1717), p. 401.)

33   Rapin, *Eclogae*, Sig. i.iijr-iiijr.

3. 1678

1   'I have completed a monument more durable than bronze, and higher than the regal structure of the pyramids; which neither devouring rain nor violent north wind can destroy, nor the innumerable succession of years, nor the passage of time.'

2   'Others will mould the breathing bronze more delicately (I for my part believe it) and will bring living features out of marble.'

3   Pope, *An Essay on Criticism* 135; Chapman's preface to his translation of Homer (*Critical Essays of the Seventeenth Century*, ed. J.E. Spingarn (3 vols., Oxford 1908-9), I, 67). For the growth in Homer's reputation (which is more notable after Oldham's day) see Kirsti Simonsuuri, *Homer's Original Genius* (Cambridge, 1979).

4   For the image, cf. Pope again: 'And but from *Nature's Fountains* scorn'd to draw' (133). In attributing to Virgil a 'boundless Mind' (130) and saying that Homer could not be 'confin'd' to rules (addition after 123) Pope is using an Oldhamesque language. We may also note in passing how unlike Oldham's formulation is Pope's more dogmatic summary: 'Learn hence for Ancient *Rules* a just Esteem; / To Copy *Nature* is to copy *them*' (139-40).

5   Waller, *Works* (London, 1730), p. 147.

6   Brooks, p. xxx n.

7   *Ibid.* p. xli, from Bodley MS Ballard XX.23.

8   See Thomas Alcock and John Wilmot, Earl of Rochester, *The Famous Pathologist*, ed. Vivian de Sola Pinto, Nottingham University Miscellany, 1 (Nottingham, 1961). Pinto dates the episode 1675-6.

9   Again Oldham is helping himself to Cowley: 'Wit that greatest *word* of Fame / Grows such a common *Name*' (*Poems*, ed. A.R. Waller (Cambridge, 1905), p. 17).

10   'Omne tulit punctum qui miscuit utile dulci', *Ars Poetica* 343.

11   Cowley, *Upon ... Verses of my Lord Broghills* (*Poems*, p. 408); Dryden, *To the Lady Castlemain* (*Poems*, p. 156); these borrowings are noted by Brooks.

12   James Howell, *Familiar Letters*, ed. Joseph Jacobs (2 vols., London, 1890-2), p. 73.

13   *The Flemings in Oxford*, ed. J.R. Magrath (3 vols., Oxford, 1904-24), I, 18.

14   Dryden, *The Speech of Venus to Vulcan*, *Sylvae* (London, 1685), p. 50; cf. 'Till all infus'd in joy he lay possest', p. 51.

15   This phrase is similar to the language habitually used of the achievement of Denham and Waller in refining the couplet, and

reminds us of Oldham's concern for smoothness when appropriate. Ovid stresses the cold of his exile and writes of the snow melting in *Tristia* III. 12.

16   'Indeed I wish that it had pleased the gods to give us an easier way of conveying our meaning than by words; a simpler way of conducting correspondence than by using letters. It grieves me much that my mind can often reach a friend no matter how far away he may be, yet cannot make itself understood without writing. But that is granted only to the angels: we, to whom such happiness is not permitted, have only this way of expressing ourselves.'

17   An image that Oldham may have taken over from Denham:

> Nor then destroys it with too fond a stay,
> Like Mothers which their Infants overlay.
> > (*Cooper's Hill*)

or from Waller:

> As careless dames, whom wine and sleep betray
> To frantic dreams, their infants overlay.
> > (*Battel of the Summer Islands*)

18   *Works of John Dryden*, VIII, 96-7.

19   'Your care is for which institutions suit the state, and you are anxious for the city.'

20   Cf. *PL* II.227.

21   *The Whole Critical Works of Monsieur Rapin*, 2nd ed. (2 vols., London, 1716), II, 132.

22   Brooks identifies the sources.

23   Samuel Butler, 'Satirical Epistle to a Bad Poet' 55-8; in his *Genuine Remains in Verse and Prose* (2 vols., London, 1759). The date of the poem's composition is uncertain.

24   See M.H. Abrams, *The Mirror and the Lamp* (New York, 1953), *passim*.

25   E.g. Thomas Randolph, *A Gratulatory to Mr Ben. Johnson* and John Dryden, *To his friend the Author on his Divine Epigrams*.

26   L.L. Whyte, *The Unconscious before Freud* (London, 1962), pp. 77-105.

27   *Art Poétique* II.192-3; p. 156.

28   E.g. Spenser, *Shepheardes Calendar*, October 107-8; Hall, *Virgidemiae* I.iii.7-8.

29   I had thought that Oldham was here echoing Theseus's speech in *A Midsommer Nights Dreame*, but Professor Brooks persuades me that — quite remarkably — Oldham shows no indubitably first-hand knowledge of Shakespeare.

30   For 'Recruits' cf. 'Till with recruited rage new Spirits boil' (Dryden, *Lucretius... Concerning the Nature of Love* 86). The last two lines of the quotation are compared by Brooks to lines 3-4 of Dryden's *Prologue to the Wild-Gallant Reviv'd*:

> As some raw Squire, by tender Mother bred,
> Till one and Twenty keeps his Maidenhead,
> (Pleas'd with some Sport which he alone does find,
> And thinks a secret to all Humane kind;)

It was presumably the sexual allusion that led Oldham to recall these lines, even though he altered their reference.

31   This was a frequent tag in the seventeenth century, and is also one of the epithets for chaos listed by Joshua Poole in *The English Parnassus* (London, 1657), pp. 70 and 277.

32   *Mysogynus, or, a satyr upon women* (London, 1682), p. 5.

33   *Works of John Dryden*, VIII, 95. The borrowing was spotted by J. Cornish, *NQ*, 4 (1851), 36.

34   Besides L.L. Whyte, see J.L. Lowes, *The Road to Xanadu* (London, 1927), pp. 58-9.

35   Cowley, *Poems*, p. 253; noted by Brooks.

36   John Spencer writes of his mind as 'a dark abyss' in his verse letter (RMS 198).

37   Milton, *PL* II. 898-902; VII. 292-7; cf. II. 887 for 'rankt in loose array'. Cowley, *Poems*, p. 253.

38   Donne, *Satyre* IIII. 163.

39   'Fortune rejoices in her grim business, and determinedly plays her callous game, changing her fickle favours — kind now to me, now to another. I praise her when she is with me: but if she shakes her restless wings I yield up what she has given: I wrap myself in my own virtue, and seek honest poverty without any dowry. It is not my way, if the mast is groaning in African storms, to hurry wretchedly to prayers, and to bargain with vows, to stop my merchandise from Cyprus and Tyre from adding riches to the greedy sea. Then the breeze, and the heavenly twins, Castor and Pollux, will keep me safe in the security of my rowing-boat through the tumults of the Aegean.'

40   As Mr J.R. Mason pointed out to me.

41   *Poems of John Dryden*, p. 48.

42   Tacitus, *Annales* I.8.

43   'Mollesse' is untranslatable, but something like Milton's 'ignoble ease, and peaceful sloath, / Not peace' raised to the status of a goddess. She is a forerunner of Dullness in *The Dunciad*, the conclusion of which is evidently a development from Boileau.

44   H.A. Mason, 'Boileau's *Lutrin*', *Cambridge Quarterly*, 4 (1969), 362-80, pp. 376-9.

45   RMS 66-80; 124-36; 66. Only Chants I-IV were available to Oldham; V-VI were printed in 1683.

46   Boileau, *Le Lutrin*, made English by N.O. (London, 1682). I have been unable to identify N.O. Geoffrey Tillotson, in his Twickenham edition of *The Rape of the Lock* calls him Nicholas Okes (p. 112) but gives no evidence.

47   He may have caught this word from Cotton's *Scarronides: or,*
       Virgile Travestie (London, 1670):

> An heifer young when she doth itch,
> With *Gad-breeze* sticking in her breech,
> From shady Brake on sudden rise,
> And with her Tail erect to th' skies . . .
>   (p. 73)

       'Breeze' is not a translation of 'guêpe' offered by the dictionaries
       available to Oldham. In the margin of his draft of this simile is
       the phrase 'with Tail exalted'. This corresponds to nothing in
       Boileau, but is close to Cotton's 'her Tail erect'. Perhaps Oldham
       read through *Scarronides* and noted this parallel simile.
48   Brooks, 'The Poems of John Oldham', p. 192.
49   Scarron, *Le Virgile Travesty en Vers Burlesques* (Paris, 1655),
       p. 17; Cotton, *Scarronides*, pp. 15, 43.
50   Cf. *Scarronides*, p. 73: 'And in her am'rous Moods and Tenses'.
51   First draft, RMS 268; second 266-7; third 66; fair copy 270-3.
52   See Benjamin Boyce, 'News from Hell', *PMLA*, 58 (1943), 402-
       37.
53   As Brooks notes.
54   Though Donne does mention 'Garnets Manes'.
55   Cowley, *Poems*, p. 247; *PL* II. 1; RMS 266, which actually reads
       'on state' and 'Monarch state'. There may also be some influence
       from *Mac Flecknoe*, for line 107, which reads 'High on a
       Throne . . .' probably read 'High on a state' in the MS that
       Oldham read and copied into RMS (from which this portion of
       the poem is now missing).
56   John Kenyon, *The Popish Plot* (Harmondsworth, 1974), p. 97.
57   RMS 260, 247.
58   Professor Brooks has identified these sources.
59   Weldon M. Williams, 'The Influence of Ben Jonson's *Catiline*
       upon John Oldham's *Satyrs upon the Jesuits*', *ELH*, 11 (1944),
       38-62; p. 48.
60   Besides John Kenyon, see John Bossy, *The English Catholic*
       Community 1570-1850 (London, 1975) and John Miller,
       Popery and Politics in England 1660-1688 (Cambridge, 1973),
       who on pp. 67-90 gives a survey of anti-Catholic propaganda.
61   *A True and Perfect Narrative of the late terrible and bloody*
       Murther of Sr Edmondberry Godfrey (1678).
62   *An Elegy on the Death of the Plot* (London, 1681). Cf. Oldham's
       The Careless Good Fellow.
63   On Godfrey's death: *The Proclamation Promoted* (1678); Oates's
       homosexuality: *Cupid turn'd Musqueteer* (n.d.); Presbyterians
       attacked: *The Humble Petitions of his Majesty's Truly Loyal*
       Protestant Subjects (n.d.) and *The True Presbyterian without*
       Disguise (London, 1680); crabbed and obscure: *The Loyal*
       Citizen (1682) and *The Old Cause's Epitaph by Anticipation*
       (London, 1683).

64   *The Penguin Book of Restoration Verse*, ed. Harold Love (Harmondsworth, 1968), p. 124.
65   See James L. Thorson, 'A Broadside by Samuel Butler (1612-1680)', *Bodleian Library Record*, 9 (1974), 178-86.
66   *An Answer to the Pamphlet called, The Loyal Feast* (London, 1682).

4. Horace

1   I have used the following editions and translations of Horace:

(*a*) *Editions*
BOND: *Quinti Horatii Flacci Poemata* ... commentarii ... a Ioanne Bond (Amsterdam, 1676).
DACIER: *Les Oeuvres d'Horace*, traduites en Francois, avec des notes et des remarques critiques sur tout l'ouvrage. Par M. Dacier (10 vols., Paris, 1681-9).
HEINSIUS: *Quintus Horatius Flaccus.* Accedunt Danielis Heinsii De Satyra Horatiana Libri duo (Leiden, 1629).
LUBINUS: *Quintus Horatius Flaccus* accuratissime emendatus, & explicatus paraphrasti nova scholastica Eilhardi Lubini (Frankfurt, 1612).
MARES: *Quintus Horatius Flaccus* ad usum et ad castos mores studiosae juventutis, accommodatus cum notis & commentarijs brevibus Rdi P. Iudoci de Mares (Cologne, 1664).
MAROLLES: *Les Oeuvres d'Horace Latin et Francois* ... de la version de M. de Marolles (2 vols., Paris, 1652).
MARTIGNAC: *Horace* de la traduction de Mr de Martignac, [3rd ed.] (Paris, 1696).
MINELLIUS-RAPPOLTUS: *Quintus Horatius Flaccus* cum notis marginalibus Johannis Min-elli et D. Friderici Rappolti (Paris, 1675).
SCHREVELIUS: *Q. Horatius Flaccus* cum commentariis selectissimis variorum ... accurante Corn. Schrevelius (Leiden, 1663).
VAENIUS[1]:   *Quinti Horatii Flacci Emblemata* ... Studio Othonis Vaeni (Antwerp, 1612).
VAENIUS[2]:   *Le Théatre Moral de la Vie Humaine* ... par le Sieur Otho Vaenius (Brussels, 1678).

(*b*) *Scholia*
Scholia Horatiana ... edidit Franciscus Pauly (2 vols., Prague, 1858-9).

(*c*) *Translations*
ASHMORE: John Ashmore, *Certain Selected Odes of Horace Englished* (London, 1621).
BROME[1]:   *The Poems of Horace*, Consisting of Odes, Satyres, and Epistles, rendered in English Verse by Several Persons (London, 1666).
BROME[2]:   *The Poems of Horace* ... 2nd ed. (London, 1671).

BROME[3]: *The Poems of Horace* ... 3rd ed. (London, 1680).
CREECH: *The Odes, Satyrs and Epistles of Horace.* Done into English (London, 1684).
DRANT[1]: *A Medicinable Morall,* that is, the two Bookes of Horace his Satyres, Englyshed ... [by] T. Drant (London, 1566).
DRANT[2]: *Horace His arte of Poetrie, pistles, and Satyrs Englished,* ... By Tho. Drant (London, 1567).
FANSHAWE: *Selected Parts of Horace, Prince of Lyricks,* ... Now newly put into English (London, 1652).
HARRINGTON: *The Odes and Epodes of Horace,* translated into English by J.H. (London, 1684).
HAWKINS: *Odes of Horace, The Best of Lyrick Poets.* Containing much moralitie and sweetnesse. The third edition ... By Sr T.H. (London, 1635).
HOLYDAY: *Horace. The Best of Lyrick Poets* ... Translated into English by Barten Holyday (London, 1652).
RIDER: *All the Odes and Epodes of Horace.* Translated into English Verse: By Henry Rider (London, 1638).
ROSCOMMON: *Horace's Art of Poetry.* Made English by the ... Earl of Roscommon (London, 1680).
SMITH: *The Lyrick Poet,* Odes and Satyres Translated out of Horace into English Verse, by J.S. (1649).
The Odes and Satires of Horace, That have been done into English by the most eminent hands (London, 1715).

2   René Bray, *La Formation de la Doctrine Classique en France* (Lausanne, 1931), p. 112. Here and in Chapter 6 I do not rework ground covered by Bray and two other studies: Jules Brody, *Boileau and Longinus* (Geneva, 1958) and A.F.B. Clark, *Boileau and the French Classical Critics in England 1660-1830* (Paris, 1925). Clark attributes rather too much to Boileau and too little to the native traditions.

3   John Dryden, *The State of Innocence, and the Fall of Man* (London, 1677), Sig. b2*v*.

4   *SNP* Sig. a3*v*. English interest in Rapin was considerable. In 1672 his *Réflexions sur l'Usage de l'Eloquence de ce Temps* was published in France, and immediately translated into English and published by Fell's press at Oxford, while Oldham was an undergraduate. In the same year Fell issued Rapin's *Comparison between the Eloquence of Demosthenes and Cicero* (first published in France in 1670), while in London Jonathan Edwin brought out the *Judgment on Alexander and Caesar* and *Observations on the Poems of Homer and Virgil.* In 1673 Edwin published the *Comparison of Plato and Aristotle* (published in France in 1671), and there was a translation of *Hortorum Libri IV* (1665). In 1674 Rapin published his *Réflexions sur la Poétique d'Aristote,* which was rapidly translated by Rymer and published by Edwin.

5   *Oeuvres Diverses du R.P. R. Rapin, Concernant Les Belles Lettres* (2 vols., Amsterdam, 1693), II, 26-7.

6   *Ibid.* II, 139.
7   *Ibid.* II, 129.
8   Dominique Bouhours, *Les Entretiens d'Ariste et d'Eugene* (Paris, 1962), pp. 125-6.
9   BL MS Harley 7319 fol. 133*r*.
10   *Poems of Horace* (1666), Sig. A5*v*.
11   *Traité du Sublime*, p. 15.
12   Professor Brooks reminds me that 'sublime' is translated by 'lofty' throughout Pulteney's rendering of the *Traité* (*A Treatise of the Loftiness or Elegancy of Speech*. Written Originally in Greek by Longin; And now Translated out of French by Mr. J.P. (London, 1680)).
13   Robert Gould, *Poems chiefly consisting of Satyrs and Satyrical Epistles* (London, 1689), p. 176.
14   *Poems of John Dryden*, p. 608.
15   The major borrowings have been listed by Brooks, and by Bernfried Nugel, *A New English Horace* (Frankfurt, 1971).
16   *Rhetoric* II.xii.6.
17   Though Dryden seems to have recalled Roscommon's phrase in his translation of the parallel passage in Juvenal X (line 306 in Dryden).
18   *Rhetoric* II.xiii.3.
19   In Minellius-Rappoltus and Schrevelius.
20   Minellius-Rappoltus and Schrevelius have the gloss 'morosus', which may derive from Horace's own 'difficilem et morosum' (*Serm.* II.v.90).
21   *Works of John Dryden*, XVII, 74-5.
22   *Oeuvres Diverses*, II, 188.
23   *Works of John Dryden*, XVII, 40.
24   [John Sheffield], *An Essay upon Poetry* (London, 1682), pp. 9-10.
25   Quoted in *Rochester: The Critical Heritage*, ed. David Farley-Hills (London, 1972), p. 146.
26   *Ibid.* p. 147.
27   *SJ* Sig. A2*r*. See Isaac Casaubon, *De Satyrica Graecorum Poesi & Romanorum Satira Libri Duo* (Paris, 1605).
28   Sheffield, *Essay upon Poetry*, p. 14. When Pope rewrites the same lines of Horace (268-9) in his *Essay on Criticism* (124-5) he changes the reference back to Homer.
29   *Works of John Dryden*, XVII, 72-3.
30   *Ibid.* 12-13.
31   Some lines here have been influenced by Boileau, *Art Poétique*, I.189-96; p. 145.
32   *The Poems of Horace* (1666), p. 230.
33   Pace Harold F. Brooks, 'The "Imitation" in English Poetry, especially in formal satire, before the Age of Pope', *RES*, 25 (1949), 124-40. I have not discussed the theories of translation prevalent at this period, because they have received a lot of attention in recent years, and a detailed examination of the

practice of translation often shows the writers deviating from their declared principles and mixing in one version supposedly rival methods.

34 Eduard Fraenkel, *Horace* (Oxford, 1957), p. 113.
35 *Ibid.* p. 114.
36 *Ibid.* p. 117.
37 *A True Account of the Royal Bagnio* ... by a Person of Quality (London, 1680).
38 '*A capite usque ad calcem*: Quum rem totam significamus, A capite usque ad calcem, dicimus. Cujus adagii triplex potest esse usus. Aut enim ad corpus referetur, aut ad animum, aut ad rem ... Horat. Talos a vertice pulcher ad imos' (*Adagiorum D. Erasmi Roterodami Epitome* (Oxford, 1666), p. 2). ('*From top to toe*: When we wish to designate the whole of something we say, "from top to toe". This adage can be used in three ways: of the body, the mind, or objects: e.g. Horace: "Handsome from top to toe" (*Epist.* II.ii.4).')
39 'Because of your anger, impatient of this sort of gauche garrulity, you immediately rebuke this talkative man and send him away.'
40 'It is good, Bollanus, that you are irascible and angry, and tolerate impositions from no one: Horace indeed used to accommodate himself to men's habits.'
41 *Theophrasti Notationes Morum.* Isaacus Casaubonus recensuit ... (Leiden, 1617), p. 136. Howard Erskine-Hill discusses the connection with Theophrastus in his 'Courtiers out of Horace', in *John Donne: Essays in Celebration*, ed. A.J. Smith (London, 1972), p. 280.
42 *Theophrasti Notationes Morum*, p. 133. For the fop asking about the going rate for commodities, cf. 'On his way down to Athens he will ask the first man that he meets how hides and salt-fish were selling' (trans. Jebb; Ἀγροικία 12).
43 The absence of inverted commas at the beginning of this line indicates that this is spoken by the fop.
44 As Brooks notes.
45 Fraenkel, *Horace*, pp. 114, 118.
46 Ezra Pound, 'Horace', *Criterion*, 9 (1929-30), 217-27, p. 226.
47 For Dryden, see H.A. Mason, 'Dryden's Dream of Happiness', *Cambridge Quarterly*, 8 (1978), 11-55 and 9 (1980), 218-71; 'Living in the Present', *Cambridge Quarterly*, 10 (1981), 91-129.
48 W.B. Yeats, *Collected Poems* (London, 1950), p. 211.
49 Oldham's interest in I.xxxi and II.xiv has some precedent. The conclusion of the former is quoted by Montaigne at the end of his essay 'De L'Experience', and the subject of the poem was dear to Burton, whose *Anatomy* has some important pages on the fear of death, unnecessary pursuit of wealth, and far-fetched food (1.2.4.7). After Oldham, II.xiv was translated by Potenger, Creech, Congreve and Johnson, all of whom seem indebted to Oldham. Oldham seems to be alone in adopting the more expansive stanza-form (an inheritance from Cowley) instead of trying to match Horace's form.

50   R.G.M. Nisbet and Margaret Hubbard, *A Commentary on Horace: Odes Book I* (Oxford, 1970), pp. 347-8. I take further points from their commentary below.

51   For the phrasing of the two lines beginning 'Not the large Crops . . .' Oldham has recalled Denham's lines on the Thames: 'No unexpected inundations spoyl / The mowers hopes, nor mock the plowmans toyl' (*Cooper's Hill*).

52   John Camden, *Britain* (London, 1637), p. 577.

53   *Ibid*, p. 617.

54   *FQ* VII.vi.53.9; *PL* IV.454.

55   Michael Drayton, *Poly-Olbion* (London, 1613), pp. 231, 102.

56   Camden, *Britain*, p. 362.

57   The *OED*'s first example of 'exhaustless' is from Blackmore (1712). Other words in '-less' that Oldham uses in his translation of II.xiv are 'avoidless', 'fruitless' and 'resistless'.

58   André L. Simon, *History of the Wine Trade in England* (3 vols., London, 1906-9), III, 322-46.

59   Cf. 'for the bruised Grapes and Liquor to fall in' and 'until the Liquor have extracted the tincture and strength of the Fruit' (W. Hughes, *The Compleat Vineyard* (London, 1670), pp. 47, 60).

60   Simon, *Wine Trade*, III, 359-60.

61   *Diary of John Evelyn*, ed. E.S. de Beer (6 vols., Oxford, 1955), II, 207.

62   Simon, *Wine Trade*, III, 274.

63   Hughes, *Compleat Vineyard*, p. 64; James Howell, *Familiar Letters*, ed. Joseph Jacobs (2 vols., London, 1890-2), p. 456; *OED*.

64   Thomas Blount, *Glossographia*, 5th ed. (London, 1681), p. 71.

65   The reference to Algiers does have a topicality: see the account in *The Case of many Hundreds of Poor English-Captives in Algier* [1679]:

> 'There hath been taken, since their last breach with us, not less than a Hundred and Forty Sail of Ships and other Vessels, many of them being richly laden, besides the great Advance they make upon the persons they take, there being at this time upwards of 1500, (besides many Hundreds who have Dyed there of the Plague,) who suffer and undergo most miserable Slavery, put to dayly extream and difficult Labour' (p. 1).

66   *The Ornithology of Francis Willughby*, translated into English by John Ray (London, 1678), p. 227. I am grateful to Professor Brooks for this reference.

67   All the seventeenth-century editions that I have seen follow Lambinus's reading '& precor', except Schrevelius, who prints 'at precor', the reading that Oldham follows in '*But* not his Reason . . .'

68   *OED* 3; the first example is from Pope's *Iliad* (1718).

69   'All things are in flux, and every shape is formed changeable. Times themselves also glide on with constant motion, not unlike a river. For neither a river nor a fleeting hour can stay still, but as one wave is driven on by another, and the one which is coming is both urged on, and urges on the one before, so times haste constantly away, and are constantly following, and are always new.'

70   *Épître* III.48; suggested by A.F.B. Clark.

71   Homer has a comparison of an army to a swarm of flies in *Iliad* II.469-73, but the generic nature of the comparison is more important than specific parallels.

72   Dryden, *Lucretius Against the Fear of Death* 77-9.

73   [Thomas Godwyn], *Romanae Historiae Anthologia*, newly revised (Oxford, 1642), pp. 65-6.

5. Juvenal

1   I have used the following editions and translations of Juvenal:

(*a*) *Editions*

FARNABY: *Iunii Ivvenalis Et Auli Persii Flacci Satyrae* (London, 1612); there is a fourth, revised edition in 1633.

LUBINUS: *D. Ivnii Ivvenalis Sutyrarvm Libri V* ... Cum Analysi & doctissimis Commentariis, partim nunc primum, partim de integro editis Eilhardi Lvbini (Hanover, 1603).

RIGALTIUS: *D. Ivnii Ivvenalis Satirarvm Libri V* ... Nova editio. Cvra Nicolai Rigaltii (Paris, 1616).

SCHREVELIUS: *D. Junii Juvenalis, Et Auli Persii Flacci Satirae*: Cum Veteris Scholiastae, & Variorum Commentariis. Accurante Cornelio Schrevelio (Leiden, 1648).

(*b*) *Translations*

DU CHESNE: *Les Satyres de I. Ivvenal d'Aquin*, traduites en Francois. Par A. du Chesne (Paris, 1607).

DRYDEN: *The Satires of Decimus Junius Juvenalis* Translated into English Verse. By Mr. Dryden, and Several other Eminent Hands ... (London, 1693).

HARVEY: J.H., *The Tenth Satyr of Juvenal* done into English Verse (London, [1694]).

HIGDEN: *A Modern Essay on the Thirteenth Satyr of Juvenal*. By Henry Higden (London, 1686).

HIGDEN: *A Modern Essay on the Tenth Satyr of Juvenal*. By Henry Higden (London, 1687).

HOLYDAY: *Decimus Junius Juvenalis and Aulus Persius Flaccus* Translated and Illustrated. As well with Sculpture as Notes. By Barten Holyday (Oxford, 1673).

MAROLLES: *D. Ivnii Ivvenalis Et Avli Persii Flacci Satirae* ... Accurante Michaele De Marolles (Paris, 1658).

MARTIGNAC: *Les Satyres de Juvenal, Et de Perse*, De La Traduction De M^r De Martignac. Avec Des Remarques (Paris, 1682).

STAPYLTON[1]:   *The First Six Satyrs of Juvenal* ... By Sir Rob: Stapylton (Oxford, 1644).

STAPYLTON[2]:   *Juvenal's Sixteen Satyrs* ... By Sir Robert Stapylton (London, 1647).

STAPYLTON[3]:   *Mores Hominum* ... By Sir Robert Stapylton (London, 1660).

DE LA VALTERIE: *Les Satyres de Juvenal et de Perse.* Traduction Novvelle (2 vols., Paris, 1680-1).

WOOD: *Juvenalis Redivivus.* Or The First Satyr of Juvenal taught to speak plain English (1683).

Details of Oldham's use of previous editions and translations, together with details of later translators' use of Oldham, are given in the appendix to my PhD thesis. A survey of seventeenth-century translations of Juvenal, with special attention to Satire X, is provided by Raman Selden, 'Juvenal and Restoration Modes of Translation', *MLR*, 68 (1973), 481-93.

2   *First Six Satyrs*, Sig. A3r.
3   *Juvenal's Sixteen Satyrs*, Sig. A2v.
4   *Ibid.*: 'Lastly there sprung up a Sect of *formall Stoicks*, little people, that for a few *wanton words* (which was all they under-stood) cast him out of their hands.' *Mores Hominum* (1660) reads: '... in our seed-plots of Learning, there sprung up ...' This implies puritan opposition to Juvenal in the universities during the Commonwealth, but I have found nothing to support this suggestion.
5   *Juvenal's Sixteen Satyrs*, Sig. A2v-A3r.
6   *Ibid.* Sig A4v.
7   *First Six Satyrs*, Sig. A3r.
8   *Juvenal's Sixteen Satyrs*, Sig. A4r.
9   *Ibid.* Sig. A5r-A6v.
10   *Decimus Junius Juvenalis*, Sig. av.
11   *Poems of John Dryden*, p. 654.
12   *Mores Hominum*, pp. 8-9.
13   *Ibid.* pp. 158-9.
14   'A Satyr against Woman' in *A Ternary of Satyrs* (1679) actually adapts Stapylton's line, 'I'm tir'd with Men, but yet not satisfy'd' (p. 38). Other references to Messalina are by Robert Gould (*Poems chiefly consisting of Satyrs and Satyrical Epistles* (London, 1689), p. 143) and the anonymous authors of 'Rochester's Farewell' and 'A Satyr which the King took out of his Pocket' (*Works of the ... Earls of Rochester and Roscommon* (London, 1707), pp. 125, 132).
15   Gould, *Poems*, pp. 243-4.
16   Juvenal VI.602-3; Gould, *Poems*, p. 289; Oldham, *SNP* 133.
17   Higden, Sig. A3r.

18   *Ibid.* Sig. A4r-v. Perhaps Dryden wrote the poem because
      Higden's translation had been borrowed and then scorned by
      Shadwell.
19   *Oeuvres Diverses du R.P. R. Rapin, Concernant Les Belles Lettres*
      (2 vols.. Amsterdam, 1693), II, 203-4.
20   Josué de Decker, *Juvenalis Declamans: Étude sur la Rhétorique
      Declamatoire dans les Satires de Juvénal*, Receuil de Travaux
      publiée par la Faculté de Philosophie et Lettres de l'Université
      de Gand, 41 (Gand, 1913), p. 139.
21   [Thomas Godwyn], *Romanae Historiae Anthologia*, newly
      revised (Oxford, 1642), p. 25.
22   Erasmus, *Adagiorum Chiliades Des. Erasmi Roterodami* (Basle,
      1559), p. 1013:

      'In the same letter Cicero (with a touch of the sententious)
      uses the phrase "In the Roman way", meaning simply and
      without dissimulation, rather than learnedly. For such were
      those early Romans, very different from the Greeks. "I
      promise you", he said, "– and I'm not speaking in the old
      way I used when I wrote to you about Milo, which you rightly
      ridiculed, but in the Roman way, when men don't use empty
      words – that there is no man more trustworthy, better,
      wiser." Pastoral plain-dealing dwelt with these Romans . . .'

23   'In this fine satire divine providence is especially demonstrated,
      which allows nothing to go unpunished to evil-doers; no bad man
      is happy, nor escapes his punishment. Which, indeed, he always
      carries about with him in his mind and conscience, sterner than
      any torturer.'
24   *Mores Hominum*, Comment.
25   *Platonis de rebus divinis dialogi selecti Graece & Latine* (Cam-
      bridge, 1673), Sig. A3r.
26   Line 251 of this poem; the fragmentary poem on Charles in RMS
      80; references throughout the *Satyrs upon the Jesuits* to killing
      kings.
27   'Εικών Βασιλική. *The Pourtracture of his Sacred Majestie in his
      Solitudes and Sufferings* (1648), p. 5; cf. pp. 10, 51, 75-6.
28   'He gives the reason for such crimes and perjuries, which he shows
      to be the impiety through which men believe that all things
      happen by chance, and nothing through divine providence: this
      follows Epicurus, who abolished God and providence.'
29   Keith Thomas, *Religion and the Decline of Magic*, rev. ed.
      (Harmondsworth, 1973), p. 127.
30   Burnet, quoted in *Rochester: The Critical Heritage*, ed. David
      Farley-Hills (London, 1972), pp. 60-4; see also Phillip Harth,
      Contexts of Dryden's Thought (Chicago, 1968), pp. 80 and 112.
31   'They do not dare to pray. For they believe God to be hostile to
      them, and they despair of his mercy: and there is no more
      wretched state than this.'
32   See H.A. Mason, 'Is Juvenal a Classic?', in *Critical Essays on*

Roman Literature: Satire, ed. J.P. Sullivan (London, 1963), pp. 93-176.

33   It is, of course, a different matter when Oldham applies these lines to Spenser's ghost in *A Satyr dissuading from Poetry*; indeed, the transposition may itself be a criticism of Boileau.

34   Dryden, *Horace Lib. I. Ode 9* 19-22.

35   *PL* II.227.

36   William Byrd, *Svperivs. Psalmes, Sonets & songs of sadnes and pietie* (London, 1588), Sig. Dr.

37   *Volpone*, I.i.77-8; I.ii.92-3; I.iiii.69-70.

38   T.S. Eliot, 'Poetry in the Eighteenth Century' in *From Dryden to Johnson*, ed. Boris Ford (Harmondsworth, 1957), pp. 271-7, p. 276.

39   F.R. Leavis, *Revaluation: Tradition and Development in English Poetry* (London, 1936), p. 118.

40   Perhaps Oldham learned here from Rochester's 'The Disabled Debauchee':

> 'I'll tell of whores attacked, their lords at home;
>   Bawds' quarters beaten up, and fortress won;
> Windows demolished, watches overcome;
> And handsome ills by my contrivance done.'
>   (33-6)

6. Boileau

1   For most details see A.F.B. Clark, *Boileau and the French Classical Critics in England 1660-1830* (Paris, 1925). 'Utile Dulci' is printed in *Court Satires of the Restoration*, ed. J.H. Wilson (Columbus, 1976), pp. 49-53.

2   *Upon a Lady . . . (PT* 90-6) was previously translated in John Bulteel's *A New Collection of Poems and Songs* (1674), which Oldham probably knew, for it includes the only printed text of Dryden's *To the Dutchess of Cleaveland*, from which Oldham may be using a phrase in the *Letter from the Country*.

3   Quoted in *The Works of Monsieur Boileau*, made English (London, 1712), I.lxii.

4   *The Letters of Saint Evremond*, ed. John Hayward (London, 1930), pp. 158-60.

5   *The Diary of Dudley Ryder 1715-1716*, ed. William Matthews (London, 1939), pp. 63, 110-11.

6   Of the many discussions of this poem, those paying special attention to the presence or absence of Boileau are by Thomas Rymer and Samuel Johnson (*Rochester: The Critical Heritage*, ed. David Farley-Hills (London, 1972), pp. 167-8 and 207); John Moore, 'The Originality of Rochester's *Satyr Against Mankind*', *PMLA*, 58 (1943), 393-401; Paul C. Davies, 'Rochester and Boileau: A Reconsideration', *Comparative Literature*, 21 (1969), 348-55.

7   'Evenness of Soul': the French is: 'Egalité d'ame'. Miège's

Dictionary suggests 'evenness' for 'égalité', and has the example: 'J'aime l'égalité de vôtre esprit: I love the evenness of your temper.'

8 Boileau is of course drawing here on Horace, *Serm.* I.i.33-8, to which Oldham has returned in his passage: he has 'Saddens the year' ('contristat ... annum' – not 'attrister la nature') and 'overcasts' ('inversum'); also 'prudent' ('sapiens'). For 'gueret' Miège gives 'fallow', Cotgrave 'fallow', or 'fallow ground'. For 'Aquilon' Cotgrave gives 'The Northern wind'.

9 Cotgrave and Miège both give 'stay' and 'prop' for 'appui'.

10 E.g. Seneca, *De Beneficiis*, VII i.7.

11 The congruence of the thoughts suggests that Pope may have recalled the 'man / scan' rhyme when he wrote:

> Know then thyself, presume not God to scan;
> The proper study of Mankind is Man.
> (*Essay on Man* II.1-2)

12 Details are given by Brooks.

13 Recalled of course by Pope (*Essay on Criticism* 694). But cf. also Basil Kennett's 'the Glory and the Scandal of the Universe', translating in 1704 Pascal's 'gloire, & rebut de l'univers' (Pascal, *Thoughts on Religion and other subjects*, translated (London, 1704), p. 185). 'Rebut' is 'refuse', 'offals'.

14 Noted by Brooks.

15 Emrys Jones, 'Pope and Dulness', *Proceedings of the British Academy*, 54 (1968), 231-63. But I believe that he is overstating, or being too selective, in talking of 'something almost hysterical in the violent response' of Oldham.

16 The comparable passage in Hall (*Virgidemiarum* II.vi) achieves much less.

17 *Reliquiae Wottonianae* (London, 1651), pp. 522-3.

18 *Les Fabulistes Latins*, ed. Leopold Hervieux (5 vols., Paris, 1884-99). Phaedrus's fable is quoted from II, 28-9 and Romulus's from II, 242-3. Phaedrus and Romulus were available in many editions: see I, 199ff and 312ff.

19 The translation itself appears to have been the work of Pierre de Boissat.

20 Oldham also takes some hints from *Aesop Improved* (London, 1673), pp. 37-8, and John Ogilby, *Aesopic's* (London, 1668), p. 113.

Epilogue

1 See Brooks, 'Bibliography'. Since Oldham's poems appeared in print fairly shortly after they were written, the number of manuscript copies is comparatively small. Some short poems were copied from the printed texts into commonplace books: the Cosmelia poems, the devotional paraphrases, the translations of Ovid's Elegies, Horace's Odes, Petronius and *The Careless*

Good Fellow. Only three poems seem to have circulated at all widely in manuscript: *Sardanapalus*, the *Satyr against Vertue* and *Garnet's Ghost*. Significantly, the last two poems were printed surreptitiously in 1679 from manuscript copies: *Garnet's Ghost* is advertised as being 'by the author of the Satyr against Vertue (not yet printed)', which implies that many customers would know of the *Satyr* from manuscript versions.

2   Cf. John Harvey on Oldham's equal abilities in translating Juvenal and Ovid (J.H., *The Tenth Satyr of Juvenal* done into English Verse (London,[1694].), Sig. B2*r*).

3   BL MS Add. 28276, fol. 89*v*. It borrows from Dryden's memorial poem.

4   *Miscellany Poems and Translations by Oxford Hands* (London, 1685), p. 60.

5   *A Satyr Against the French* (London, 1691), pp. 24-5.

6   BL C.45.a.1. The note on the endpaper was printed in Thompson's edition of Oldham.

7   Joseph Spence, *Observations, Anecdotes, and Characters*, ed. James M. Osborn (2 vols., Oxford, 1966), I, 202.

8   See the notes in the Twickenham edition.

9   *Imitations of Horace, Ep.* I.vii.62; II.ii.241; II.ii.257; *Epistle to Bathurst* 40.

10   *Imitations of Horace, Ep.* I.vii.62-4.

11   *Ibid. Ep.* I.i.62; *Dunciad* B, IV.501. The former example comes in a passage whose rhetorical structure is a figure frequently used by Oldham:

> Be furious, envious, slothful, mad or drunk,
> Slave to a Wife or Vassal to a Punk,
> A Switz, a High-dutch, or a Low-dutch Bear —
> All that we ask is but a patient Ear.

12   Pope, *The Fourth Satire of Dr John Donne versified* 224-5. The second line may also be an echo of Juvenal III.182-3: 'hic viuimus ambitiosa / Paupertate omnes' ('here we all live in ambitious poverty').

13   As noted by Felicity Rosslyn, 'Pope and Cowley', *NQ*, 222 (1977), 237-8.

14   Lines 19-25; 176-8; 290-2; 484-9.

15   Some of the following points are made at greater length by Dustin Griffin, 'Dryden's "Oldham" and the Perils of Writing', *MLQ*, 37 (1976), 133-50.

16   *Sylvae*, Sig. A8*r*.

17   Earl Miner, *Dryden's Poetry* (Bloomington, 1967), p. 248.

18   Hebrews xii.1; the point is partly made by Griffin.

19   Abraham Cowley, *Essays, Plays and Sundry Verses*, ed. A.R. Waller (Cambridge, 1906), pp. 399-400. The use of 'slippery' with these connotations can be paralleled in Shakespeare (*King John* III.iv.137; *Coriolanus* IV.iv.12; *Troylus and Cressida* III.iii.84) and widely in the seventeenth century.

20   *Sylvae*, Sig. A8*r*.

BIBLIOGRAPHY

I. Works of Oldham

For full details see Brooks's 'A Bibliography of John Oldham', listed below.

Garnet's Ghost, addressing to the Jesuits, met in private Caball, just after the Murther of Sir Edmund-Bury Godfrey ([London, 1679]).
A Satyr against Vertue (London, 1679).
Satyrs upon the Jesuits (London, 1681).
Satyrs upon the Jesuits ... The second edition more corrected (London, 1682).
Some New Pieces never before publisht (London, 1681).
Poems, And Translations (London, 1683).
Remains of Mr. John Oldham in Verse and Prose (London, 1684).
Remains of Mr. John Oldham in Verse and Prose, 2nd ed. (London, 1687).
The Works of Mr. John Oldham, together with his Remains (2 vols., London, 1722).
The Compositions in Prose and Verse of Mr. John Oldham, ed. Edward Thompson (3 vols., London, 1770).
The Poems of John Oldham, ed. with a memoir by Robert Bell (London, [1854]) *[a highly corrupt text]*.
'The Complete Works of John Oldham (1653-1683)', ed. Harold F. Brooks (4 vols., unpublished DPhil dissertation, Oxford, 1939).
Poems of John Oldham, with an introduction by Bonamy Dobrée (London, 1960) *[text reprinted from Bell]*.
John Oldham, *Selected Poems*, ed. with an introduction by Ken Robinson (Newcastle, 1980) *[text contaminated from Bell]*.

II. Works on Oldham

This section includes more general books that have a substantial discussion of Oldham's work.

Brooks, Harold F. 'Attributions to Rochester', *TLS* (9 May 1935), 301.
　　'A Bibliography of John Oldham the Restoration Satirist', *Oxford Bibliographical Society Proceedings & Papers*, 5 (1936-9) (Oxford, 1940), pp. 1-38.
　　'The Chief Substantive Editions of Oldham's Poems, 1679-1684', *Studies in Bibliography*, 27 (1974), 188-226.
　　'The Family of John Oldham', *NQ*, 167 (1934), 30-1.
　　'The Family of John Oldham the Poet', *Miscellanea Genealogica et Heraldica and the British Archivist*, 5th series, 5 (1932-4), 323-6.

'The "Imitation" in English Poetry, especially in formal Satire, before the Age of Pope', *RES*, 25 (1949), 124-40.

'John Oldham', *TLS* (12 July 1934), 492.

'John Oldham', *Bulletin of the Institute of Historical Research*, 18 (1940-1), 135-6.

'John Oldham: some problems of biography and annotation', *PQ*, 54 (1975), 569-78.

'John Shepheard, Master of Whitgift School when John Oldham the Poet was Under Master', *Notes and Queries for Somerset and Dorset*, 30 (1979), 435-44.

'Oldham and Phineas Fletcher: an unrecognized source for *Satyrs upon the Jesuits*', *RES*, 22 (1971), 410-22 and 23 (1972), 19-34.

'The Poems of John Oldham' in *Restoration Literature: Critical Approaches*, ed. Harold Love (London, 1972), pp. 177-203.

'When did Dryden write *Mac Flecknoe*?', *RES*, 11 (1935), 74-8.

Cable, Chester H. 'Oldham's Borrowing from Buchanan', *MLN*, 66 (1951), 523-7.

Engel III, Wilson F. 'John Oldham and the Threat of Building Pauls', *NQ*, 222 (1977), 522-3.

Hammond, P.F. 'A Commonplace Book owned by John Oldham', *NQ*, 224 (1979), 515-18 and 226 (1981), 51-2.

'John Oldham: a critical study of the origins and development of his work, with special reference to his translations' (unpublished PhD. thesis, Cambridge, 1979).

Hill, J.L. 'John Oldham', *St Edmund Hall Magazine*, 1 (1922), 19-27.

'A John Oldham Manuscript', *St Edmund Hall Magazine*, 3 (1931), 60-8.

Korshin, Paul J. *From Concord to Dissent* (Menston, 1973).

Mackin, Cooper R. 'The satiric technique of John Oldham's *Satyrs upon the Jesuits*', *SP*, 62 (1965), 78-90.

O'Neill, John H. 'Oldham's "Sardanapalus": A Restoration Mock-Encomium and its Topical Implications', *Clio*, 5 (1976), 193-210.

Robinson, K.E. 'The Family of John Oldham', *NQ*, 219 (1974), 414-15.

'John Oldham and "The Art of Sinking in Poetry" ', *NQ*, 219 (1974), 48.

'John Oldham, St Paul's and the Imitation', *NQ*, 224 (1979), 515.

'Juvenal, Oldham and Dryden', *NQ*, 224 (1979), 518-20.

Rosenfeld, Sybil. 'The Family of John Oldham', *NQ*, 164 (1933), 112-13.

Selden, Raman. 'Oldham's Versions of the Classics', in *Poetry and Drama 1570-1700: Essays in Honour of Harold F. Brooks*, ed. Antony Coleman and Antony Hammond (London, 1981), pp. 110-35.

Sharrock, Roger. 'Modes of Satire', in *Restoration Theatre*, Stratford-upon-Avon Studies, 6 (London, 1965), pp. 108-32.

Trickett, Rachel. *The Honest Muse* (Oxford, 1967).

Vieth, David M. 'John Oldham, the Wits and *A Satyr against Vertue*', *PQ*, 32 (1953), 90-3.

Williams, Weldon M. 'The Genesis of John Oldham's *Satyrs upon the Jesuits*', *PMLA*, 58 (1943), 958-70.

'The Influence of Ben Jonson's *Catiline* upon John Oldham's *Satyrs upon the Jesuits*', *ELH*, 11 (1944), 38-62.

INDEX

243